D1251736

Poisoned

Poisoned

CHICAGO 1907.
A CORRUPT SYSTEM,
AN ACCUSED KILLER,
AND THE CRUSADE TO SAVE HIM

Steve Shukis

Title Town
PUBLISHING

Library of Congress Cataloging-in-Publication Data-On File

ISBN: 978-0-99119-381-3

For inquiries about volume orders, please contact:

TitleTown Publishing, LLC
PO Box 12093
Green Bay, WI 54307-12093
920-737-8051

Published in the United States by TitleTown Publishing
http://www.titletownpublishing.com

Distributed by Midpoint Trade Books
www.midpointtrade.com

Printed in the United States of America

Interior design by Neuwirth & Associates, Inc.
Cover Design by Michael Short

Contents

•

"Those who cannot remember the past are condemned to repeat it."

George Santayana
The Life of Reason (1905)

"Capital punishment will become a thing of the past in Illinois if a bill to abolish it, which passed the House today, succeeds . . . .In urging the passage of the measure Representative Chiperfield referred to the memorable Billik case in Chicago."

New York Times
May 28, 1909

"Declaring the state's capital punishment system 'haunted by the demon of error' and citing the state legislature's failure to reform it, Gov. George Ryan on Saturday commuted the sentences of every inmate on Illinois' Death Row."

Chicago Tribune
Jan 12, 2003

Cast of Characters

●

Barbour, James: Assistant State's Attorney, prosecuted Knute Knudson; took part in Henry Niemann Inquest

Barnes, Hon. Albert C.: Cook County Circuit Court Judge; presided over Billik trial

Barrett, Charles V.: Assistant Cook County Coroner; helped conduct Vrzal Inquest

Billik, Edna: daughter of Herman Billik; 9 years old at the time of her father's trial

Billik, Emil: youngest son of Herman Billik; 11 years old at the time of his father's trial

Billik, Frank: oldest son of Herman Billik; 15 years old at time of his father's trial; lived in Cleveland

Billik, Herman: Bohemian fortune teller charged with murdering six members of the Vrzal family

Billik, Herman Jr.: son of Herman Billik; just turned 14 years old when his father's trial began

Billik, Mary Cermak: wife of Herman Billik

Burres, Joseph R.: Attorney who successfully defended Knute Knudson and Mary Sladek

Cermak, Mary (see Mary Cermak Billik)

Christison, Dr. John Sanderson: Medical doctor / criminologist; tried to prove Billik's innocence

Cooney, Joseph P. "Tip": Former boyfriend of Emma Vrzal

Davies, Will: Cook County Jailer; oversaw executions

Davis, Ross Wade: Public Defender; represented Billik at criminal trial

Deneen, Charles S.: Governor of Illinois; ruled on Billik's plea before the Board of Pardons

Dunne, Edward F.: Former Judge and Mayor of Chicago; fought to save Billik's life

Edwardson, Leonard G.: Editor, *Chicago Examiner*; investigated Vrzal / Niemann murders

Engelthaler, Kate: cousin of Rose Vrzal, with whom Rose, Jerry, and Bertha lived at the time of Rose's death

Gregory, Stephen S.: Attorney; represented Billik before Board of Pardons

Hadley, Charles W.: DuPage County State's Attorney; investigated the murder of Henry Niemann

Haines, Dr. Walter S.: Professor of Chemistry / toxicologist; conducted chemical analysis on Vrzals

Healy, John J.: Cook County State's Attorney; oversaw Billik prosecution

Hinckley, Francis E.: Public Defender, represented Billik at criminal trial and appeals

Hoffman, Peter M.: Cook County Coroner; conducted Vrzal and William Niemann Inquests

Holt, Robert N.: Cook County Assistant State's Attorney; prosecuted Billik, testified at Pardon Board Hearing

Knudson, Knute: Charged with murdering his wife by arsenic poisoning

Kolar, Otto: Billik Defense Attorney through Coroner's Inquest

Landis, Hon. Kenesaw M.: Federal Judge; Ruled on Billik's appeal

Mech, Louise Niemann: sister of William Niemann; helped care for her father Henry

Moyer, Dr. Harold: Alienist for Cook County; participated in Vrzal and Niemann investigations

Napieralski, Dr. Emanuel F.: Doctor who treated Vrzal family for gas poisoning incident

Niemann, Emma Vrzal: eldest daughter of Vrzal family, married William Niemann

Niemann, Fred: brother of William Niemann

Niemann, Henry: father of William Niemann; died in DuPage County August 21, 1905 at the age of 77

Niemann, Henry: son of William Niemann and Louise Runge Niemann; age 13 when his father died in 1907

Niemann, Louise: (see Louise Niemann Mech)

Niemann, Louise Runge: first wife of William Niemann; died August 29, 1903 at the age of 31

Niemann, William: Dairy farmer / widower; married Emma Vrzal; died Nov. 4, 1907 at the age of 39

Niemann, Willie "Bill": son of William Niemann and Louise Runge Niemann; age 9 when his father died in 1907

O'Callaghan, Fr. Peter J.: Pastor St. Mary's Church; organized protests to try to save Billik from execution

Parkison, Benjamin: Billik's nephew, adopted son of Elsa Schmidt; lived with Billik at time of Rose Vrzal's death

Popham, George M.: Assistant Cook County State's Attorney; prosecuted Billik

Reinhardt, Henry G.W.: Cook County Assistant Coroner's Physician; conducted autopsy of William Niemann

Runge, Louise (see Louise Runge Niemann)

Runge, Magdalena: mother of Louise Runge Niemann

Schmidt, Dr. Emil: brother-in-law of Herman Billik; lived in Cleveland

Schmidt, Elsa Zajicek: (step-?)sister of Herman Billik; married to Dr. Emil Schmidt

Shippy, George M.: Chicago Police Inspector / Chief of Police; oversaw Vrzal murder investigation

Sladek, Mary: Charged with poisoning her family with arsenic

Vrzal, Bertha: youngest of Vrzal children, survived; 7 years old when her mother died in December 1906

Vrzal, Ella: daughter of Rose and Martin Vrzal; died November 30, 1906 at the age of 12

Vrzal, Emma (see Emma Vrzal Niemann)

Vrzal, Jerry: only son of the Vrzal family; survived; had just turned 17 when his mother died in December 1906

Vrzal, Martin: husband of Rose Vrzal; died March 26, 1905 at the age of 47

Vrzal, Mary: daughter of Rose and Martin Vrzal; died July 27, 1905 at the age of 21

Vrzal, Rose Matous: wife of Martin Vrzal; died December 5, 1906 at the age of 44

Vrzal, Rosie: daughter of Rose and Martin Vrzal; died August 31, 1906 at the age of 14

Vrzal, Tillie: daughter of Rose and Martin Vrzal; died December 22, 1905 at the age of 18

Timeline of Events

•

AUGUST 29, 1903

Louise Runge Niemann dies at the age of 31; she is diagnosed with tuberculosis.

MARCH 26, 1905

Martin Vrzal dies; he is diagnosed with gastritis and rheumatism.

JULY 27, 1905

Mary Vrzal dies at age of 21; she is diagnosed with an ulcer of the stomach.

AUGUST 21, 1905

Henry Niemann dies at the age of 77; he is diagnosed with heart trouble and alcoholism.

DECEMBER 22, 1905

Tillie Vrzal dies at the age of 18; she is diagnosed with typhoid fever.

JULY 1906

Gas is turned on in the Vrzal home; Bertha, Ella, and Tille Vrzal survive.

AUGUST 31, 1906

Rosie Vrzal dies at age 14; she is diagnosed with heart problems.

NOVEMBER 2, 1906

Rose Vrzal sells milk depot. She, Jerry, Ella, and Bertha move in with her cousin Kate Engelthaler.

NOVEMBER 30, 1906

Ella Vrzal dies at the age of 12; she is diagnosed with Addison's disease.

DECEMBER 2, 1906

Chicago Police begin investigating suspicious deaths in Vrzal family.

DECEMBER 5, 1906

Rose Vrzal dies from poisoning; authorities presume her death to be self-inflicted.

DECEMBER 6, 1906

A Coroner's Inquest is launched to determine the cause of the Vrzal deaths.

DECEMBER 7, 1906

Herman Billik is charged with the murders of Martin, Mary, Tillie, Rosie, and Ella Vrzal.

DECEMBER 8, 1906

Herman Billik is charged with the murder of Rose Vrzal.

JANUARY 4, 1907

Coroner's Inquest declares arsenic poisoning the cause of deaths of Mary, Rosie, and Ella Vrzal.

FEBRUARY 21, 1907

Coroner's Inquest declares arsenic poisoning the cause of the deaths of Martin, Rose, and Tillie Vrzal.

JULY 3, 1907

Herman Billik is put on trial for the murder of Mary Vrzal.

JULY 18, 1907

Herman Billik is convicted of murdering Mary Vrzal and is sentenced to death by hanging.

NOVEMBER 4, 1907

William Niemann dies at the age of 39.

NOVEMBER 18, 1907

Coroner's Inquest declares William Niemann died from a combination of natural causes.

MAY 8, 1908

Dr. J. Sanderson Christison dies under suspicious circumstances, ruled to be accidental or suicide.

JULY 24, 1908

The body of Henry Niemann is exhumed for testing.

SEPTEMBER 25, 1908

DuPage County Coroner declares Henry Niemann's death to be murder by arsenic poisoning.

This book is dedicated to my father, Gary Shukis, for teaching me the beauty and power of the written word.

Part I

The
Investigation

Vrzal family grave monument, Bohemian National Cemetery, Chicago.
Author's photo.

1

A Mystery

In early December of 1906, the Chicago Police received an anonymous message at the Twentieth Precinct. They were told to look into the recent death of a young girl who might have been poisoned. Twelve-year-old Ella Vrzal (pronounced "Ver-zuhl") had died just a few days earlier, on Thanksgiving.* Her death didn't appear particularly suspicious; she was known to suffer from Addison's disease, which could be fatal, and had been under the care of a doctor. Police checked to see if there were any other recent deaths in the family, as was claimed in their "tip." They discovered that there were—several more. In fact, in the previous two years a total of five Vrzals had died: four girls and their father, Martin.

It all started in the spring of the previous year when Martin Vrzal became ill. He was diagnosed with gastritis, an inflammation of the stomach, and died on March 26th, 1905. He was only forty-seven years old, and left behind a wife and seven children. Just four months later, on July 27th, his twenty-one-year-old daughter, Mary, died of an ulcer of the stomach. Her eighteen-year-old sister, Tillie, died of typhoid fever on December 22nd that same year. The following year, on August 31st, 1906, fourteen-year-old Rosie

---

* Official date of death early a.m. Friday, November 30, 1906

Vrzal* died from a condition known as endocarditis, an inflammation of the lining of the heart. Now, just a few months later, young Ella's death prompted the message to police. While there appeared to be a valid explanation for each, the fact that five family members died within just twenty months compelled detectives to take a closer look. Inspector Shippy was apprised of the situation.

With a large frame and broad mustache, Inspector George M. Shippy was Chicago's "super sleuth." He had recently garnered a national reputation by uncovering the crimes of Johan Hoch, "Chicago's Bluebeard." Hoch had married, then swindled, as many as fifty women, murdering an unknown number in the process. Shippy had followed his trail tirelessly in an epic investigation, uncovering victims across the country, from New York down to Missouri and out west to California. Police finally brought the killer to justice after Shippy gathered the evidence to convict him of killing a Chicago woman, and Hoch was hanged. Indeed, if anyone was prepared to uncover a poison plot, it was Inspector Shippy. He summoned Mrs. Rose Vrzal, the widowed mother of the deceased, to the Twentieth Precinct Station.

Rose Vrzal was forty-four years old, though she looked far older. She was a small but sturdy woman, with a weathered look that reflected years of hard work and the stress of losing a husband and four children. She was born Rose Matous in Bohemia, now a region in the Western part of the Czech Republic. Rose married Martin Vrzal in 1880 and they immigrated to the United States the following year. The Vrzals settled in Chicago's near-West Side, in a section known as Pilsen. It was named after the Bohemian city of Plzen, probably best known today as the birthplace of Pilsner beer. Pilsen was a bustling, working-class neighborhood as well as a center of labor activism. It was home to tens of thousands of Bohemians, as well as many other recent immigrants, mostly from eastern Europe. The streets were crowded and the air was filled with noise: the cacophony of foreign tongues, horse hooves pounding cobblestone streets, trolley cars screeching against rails and ringing their bells, and the barking

---

* For clarity, I will refer to Mrs. Rose Vrzal as "Rose," and to her daughter as "Rosie."

of newsboys and peddlers offering a countless variety of goods and services. Carl Sandburg described it in his poem "Blue Island Intersection," named for one of the area's main thoroughfares, Blue Island Avenue, which cuts on an angle through the heart of Pilsen:

Six Street ends come together here
They feed people and wagons into the center
In and out all day horses with thoughts of nose-bags
Men with shovels, women with baskets and baby buggies
Six ends of streets and no sleep for them all day
The people and wagons come and go, out and in
Triangles of banks, and drug stores watch
The policemen whistle, the trolley cars bump
Wheels, wheels, feet, feet, all day[1]

It was amid this chaos that the Vrzals raised a family. They had seven children:* Emma, Mary, Tillie, Jerry, Rosie, Ella, and Bertha. The couple spoke no English, but that was hardly necessary in a neighborhood filled with Bohemian immigrants. Chicago was a city of immigrants, but it was far from the proverbial melting pot. It was more of a patchwork, a city of neighborhoods defined by class and ethnicity, with each group having its own stores, churches, and fraternal organizations.

After almost twenty years of hard work as a carpenter and cabinet-maker, Martin Vrzal saved enough money by 1900 to buy a small milk depot right in the heart of Pilsen, on 19th St. just west of Paulina St. The business, which Rose and the children helped operate, was on the lower level, and the family lived above it. There was also an upper-floor apartment that they rented out. In the rear of the property was a small barn where they kept chickens, a pig or two, and their prized draft horse, which made the daily runs with Martin to pick up their milk shipments at the train station each morning. The Vrzals were living the American dream. Then, in late 1904, their troubles began.

---

* An eighth child, Anna, died as an infant in 1897.

One afternoon their dog, a large and playful St. Bernard, became ill. He threw up everything he had eaten, and started whining incessantly. Over the course of the next few days, he refused to eat even a single bite. The family could do nothing but watch as he gradually wasted away. He became so weak he could barely lift himself to walk. After several weeks, he died. It was an omen of worse things to come.

Not long after, Martin, a stout and healthy man who was rarely, if ever, sick, started feeling an aching in his joints. It grew worse. When the family doctors couldn't help him they called in specialists, but nothing they did seemed to work. The pain was tremendous. He grew weak, and suffered horrible soreness in his throat and mouth. Eventually, he was bed-ridden and nearly blind. He died in the spring of 1905. Mary Vrzal, now twenty-one, became sick a short time later. She also suffered terribly, with stomach pain and nausea. She died after only a few weeks. About three months later, in October, Tillie Vrzal came down with typhoid. She died just before Christmas 1905.

For a short time, things seemed to return to normal. Rose and the children managed to keep the milk depot going, and occasionally found time for fun, like taking in a vaudeville show downtown, or a day trip out to the country. Then in the spring, it started again. One of the children found several chickens dead in the yard. A short time later, the rest of chickens died. A pig they kept for meat suffered a similar fate, writhing in pain before expiring a few days later. By the summer of 1906, both Jerry and little Rosie were diagnosed with serious heart conditions. It seemed as if some terrible curse had befallen the Vrzals. Jerry managed to recover, but Rosie only got worse. She weakened, and died at the end of August. Ella was next. She was diagnosed with Addison's disease within a few months of Rosie's death.

Perhaps hoping to escape whatever malevolence had engulfed their lives, in early November 1906 Rose sold the property and milk business on 19th St. to her son-in-law William Niemann, the husband of her oldest daughter Emma. Rose and the three younger children, Jerry (17), Ella (12), and Bertha (7), moved in with her cousin a few miles away. But the darkness followed them. They had barely settled in to their new home when Ella died on Thanksgiving. Now, two days after the young girl's funeral, Rose was at the police station answering questions.

December 3, 1906

Inspector Shippy and his second-in-command, Lieutenant O'Brien, interviewed Mrs. Vrzal for several hours. They conferred with family physicians Dr. Frank Novak and Dr. Charles Caldwell, and eventually came to the conclusion that the whole matter was no more than a series of tragic coincidences. "We are convinced that the deaths were due to natural causes," reported Lieut. O'Brien. "We have investigated the reports of heavy insurance on all of the members of the family and found them untrue."[2] Dr. Novak said the deaths were from gastritis and that he didn't connect any mystery to them at all. The Cook County Coroner was not even officially notified. It seemed to be a closed case.

2

Find Herman Billik

Shortly before two o'clock the following afternoon, doctors received a frantic phone call. Rose Vrzal was critically ill. They raced to the home. When they arrived, they found a chaotic scene. Rose was lying in bed unconscious, the apartment abuzz with friends, neighbors, and family. They found a cork in her bed, and among the crowd that had gathered there was talk about a suspicious bottle, possibly smelling of chloroform, which had been spotted at her bedside earlier. It looked like a suicide attempt. The group searched the house frantically, both inside and out, looking for the mysterious bottle, to no avail. Police were notified.

Doctors worked on Rose throughout the night. They managed to revive her at about 2 a.m. She had intense pain in her stomach and was throwing up violently. With her cousin, Kate Engelthaler, translating, Dr. Caldwell asked Rose whether she had taken any poison. "Nay, nay," she barked. Believing the symptoms were all too obvious, he asked her what type of poison she had taken. She looked irritated and shook her head that she hadn't taken any, raising her hand as if to swear to it. "They accuse you of poisoning your children," Caldwell said. She raised her hand again to swear and said firmly, "Nay, nay." She again shook her head.[3] Then she lapsed back into unconsciousness. Despite all of their efforts, she never recovered. Rose Vrzal was dead. Police discovered what appeared to be a will that she had recently written, possibly on her deathbed. In it, she had left $1,000 each to her younger children, Bertha and Jerry, and twenty-five dollars to Emma.

As police continued taking statements and searching the house for clues, Inspector Shippy sent Lieut. O'Brien to another location: 677 W. 19th St.,* the Vrzal's former home and milk depot, currently occupied by their daughter Emma and her husband, William Niemann. Emma had shown up at the police station the night before, when her mother was being interviewed. She had told Inspector Shippy that she was suspicious about an acquaintance of the family who had borrowed money from them. Police didn't pay much attention to her at the time, but they certainly were now. Lieut. O'Brien picked up Emma and brought her to her mother's house, never telling her that her mother was dead. When they arrived, Rose's body was covered. Then, as they stepped into the bedroom, an officer suddenly lifted the cover, exposing her lifeless body. He bluntly asked Emma what she knew about her mother's death. She staggered, and fainted.

Shippy was known to use such dramatic tactics to try to startle witnesses and suspects into talking. He had once even propped up the corpse of a murdered man in his tomb, extended the man's arm and fixed his hand to point an accusing finger, then paraded a group of suspects inside.[4] He thought that the real murderer would be so frightened that the victim had apparently come up out of his grave to identify him that he would confess. The men were frightened and traumatized, but no one confessed.

When Emma regained consciousness, she told the officers, "Now you must get that man . . . Billik . . . I want him hung."[5] O'Brien asked her what she was accusing him of, but she couldn't speak. She motioned for a pencil and paper, and wrote, "Billik gave father medicine—and gave some to Mary."[6] Then she fainted again. When Emma was revived a second time, she was able to provide a few more details. "Billik" was Herman Billik, a Bohemian fortune teller

---

* Address is from old City of Chicago street numbering system. They were renumbered in 1909.

living in Pilsen. Emma said that he gave her father some type of brown medicine before his death, and gave her sister Mary a white colored medicine a few days before she died. Emma was weak and shaking, and investigators decided to interview her further at the station after she had a chance to recover. Police were dispatched to bring this "Billik" in for questioning.

Herman Billik* was a large man, with a large presence. He was rather plump, with a round face and double chin, but he was also by all accounts handsome, with piercing hazel eyes, wavy brown hair, and a thick mustache that was twisted and curled at the ends, as was the style of the day. His words purred in a thick Bohemian accent, and his manner was described by some as "oily."[7] He was a charismatic, unforgettable figure. Billik was listed in the Chicago city directory as a "palmist,"[8] or palm reader, but he did much more—he was a fortune teller, adviser, clairvoyant, hypnotist, medicine man, and all-around mystic. He sometimes used the title "Professor," though it was apparently self-bestowed. Billik was about forty years old. He was born in Germany, to Bohemian parents. He came to the U.S. in the 1880s and settled in Ohio, but moved to Chicago by 1900.

It was about two-thirty in the afternoon when officers arrived at Herman Billik's tiny storefront apartment at 19th St. and Blue Island Ave. Jerry Vrzal had gone with them to help locate him. Jerry knocked at the door and let him know police wanted to talk with him. "Tell them I'm not here!" bellowed the big Bohemian. Detectives then stepped forward to inform him that he would be going with them, either voluntarily, or otherwise. By the time he was brought in to the station, Emma Niemann was relating the details of a bizarre story to police. She said that Billik had been an adviser to her family for years, and at various times had worked charms and spells for her parents and the children, including herself. Emma

---

* His last name was originally "*Zajicek,*" (pronounced something like "Sighsec," and spelled many different ways). He changed it to "Billik," which was his step-father's name, simply because it was easier for people to say and spell. Variations include: *Zaijcek, Seitsek, Seidzek, Sizek, Ciecek, Ceicek,* and *Zeischek.*

believed that he still held some special power over them. She said he had borrowed money from them many times, adding up to a significant sum, and that she had protested, but her mother told her not to interfere. She claimed he was once in love with her, but she had discovered that he had a wife and children, and began to despise him. She said that after she married William Niemann, Billik began "making passes"[9] at her sister Mary. Emma told police about the mysterious bottle spotted at her mother's bedside. She said that her mother had shown it to her a year earlier and told her that she was going to take it when her troubles became too much to bear.[10] Emma also recounted how Billik treated both her father and her sister Mary with strange medicines not long before they died.

Inspector Shippy made it clear to Billik that he was now a suspect in the deaths. Billik became indignant. He shouted and protested his innocence. He claimed Emma must be hysterical, and that it would be proven that the family members died of natural causes. But the interrogation went on for hours, and eventually he began making some incriminating statements. He admitted that he treated Martin Vrzal and some of the children with medicine before their deaths, though he swore he never gave them anything more than saltpeter occasionally mixed with whiskey. He also admitted that he was alone with Rose Vrzal not long before she was found unconscious, but denied harming her. He claimed that Rose and her daughter Emma were both in love with him, not the other way around. Emma and Rose insisted on asking his advice on everything, he said, and for that he took money from them on many occasions, in amounts between ten and fifty dollars at a time.

Detectives went over Mrs. Vrzals financial records. Though she had only recently sold her house and the milk business for almost $2,000, and had collected another $2,400 or so in insurance money from the deaths of her husband and children, she appeared to have died almost penniless. The $2,000 she left in her will was the amount of her own life insurance. After figuring the amount spent on funeral and burial expenses and doctors bills, police determined that almost $1,900 was unaccounted for. They decided they had enough evidence to hold Billik in custody, and he was locked in a cell. The coroner's office was conducting a postmortem exam on Rose. They suspected she died from an overdose of either chloroform or laudanum (an opiate).

Investigators continued searching for clues late into the evening. They scoured Billik's apartment at 613 Blue Island Ave.* and discovered a satchel containing several letters written in Bohemian. They were addressed to Billik, and at least some appeared to be from Rose Vrzal. Police took them as evidence. They also took Billik's wife Mary and their thirteen-year-old son, Herman Jr., in for questioning.

When police had the letters translated, they realized they had unearthed a bombshell. They sounded like love letters. Some discussed borrowing money and, apparently, poisoning Billik's mother in Cleveland. One was addressed to Billik and signed, "With ten thousand kisses—Rosa."[11] Another, which wasn't signed, reportedly contained the passages, "Poison your mother in Cleveland. She has lots of money,"[12] and, "You would better give the old lady poison now . . ."[13] Mary Billik said the letters were written by Rose Vrzal.

In an effort to get her to talk, Shippy told Mary (falsely) that her husband had implicated her in a poison plot. She broke down and cried. She said that she had numerous arguments with her husband about his relationship with Rose Vrzal and her family, but she denied any knowledge of a plan to poison anyone. The police grilled Herman Billik into the early morning. He admitted to having talked with Mrs. Vrzal about poisoning "certain persons."[14] He said that Rose and Emma had at various times suggested he kill his mother, and even his wife, but he still denied involvement in any of the deaths.

The press had a field day. It was instantly a national story, covered by the likes of the *New York Times* and *Washington Post*, each eager to share every detail. Six members of a family lay dead, and "Professor Herman" was the perfect villain: "The

---

* Pre-1910 address.

prisoner is a man of the type of Johann Hoch, the wife murderer. He is fat and suave and appeared little troubled by his
arrest," read the *Chicago Daily Tribune*.[15] Many comparisons
were made between Hoch and Billik. Ironically, one could just
as easily have compared Inspector Shippy to either man, as they
were all heavy-set, mustachioed, and charismatic. But Billik
had an air of pomp and mystery that made him stand out, even
among those men. He was called a "G*psy sorcerer" and a "nec-
romancer," among many other colorful monikers. The story was
a major topic of conversation among Chicagoans, and the Bohemian community in particular. Popular theory held that Billik
had Mrs. Vrzal under a hypnotic spell and persuaded her to kill
her family, then herself.

Herman Billik
and unidentified
police officer,
Hyde Park
Station. *Photo
courtesy of the
Chicago His-
tory Museum,
DN-0004382.*

3

The Inquest Begins

The coroner convened an inquest to determine the cause of Rose Vrzal's death. An inquest was less formal than a trial, held sitting at a table at the neighborhood police station rather than in a courtroom. There was no actual judge; Coroner Peter Hoffman had that role. Hoffman was a portly fellow, with a thick, bushy mustache, and enjoyed chomping a fat cigar much of the time. He ran the proceedings with an iron fist. He determined who could talk, when, and for how long. Suspects did not have any specific right to testify, or to ask questions of anyone. It was strictly up to the coroner as to who testified and what evidence was considered. But Hoffman wasn't a lawyer. In fact, he wasn't a doctor either. The Cook County Coroner was an elected office, and Peter Hoffman was a pure politician. He had been a clerk for a railroad for seventeen years before being elected a County Commissioner from suburban Des Plaines. He always brought out a big Republican vote in the northwest suburbs, so Republican political bosses slated him to run for Coroner in 1904. He was elected in a Republican landslide in November of that year.

A jury of six men (chosen by Hoffman, naturally) was assembled at the station. It was their job to decide the "cause and manner of death."[16] Coroner's juries could also identify parties responsible for homicides, or assign blame in accidents.[17] They began by hearing testimony from Emma Niemann. At twenty-five, Emma was the oldest of the Vrzal children, and was rather plain-looking, though not particularly unattractive: she was thin, with long, dark brown hair, which she normally wore pulled back and tied into a bun. Emma slouched in her chair, her long winter coat appearing to weigh her down like an anchor. She looked worn and tired, with dark circles under her eyes. She conveyed her story in dramatic fashion, in between fainting spells.

She said that the family first met Billik in the fall of 1904, when he lived down the block on 19th St. and started buying milk from them. Billik was a regular customer, often stopping by several times in a day.* The Vrzals got to know him well. They discovered he was a fortune teller, and he did readings for all of them. Emma said he impressed them with his powers and soon became very friendly with both her father and mother. Emma talked of Billik's hypnotic powers, and his growing influence over their family. At times he would tour the country and telegraph them from various places, requesting sums of money to be forwarded to him. She said they would always comply, though it became increasingly difficult to raise the funds. She thought he had taken as much as $3,000 from the family, and possibly some of the life insurance money, too.

She stated clearly that Billik had robbed them, but when pressed to make a direct accusation of murder, Emma would only say that she wanted police to find out what was in the medicine he had given them. When her father was sick with rheumatism, Billik gave him a concoction which Emma described as a brownish liquid with a white powder in the bottom. A month and a half later he died. She said Billik also gave her sister Mary some type of medicine shortly before her death, and that he provided other family members with powders and potions at times. She said he gave her some

---

* At the time, pasteurization was costly and uncommon, and many of Pilsen's poor didn't even have an ice box (the home refrigerator was still decades away). A trip to the neighborhood milk dealer, sometimes several times a day, was the only way to get fresh milk.

Emma Vrzal Niemann testifies at coroner's inquest. Herman Billik can be seen seated behind her, listening closely. *Photo courtesy of the Chicago History Museum, DN-0004528.*

white pills when she was sick once, but she was suspicious and only pretended to take them.

She talked of being "drawn" into following Billik on a trip to Cleveland with her mother at one point. She said both she and her mother kissed him when he met them near the train station, feeling strangely compelled to do so. She also told of visiting Billik in July of 1905 at suburban Riverside, where he was telling fortunes. Riverside was a beautiful rural community of oak-hickory forest and green space along the DesPlaines River.* It was a popular day trip and weekend picnic spot for Chicagoans, particularly Bohemians.

---

* Riverside was designed by famed landscape architect Frederick Law Olmsted, who designed New York's Central Park, and the spectacular Midway of Chicago's 1893 World's Fair.

Emma went with a friend, and the two sat at a small table in Billik's tent as he told their fortunes with cards. It was just three months after Emma's father had died. She said that Billik predicted that she would be married soon, but that she also would be in mourning again. The prediction was fulfilled, she said, when she married William Niemann and her sister Mary died, all within just a few weeks of the prophecy.

In addition to Emma, two other Vrzal children survived: Bertha, 7, and Jerry, 17. Jerry was the next to testify. He was tall, but slight and somewhat frail. He was, nonetheless, handsome, with short dark hair, that was slicked and combed to one side. He was reported to have some type of heart condition, for which he was treated periodically. Jerry had spent much of the day with his mother before she took ill. He originally told Lieutenant O'Brien and the doctors on the scene that he didn't know anything about her death. He now claimed to have actually seen her with a bottle of poison in her hand. He said he had just returned from an errand and found her holding a bottle he thought contained chloroform. He said it was approximately a four-ounce bottle, with a skull and crossbones on it, marked "John Novak."* Mrs. Vrzal was known to keep a bottle of chloroform in the house, prescribed by Dr. Novak for toothaches. Jerry described struggling with his mother, trying to take it away from her, but he claimed that she overpowered him and pushed him against the wall. He said that she went into the bedroom and closed the door, then came out after a short time, still holding the bottle. She took a drink, then threw it into the stove. Inspector Shippy wondered why Jerry hadn't mentioned the incident before. Was he hiding something, perhaps out of fear of Billik, or even due to some special power the hypnotist held over him? Shippy noted that the boy had seen Billik just before being interviewed the first time, and was probably influenced to keep quiet.

Jerry mentioned traveling with Billik and his son to faraway cities. He assumed that his mother had financed the trips. He said

---

* John Novak was a druggist, and brother of Dr. Frank Novak, the Vrzal's family physician.

Billik would travel frequently, and telegram requests for money to the Vrzals along the way. He said his parents had mentioned that "someone" owed them a good deal of money, but never told him who it was. He thought maybe it was Billik, but wasn't sure.

Dr. Caldwell was the final witness for the day. He said that the symptoms he observed in Ella and little Rosie were consistent with arsenic poisoning, but that the only way to be certain would be to conduct autopsies. Hoffman adjourned the inquest. He wanted the bodies exhumed. Billik remained adamant that all he ever administered was whiskey with saltpeter. "I court investigation," he said. "I would like to have all the bodies exhumed and searched for poison."[18]

DECEMBER 7, 1906

The following morning, prosecutors went before the Municipal Court to swear a complaint saying they believed Billik had poisoned Martin Vrzal and his four daughters.[19] Undertakers confirmed that no arsenic was used in the embalming process. If any were found, it would prove poisoning. The judge ordered the coroner to exhume the bodies of the entire Vrzal family.

Late that afternoon, Coroner Hoffman, two of his assistants, and two plainclothes officers headed for the Bohemian National Cemetery on the city's far Northwest Side. They rumbled past the iron gates and imposing Gothic-style gatehouse, and arrived at the main office at about 5 p.m. They obtained affidavits from cemetery officials and undertakers certifying the identities of those buried, and the precise locations of the graves. Everything was carefully documented. It was six o'clock and already dark when Hoffman and his men, along with three gravediggers, set out for the Vrzal grave-site. In an eerie scene deep in the center of the vast cemetery Hoffman's men held lanterns as the gravediggers secured ropes and slowly raised the coffins of Mary, Rosie, and Ella Vrzal. The caskets were sealed with wax to prevent any tampering, and were removed to the county morgue. They would be opened in the morning in the presence of witnesses. "If the poison is found in their stomachs," Inspector Shippy declared, "I believe we have conclusive evidence against Billik."[20]

4

Hypnotism, Dead Chickens, and More Victims

DECEMBER 8, 1906

As doctors prepared to examine the bodies, a detective brought them two of the most perplexing clues: a package filled with ashes, and a dead chicken. He had found them at Rose Vrzal's residence. It wasn't uncommon for people to keep chickens in early 20th century Chicago, but the officer's attention had been drawn to several *dead* ones he had spotted in the back yard. When he had looked closer, he had noticed they were near a pile of ashes that the animals had apparently picked over. The ashes, he learned, had been thrown out from the kitchen stove the morning after Rose Vrzal died. He had wisely gathered up the evidence, knowing that the bottle containing the poison Mrs. Vrzal had taken was thrown into the stove. He had assumed the chickens died after eating from the ashes. Doctors confirmed that the ashes contained traces of some unspecified poison, but they would need to complete further tests.

For now, the coroner's office already had their hands full. At the morgue, a team of top doctors was assembled to handle the autopsies of the Vrzal girls. They expected it would take many days to complete full examinations, including dissecting the internal organs for chemical analysis. As the team started their work, funeral services for the girls' mother, Rose Vrzal, were getting underway.

In those days wakes and funerals were commonly held in the home of the deceased, with visitation in the parlor before the body was removed to the cemetery for burial. Friends and family gathered at the home at 1536 W. 50th St.,* where Rose had been living at the time of her death. A crowd of curious onlookers gathered outside. Some followed the procession, which made its way some fifteen miles north across the city to the Bohemian National Cemetery. When they got there, the family was notified that Rose's body would have to be taken to the county morgue immediately after the services. Emma and Jerry became hysterical. They sobbed, and yelled, and even talked about going down to the morgue and protesting. At noon, officials from the cemetery notified Coroner Hoffman that they thought the two might make a scene at the morgue. Hoffman said they would not be allowed in, and even had officers stationed around the building to make sure. He feared that if they happened to view the bodies of their family being autopsied it would be too traumatic for them, maybe even fatal to Jerry considering his health problems. Eventually the two calmed down, and the services at the cemetery were completed. Rose Vrzal's body was delivered to the morgue without incident. And when Jerry composed himself, Hoffman asked him to talk with investigators again.

Both Shippy and Hoffman considered Jerry an important witness, and they wanted to get at the truth of his conflicting statements. "I believe the boy is the key to the situation," said Hoffman. "He already has given indications of knowing several things of the utmost value, and had it not been for the necessity of handling him carefully on account of his weak heart I think we might have arrived at a solution."[21] Shippy asked Jerry again about the day his mother died. Jerry said Billik had pressured him into saying that he didn't know anything about his mother's death, or the bottle of poison. He said Billik had visited with his mother that morning, then stopped by later to see how she was doing.

---

* Pre-1910 address.

At the morgue, coroner's physicians discovered arsenic in Rose Vrzal's stomach. Herman Billik was brought before a judge and arraigned for her murder, the only one of the six deaths with which he hadn't already been charged. He was ordered to be held without bail, as was Mary Billik, though she hadn't been charged with anything. The judge declared her a material witness, and said she would be held until the investigation was completed. She was questioned again for several hours, and said that her husband had once warned her not to eat at the Vrzal home, that she would be poisoned. She said he had told her that Mrs. Vrzal and Emma had both suggested that he poison her and his mother, but he wouldn't do it.

When they were done with Mrs. Billik, investigators directed more questions at Herman. By this point, he had been interrogated for hours at a time in Shippy's office, and it was beginning to wear on him. New details emerged. He admitted he had been conning the Vrzal family for years. He said he "borrowed" money from them to travel the country in search of rare herbs, which he needed in order to brew a mystic love potion for Emma, who was still unmarried at the time. She was supposedly interested in a wealthy young butcher from the West Side, and the potion, said Billik, would make him fall madly in love with her. Billik contacted the family from various points for more money to continue his search for the ever-elusive herbs.

He acknowledged that Mrs. Vrzal sent him money numerous times. "I admit that I am a bad man and that I conned the woman. I swindled her out of eighteen hundred dollars, but I did not poison any member of the family. The woman was in love with me and wanted to marry me. She wanted me to poison my wife."[22] But Billik steadfastly denied having a hand in any of the deaths. Police told him that the evidence was mounting against him. "Well, go ahead and hang me," he declared. "I have done nothing and you cannot make me say that I have."[23]

As the police probe continued over the following weeks, the story grew more bizarre. Assistant Police Chief Schuettler, described as an "authority" on the subject of hypnotism,[24] was called in. He was reputed to possess a "hypnotic eye," able to fix his stare upon suspects until they invariably confessed. A man once even appealed a murder conviction on the grounds that Schuettler had hypnotized him into confessing.[25] Schuettler was absolutely enormous: tall and wide, a virtual giant. He was probably the only man on the force who could make the 6'2," 240-pound Shippy look like a schoolboy in comparison. Scheuttler wanted to determine if Billik had used hypnotism to carry out his crimes.

Jerry Vrzal told Scheuttler that Billik had warned him not to let anyone know that he had been at the house the day Rose took poison, and that Billik had asked what happened to "the bottle" (presumably the one containing the poison that killed Rose). Jerry reiterated much of what Emma had said about Billik giving potions and pills to members of the family, and working various types of spells. "That Billik used hypnotism is more than probable," [26] declared Schuettler when he was finished. After going over all the evidence, he was not impressed by Billik's denials. "He is a criminal by his own admission and admits only such things as we can prove," said the Assistant Chief. "The whole case now rests on the examination of the bodies."[27]

Schuettler wondered if Jerry might actually be suffering from symptoms of arsenic poisoning himself. Dr. Harold Moyer from the coroner's office examined him. He decided that Jerry could well be the victim of some type of poison, administered in small doses. But he couldn't—or wouldn't—be any more specific, other than to say he had witnessed some outward signs of heart trouble. Schuettler and Shippy also learned that on at least one occasion some of the Vrzal girls were almost asphyxiated by gas in their home. Fortunately, a neighbor had called for a doctor, who rushed to the scene just in time to save them.

The press capitalized on the story's mix of the occult and macabre to publish the most fantastic reports. All the attention brought more people forward with clues and suspicions. Some claimed to have information about other crimes, even murders, Billik might have committed. Lieut. O'Brien was told by one informant that, five years earlier, Billik was engaged to a wealthy young woman named Mary Tonek, who died under suspicious circumstances. She reportedly suffered from symptoms similar to those of the Vrzal family, including stomach and heart problems, and collapsed suddenly. Billik left Chicago to return to Cleveland very abruptly right around the time of the girl's death. Shippy began fearing they might find a trail of murders, maybe even another Johan Hoch case. He sent much of the same team of detectives that had worked on the Hoch investigation to Cleveland to look into Billik's background and dealings there.

Billik came to the U.S. in the late 1880s to join his mother Barbara in Ohio. She was a well-known clairvoyant and occultist in the Cleveland area, and Herman learned the "black arts" from her. He married Mary Cermak in Cleveland in 1890. Mary was from a prominent Bohemian family, who reportedly disowned her after she married Billik. Herman and Mary had four children. The family moved to Chicago in the late 1890s, but occasionally traveled back and forth between the cities, and still had family and contacts in Cleveland.

Shippy's team soon discovered that Rose Vrzal had sent Jerry and little Rosie to Cleveland within the past year, and that they were treated there by Billik's brother-in-law, Dr. Emil Schmidt, who saw them as a favor to Billik. Police said they both became ill and returned home to Chicago, where Rosie died within a few months. Police wondered if Schmidt was somehow involved in the Vrzal deaths. Newspapers reported that Dr. Schmidt was under indictment in Cleveland for performing an "illegal operation"[28] (i.e. an abortion), so his character was already in question.

Police also secured information that Billik might have been involved years earlier in the death of a man named Standish York, a wealthy hardware merchant from Ohio. It was reported that Billik held séances at the York home, conjuring spirits and telling fortunes. Mrs. York had also called upon Barbara Billik, Herman's mother, on occasion. Mr. York died in January of 1898. He had become ill suddenly, and in a matter of weeks lay dead. He was diagnosed with bilious fever, a vague term for a fever accompanied by persistent vomiting.

Police spoke to the doctor who had treated York. He had demanded a postmortem exam, and said he was still not convinced that the death had been fully explained. The life insurance company contested paying the policy, and litigation followed. Mrs. York eventually won the case, and inherited a large sum. Investigators believed Billik had visited her new home in California several times in recent years. They also discovered that Mrs. York's sister was in prison for embezzling a fortune from an Ohio bank. Detectives wanted to talk to both women to see what they knew about Herman Billik, and the death of Standish York.

Back in Chicago, Inspector Shippy discussed another bit of disturbing news, which he said indicated that the Vrzal murders were planned out in advance: "Billik tried the arsenic first on a dog that he brought from Cleveland," the Inspector announced, referring to the St. Bernard that Billik had given to Jerry as a gift a few years earlier. "The animal got weaker every day and finally died. Then it was Martin's turn . . ."[29]

December 13, 1906

Just a week into the investigation, Chicago Mayor Edward F. Dunne ordered a shake-up of the police department, transferring more than sixty-five men. In the move, Inspector Shippy was sent to the Des Plaines Street Station. At one time, commanding officers were routinely fired with every change of administration. Shippy himself once bragged that he was "hired and fired more often than any policeman in Chicago."[30] But he had only recently taken over the Twentieth

Precinct (also known as the Hyde Park Station), so many wondered what was behind the decision. Dunne said officers were going to be moved regularly to help curb graft, or payoffs between police officers and the criminal underworld. While Dunne had clearly heard about Shippy's sometimes cozy relationship with certain gambling bosses, he said that he simply wanted "a good man"[31] in the Hyde Park District. It was an obvious slap at Shippy, and must have made the big lawman's blood boil. He was allowed to remain in charge of the Vrzal case until it was completed, but it was clear that Mayor Dunne did not completely trust Shippy.

Meanwhile, Shippy's sideshow of an investigation continued. He opened inquiries into the deaths of Simon and Emilia Kubera, patrons of Billik who had died just a few months earlier only about four weeks apart. He also started looking into the death of Billik's mother-in-law, Mary Cermak, who had recently died in Cleveland. There seemed to be no end to the list of potential victims.

On Christmas Eve, Mrs. Barbara Herr brought a large jar of pickled mushrooms to Inspector Shippy at his new office at the Des Plaines St. Station. He hoped it was a gift for him and his men to enjoy over the holidays. He soon found out he was not so lucky. Mrs. Herr said she was given the mushrooms by Herman Billik. When she heard about the deaths in the Vrzal family, she began fearing the food might have been poisoned. She said that Billik lived next door to her for a time, and when he left he owed her money. He said he didn't have any money, but that he wanted to give her something to show his appreciation, and brought the mushrooms to her as a gift. The jar was sent to the lab, which by this time was quite busy.

They had just finished the chemical analysis of the internal organs of the Vrzal girls. Conducting the work was Professor Walter S. Haines of Rush Medical College, who had a reputation for very accurate and deliberate work. Haines' expertise had been instrumental in the conviction of Johan Hoch a few years earlier. Professor Haines announced that in the cases of Ella, Mary, and fourteen-year-old Rosie Vrzal, he found enough arsenic to have caused their deaths. "The case in many respects is a complicated one—more complicated than the Hoch case," Haines explained. "The most poison was found in the liver and only traces in the stomach. This shows that the arsenic was not administered in large doses, but little by little, day by day."[32] There was now evidence of three murders. Plenty of questions remained, however, and three more bodies were yet to be examined. The last of them were exhumed, and Haines and his team went back to work.

December 26, 1906

The day after Christmas, Billik was moved to the Cook County Jail downtown. The jail and adjacent Criminal Courts Building occupied an entire block, and was bordered by Illinois St. Hubbard, Clark, and Dearborn. The jail was on the south side of Illinois St. directly behind the courthouse, which still stands at 54 W. Hubbard. There were two wings of the jail—the first was built in 1872 and another was added in 1895 to ease overcrowding. When Herman Billik arrived, the "old wing" still housed the gallows, where the county would hang those condemned to die. The massive scaffold had actually been modified in 1887 to accommodate the simultaneous execution of four of the Haymarket "rioters." *

---

* In that incident, commonly referred to as the "Haymarket Affair," eight policeman and at least four demonstrators were killed after a bomb was thrown in the middle of a labor protest in Chicago's Haymarket Square, where workers had gathered to demand the institution of an eight hour work day. Police rounded up leaders and organizers, and charged them with inciting the incident, though the actual bomber was never identified. The trial was somewhat of a farce but, in a frenzy of public fear, eight men were convicted. Four were executed, and another defendant committed suicide before he could be hanged. In 1893 Governor John Peter Altgeld, convinced of their innocence, effectively ended his own political career by pardoning the three surviving defendants.

Following the Haymarket incident, the Cook County gallows became the ultimate symbol of injustice to labor activists and opponents of capital punishment. Herman Billik was undoubtedly familiar with that recent history. And he must have been painfully aware that those same gallows, from which the Haymarket convicts and murderers such as Johan Hoch had hung, could also represent his ultimate fate.

Billik was placed in an eight-by-six-foot cell, much of which was taken up by a bed that hung from the side of the cell wall and supported a straw mattress. There was a small toilet and sink at the rear. It was dark, and air circulation was poor. The jail was plagued by appalling conditions and allegations of improprieties. It only held prisoners awaiting trial. Upon conviction, they were transferred to state prisons. The proximity of the courthouse facilitated taking inmates to and from court. There was actually a bridge connecting the two buildings so prisoners would never even need to be taken outside. Those who were sentenced to death would never leave the complex. They were held in the jail's "murderer's row" until their execution, which was carried out right inside the facility.

5

The Inquest Resumes

The Vrzal inquest resumed after the holidays in earnest. Josephine Riha had once worked at a downtown tailor shop with the late twenty-one-year-old Mary Vrzal. Josephine said that about two weeks before her death, Mary had shared a lunch with her, which she described as a kind of meatloaf. Riha became quite ill afterward and said she never really felt right since. She said Mary had told her that the dish had been prepared by Herman Billik. Riha also claimed that Mary said that when Mr. Vrzal was sick, the family had found powder sprinkled around the floor near his bed and Billik told them it was poison placed there by the rival milk dealer from across the street.

Vrzal family physician Dr. Charles Caldwell and his young assistant, Dr. Patrick Murphy, also told of their dealings with the family. Caldwell, who had been in practice for some thirty years, said he treated fourteen-year-old Rosie over the month of August 1906. He discovered that she was anemic and had a slight heart murmur. She also complained of a sore throat, which he diagnosed as tonsillitis. He told the family she wasn't in any immediate danger. A few days later, Rosie was dead. Caldwell said he was "very much surprised,"[33] and that the idea that he might have missed something had bothered him for weeks. He figured the heart murmur must have been worse than he thought, and declared the cause of her death to be myocarditis, an inflammation of the heart. He now noted that her symptoms were consistent with arsenic poisoning, and would appear if arsenic "was given for three or four weeks . . . in small quantities."[34]

In early October, just weeks after Rosie died, Caldwell was again called upon by the Vrzals. This time, it was for twelve-year-old Ella. He described watching a chubby, stout little girl slowly weaken and waste away over the course of the next two months, until she finally died on November 30th. He treated her more than a dozen times, both at the house on 19th St., and at 50th St. after they moved. The first time, he said, she seemed "full of vivacity and full of health,"[35] only complaining of a general weakness. He gave her some iron, and thought she would be fine. Within a month, she was too weak to even walk. When the family moved, in early November, Ella had to be carried in to their new home.

Caldwell said the girl displayed symptoms which both he and Murphy diagnosed as Addison's disease, an affliction of the adrenal glands: vomiting, severe weakness, anemia, diarrhea, difficulty swallowing, a gradual wasting of the body, and pain in the stomach area. In addition, Caldwell said, a little more than two weeks before Ella died he started noticing her skin gradually darkening all over her body. Caldwell noted that this "bronzing" of the skin is one of the most unique and visible symptoms of Addison's disease, but the symptoms are "almost identical"[36] to those of chronic arsenic poisoning. He considered that possibility at the time but, he explained, "The mother always seemed very apprehensive and anxious to do everything she could for [the children]. There was nothing to exact any suspicion at all, outside of the fact of the number of deaths that occurred."[37] Looking back, however, he said he had "very grave doubt"[38] about his original diagnosis. "The gradual feeding of arsenic will produce all the symptoms that she had,"[39] stated Caldwell.

Caldwell then ran through the events of the day Mrs. Vrzal died. He remembered Herman Billik coming to his office early that morning, at around eight-fifteen, saying that he had read in the newspaper about the deaths in the Vrzal family, and that he was suffering from similar ailments. Caldwell said that Kate Engelthaler (Rose Vrzal's cousin) came into the office at about the same time. She wanted Caldwell to come see Mrs. Vrzal, who was distraught over news reports that suggested she might be responsible for her husband and children's deaths. Caldwell said that Billik and Mrs. Engelthaler left together.

Dr. Caldwell went to see Mrs. Vrzal around noon. He said she was in bed crying. She seemed nervous, but otherwise was "perfectly healthy,"[40] with no fever or rise in pulse. He prescribed only a tonic, and left. He said he returned to his office, only to receive a call a little before two o'clock from one of the Vrzal's neighbors saying that Mrs. Vrzal was unconscious. He was busy, so he sent Dr. Murphy to check on her.

Murphy arrived at the residence at about two o'clock. Mrs. Engelthaler, Jerry, and the upstairs neighbor, Mrs. Dundel, were all there. Murphy described Rose's condition as comatose. She had a weak pulse and was vomiting. He pumped her stomach to cleanse her of any possible poison, but wasn't really sure what she had taken.

Caldwell got to the home himself around five o'clock. Mrs. Vrzal was still unconscious. He said he didn't see specific evidence of poison, but Dr. Murphy told him that he thought he smelled chloroform on her breath and had found a cork that appeared to be from some type of medicine bottle under her pillow. Caldwell said that Rose was throwing up coffee-colored black vomit, which indicated arsenic poisoning to him. He and Dr. Murphy decided she could have taken a combination of arsenic and chloroform. He recounted how she denied having taken any poison or poisoning the children, before quietly slipping away.[41]

Dr. Emanuel Napieralski, a physician from the Pilsen neighborhood, then described an incident that had occurred about five months earlier, near the end of July. He said he got a phone call at around 9 p.m. from a frantic woman telling him to go to the Vrzal house on 19th St. right away. When he arrived, he walked down the stairs from the sidewalk to the main entrance (which was below street level)* as a man hurried past him out the door. He said it was very dark, and he didn't get a look at the man's face. He described him only as "large."[42] Assistant Coroner Charles Barrett pointed to Billik, who was seated a few rows behind the doctor, and asked, "Was it this gentleman sitting right here, Mr. Billik?"[43] Napieralski looked at the big Bohemian, and said he could not say that it was; he only saw the back of the man.

Napieralski said he also saw "a young fellow"[44] leave from the side entrance of the house at the same time, but he didn't see any faces, and there was a lot of excitement as he arrived. He said when he walked inside it was "like the house was on fire, smothering."[45] He smelled gas, and found two girls half-conscious in a bed in the kitchen, with Mrs. Vrzal standing beside them. He noticed the gas jet in the room was still on about half way,† and yelled for Mrs. Vrzal to open the windows. She was slow to do anything, so he turned the gas off himself. He didn't see anyone in the house except for Mrs. Vrzal and the girls, and said Mrs. Vrzal was the only one he spoke to at all. He said she asked if she could wait until morning to get the medicine he prescribed, even though the drugstore was just across the street. Napieralski said he insisted that she go right away and the girls started recovering within about a half hour.

While Dr. Napieralski's story was intriguing, the star witness

---

* This illustrates the peculiar Chicago phenomenon of "vaulted sidewalks," which resulted from construction of the city's first underground sewer system. When it was determined that street levels were too low to dig sewers that would provide adequate drainage, Chicago's answer was to, quite literally, raise the city. Over the course of about 20 years, the street grade was raised between four and eight feet, along with adjacent buildings, which were raised one by one, by dozens of men turning jacks in unison. Some homeowners couldn't afford to raise their homes, and instead simply built staircases leading from the sidewalk down to the original first floor, or up to new entrances on the second floor. Vaulted sidewalks, with houses having their first floor below sidewalk level can still be seen throughout Pilsen and other older Chicago neighborhoods.

† While the city's streetlights were electrified by this time, only the wealthy actually had electricity in their homes. Most people still used illuminating gas for lighting.

turned out to be Herman Billik's son, Herman Billik, Jr. He identified himself as being sixteen years old, but was in reality only
thirteen.[46] He most likely lied because he didn't go to school,
and instead worked as a delivery boy for a clothiers at 18th and
Blue Island.* Apparently, no one questioned his claim. One wonders, though, whether police and prosecutors would have treated
a thirteen-year-old witness the same way they did a supposed
sixteen-year-old.

Herman Jr. had a round face like his father, with big blue eyes
and light brown hair. He spoke very softly. He sat directly across a
small wooden table from Coroner Hoffman, Inspector Shippy, and
Assistant Coroner Barrett. His father was seated directly behind
him, trying intently to follow his testimony. The first question was
whether or not he knew Dr. Napieralski. Herman Jr. said that he
did, but, when asked, Napieralski said he didn't recognize the youth.
Herman Jr. then went on to explain where he had seen the doctor
before. He said he had gone with his father to the Vrzal's house late
one evening and heard Mrs. Vrzal ask his father to turn on the gas.
When his father refused, Mrs. Vrzal turned on the gas jets in the
kitchen. He said the woman who lived upstairs, Mrs. Mary Lorenz,
came down for some milk at that time. She smelled gas and went
for a doctor. Herman Jr. said he and his father then left the house
from separate exits just as Dr. Napieralski was coming in the front
door. This explained the two figures Napieralski saw leaving when
he arrived.

Assistant Coroner Barrett was relentless in his questioning,
often rattling the young witness and getting conflicting answers.
The boy was clearly nervous. Shippy and Hoffman jumped in occasionally when he appeared to contradict himself. Shippy noted
that the child had told him before that he had heard his father tell
Mrs. Vrzal to turn on the gas. Now, he claimed his father remained
silent throughout the incident.

---

* llinois' Child Labor Law, enacted in 1903, was one of the first and most
stringent in the nation. It not only prohibited children under the age of 14 from
working, it also required them to attend school for a minimum number of days.

Billik and his attorney, Otto Kolar, leaned forward to listen. At one point something caught Billik's attention, and he spoke rapidly to Kolar in Bohemian. Hoffman wasn't pleased. "Gentleman, if you want to carry on a conversation you'll have to go back further,"[47] he scolded. He was not only annoyed, but also afraid they might influence the testimony. "I don't want the witness hampered in any shape. He is only a boy."[48]

"I think that ought to apply to everybody,"[49] Kolar retorted.

"It does. You may sit there, but I don't want you to intimidate him, to say the least," warned Hoffman.[50] His admonishment was a bit ironic, in that the three men conducting the questioning (including Hoffman himself) were all extremely large and imposing men who were obviously causing the child anxiety. Herman Jr. wasn't exactly helping his father's case. He said they had traveled to San Francisco twice in the last few years, and that he remembered looking up Mrs. Standish York on one of the trips. He said his father told him that she was rich and they could probably get some money from her. Shippy was sure Billik was involved in Mr. York's death, and took note of the statement.

Herman Jr. said his father occasionally asked him to run errands, and that he had delivered many messages to Mrs. Vrzal, all requests for money. Hoffman showed him several notes and a telegram, in which the elder Billik repeatedly told Mrs. Vrzal that he needed more money to complete his "work." Herman Jr. said that the "work" was a plan between his father and Mrs. Vrzal to "kill grandmother"[51] (Herman Sr.'s mother Barbara, who lived in Cleveland). Mrs. Vrzal was to be repaid the money that Billik owed her from his mother's supposedly large estate. Herman Jr. said he heard Mrs. Vrzal ask his father to kill the woman on numerous occasions, and that she always wanted to know when the "work" would be done. Billik would always tell her it would be finished "soon," but Herman Jr. said his father had told him privately that he didn't really plan on carrying it out.

As part of the ruse, Billik had letters professionally typed, sometimes dated from other cities, such as Saratoga or Cleveland, telling Mrs. Vrzal that he was finishing "the work." Sometimes he really was in those places, but much of the time he was hiding out from her in his apartment on Blue Island Ave. Herman Jr. described the elaborate stories his father made up to continue getting money from Mrs. Vrzal. He told her that he had left his wife, and even once pretended that his mother had actually died. That prompted Mrs. Vrzal and Emma to go to Cleveland to collect their money. They arrived, only to find the "dead" woman very much alive, and living in apparent poverty.

Herman Jr. said that on the day that Mrs. Vrzal died, he came home from work for lunch around eleven-thirty. His parents were both home. His father wanted his mother to pretend that they had separated, and to tell Jerry Vrzal that they were no longer living together. His mother refused, and the two argued. Herman Jr. said his father then threatened to kill himself. Mrs. Billik eventually gave in and agreed to talk to Jerry, who was standing on the corner near their house. She acted like she was going to the store for a loaf of bread, and when she saw Jerry she told him that she didn't know where her husband was. She even asked him, "Have you seen Herman?"[52] A little while later, at about three o'clock, Herman Jr. and his father went to visit Mrs. Vrzal. When they got there she was unconscious, and they didn't stay long. Herman Jr. said Jerry told them his mother had taken chloroform and that he had thrown the bottle into the stove. Barrett suggested the boy was confusing things, but Herman Jr. repeated himself: "Yes, Jerry threw the bottle into the stove."[53]

Barrett more or less insisted that he had things mixed up. "Isn't that what your father told Jerry to say?"[54] asked the burly attorney. But young Herman wouldn't change his answer. "No sir, Jerry told my father not to say [anything about Jerry throwing the bottle into the stove] because there would be more trouble."[55] Barrett didn't pursue it any further. Instead, he asked about claims that Billik told people not to tell police or doctors that he had been to the Vrzal's house that day. Herman Jr. acknowledged that his father told Jerry not to tell the doctors he was there, but claimed he didn't say anything about the police. That same evening, he said, his father asked him to get a fifty-dollar bill changed, and then took him out for a steak dinner. Later the whole family went to the theater, though Billik was so nervous and sick he had to step outside for a short time.

Some of Herman Jr.'s most interesting stories were about his father working magic spells, or "charms" as he referred to them, using mysterious potions and a "magic box." He described how his father would take various powders, roots, and herbs, place them inside the box, then mix them with water. To make the spell work, someone would have to spill out the contents along the sidewalk, or on the target's property. Herman Jr. often assisted in that regard. He said his father was once hired by the Vrzals to work a charm against the rival milk dealer across the street, Frank Dunovsky. Billik's magic was supposed to spoil his business, and bring his customers across the street to the Vrzals. Billik bought some milk from Dunovsky, then mixed it with bloodroot and put it into the "magic box." He told Jerry to spill it out at night around Dunovsky's depot. Business soon picked up for the Vrzals, helping to convince them of Billik's powers.

Another time, Herman Jr. said, his father took him and Jerry Vrzal on the train out to the western suburb of Downers Grove to work a charm on a man named William Niemann, whose family owned a dairy farm that the Vrzals purchased milk from. The Vrzals hired Billik to "charm" Niemann into marrying Emma. Herman Jr. said they got off the train and walked down the block. His father had him sprinkle some sort of potion across the road, then they headed back to the train and returned to Chicago. Again the magic seemed to work; William Niemann did eventually marry Emma Vrzal.

Herman Jr. said he brought medicine to the Vrzal's house on two occasions before Martin died. Barrett kept insisting that he carried the medicine in the "magic box," but Herman Jr. said it was in bottles, about the size of a beer bottle. He denied ever bringing medicine to anyone any other time.

When Barrett was finished with his questions, Hoffman gave Billik's attorney a chance to clear up what it was that had upset his client during the testimony. "What was that question you wanted asked?"[56] Hoffman offered.

Kolar addressed Herman Jr. "So far as that gas episode is

concerned . . . I asked you about that after you had talked with Inspector Shippy . . . isn't that so Herman?"[57]

"Yes, sir,"[58] responded the boy, a bit sheepishly.

"You told me at that time you didn't know anything about this, didn't you? You told me this forenoon you didn't know anything about this gas episode . . ."[59]

Hoffman cut in before the boy could answer. "You put that question to me that you are going to ask,"[60] he ordered sternly.

The young attorney tried to put the question as succinctly as possible: "Ask him . . . if he didn't tell me he didn't know anything about this [gas] affair . . ."[61]

Hoffman apparently didn't like the question. "Did Mr. Kolar ask you to tell the truth?"[62] he asked Herman Jr.

"Yes, sir."

"And you have told nothing here but the truth?"

"Yes, sir."

"That is all."[63] Hoffman then excused the witness.

Herman Billik Jr. (back to camera) being questioned by Coroner Hoffman and Asst. Coroner Barrett at the coroner's inquest. Herman Billik Sr. on far left. *Photo courtesy of the Chicago History Museum, DN-0004581.*

6

Intent to Kill

The next morning, Rose's cousin, Kate Engelthaler, testified. She and her husband owned the house where Rose had moved with the children a month before she died. It was several miles south of Pilsen, on 50th St., just a few blocks from the mammoth Union Stockyards, where most all of the nation's meat supply was butchered and processed.[64] A foul smell permeated the air throughout the neighborhood, which was unbearably crowded, housing the majority of the 25,000 (mostly immigrant) workers who staffed "the yards" including Mr. Engelthaler and the couple's two sons. The area was also home to several disease-infested garbage dumps, and one fork of the Chicago River that was used by packing companies as an open air sewer known to this day as "Bubbly Creek" for the gases that rise up from the mountain of decaying animal matter at its bottom.*

Mrs. Engelthaler said that she had gone to Dr. Caldwell's office the morning Rose took ill to ask him to come check on her. There, she ran into Billik. She said she had never met him before, but

---

* The deplorable conditions for both workers and residents around the yards had just come to light in 1906 with the publication of Upton Sinclair's exposé *The Jungle*, in which he portrayed the exploitation of workers as well as the corruption among officials that created the appalling situation.

chatted with him while waiting to see the doctor. She mentioned her cousin, and it became apparent that Billik also knew her. After they saw the doctor, Billik accompanied her on the streetcar back to the house. When they arrived at about nine o'clock, Jerry was home, and Kate decided to run a few errands back on the West Side in Pilsen. One happened to be right across the street from where Herman Jr. worked, so Billik asked her if she could stop there and ask for Herman Jr. to come join him. It was right on her way, so she agreed and headed for 18th and Blue Island. She said that when she got to that corner, she saw Jerry standing there. Asst. Coroner Barrett had to ask her to repeat herself to make sure there wasn't a miscommunication. She realized it was strange, and said, "Yes, I left home and left Jerry home and when I got on the West Side Jerry was there too . . . [I said] 'What you doing here?'"[65] They didn't have much conversation, but she said Jerry told her *he* was going to get Herman Jr., and that Mr. Billik was also nearby.

Mrs. Engelthaler went about finishing her errands. When she returned home at about two-thirty or three o'clock, there was a commotion at the house. Doctors and neighbors came and went. Mrs. Dundel told Mrs. Engelthaler that she had gone to the drug-store to get the prescription from Dr. Caldwell filled, and when she came back she had found Rose unconscious. Engelthaler said Jerry told her that "maybe" his mother had taken poison; she had fallen asleep and he couldn't wake her.[66] She said Billik came by with Herman Jr. later that afternoon, around four o'clock. They saw Mrs. Vrzal was unconscious, and left. Barrett asked Mrs. Engelthaler if Rose ever spoke to her about having insurance on the children. "She said that insurance don't cover for the funeral and for the sickness," replied Engelthaler.[67]

Engelthaler's son Albert spoke next. He worked as an errand boy at the stockyards, and left the house early in the morning. He said that on the day Mrs. Vrzal died, he came home at about ten o'clock for lunch and saw Billik sitting alongside her bed talking with her. He said Jerry was also in the room for most of the time, but stepped out for about fifteen minutes, leaving Rose and Billik alone. Albert said Jerry and Billik left together around ten-thirty.

When Albert left to go back to work at about one o'clock, Mrs. Dundel was caring for Rose. Mrs. Dundel was with her most of that day and into the night, and must have known quite a bit about the critical time period in which Rose swallowed poison. Unfortunately, and inexplicably, she was not called at the inquest.

Later, the jury heard from a young man named Benjamin Parkison, Billik's nephew. He was twenty-one years old, the adopted son of Billik's step-sister* Elsa and her husband, the aforementioned Dr. Emil Schmidt. They lived in Cleveland, but Parkison had been staying with the Billiks in Chicago for the past five months. He said that on the day Mrs. Vrzal died, Herman Billik was so upset that he threatened to kill himself. Parkison had also heard of the proposed plot in which Billik was to kill his own mother. He said that Mrs. Billik told him that Emma Vrzal had told Herman to get rid of both his wife and mother by poisoning them, but that Billik refused. Parkison said Billik told him, "[Emma] must be a darned fool"[68] to make such a suggestion.

Jerry Vrzal had already testified, but was called again. He answered rapid-fire questions from Assistant Coroner Barrett. This time, Jerry said Billik had taken the Vrzals' entire savings. He figured it could have been as much as $7,000. He said that Billik claimed that his mother in Cleveland had property and a huge life insurance policy, and that when she died he would inherit a fortune and pay the Vrzals back. But it didn't sound like they were willing to wait for her to die a natural death. Jerry said he frequently heard his mother and Billik discussing "the job" that Billik was supposed to finish, and that Billik repeatedly asked her for more money so he could complete it. Jerry, like the other boys, claimed the "job" was for Billik to kill his own mother.

---

* Elsa is variously referred to as Billik's step-sister or his half-sister. Shippy stated at the Inquest that she was actually his step-aunt. Whatever the biological relationship, they were raised together, and considered one another brother and sister.

Jerry described traveling with Billik and Herman Jr. to Cleveland and Niagara Falls, sleeping in private rail cars and fancy hotels along the way, all on Mrs. Vrzal's money. The purpose of the trips wasn't clear, but usually revolved around spells and magic. Jerry said that after he complained about Billik's frequent requests for money, his mother sent him to Cleveland, where he stayed with Billik's family for several months. There, Billik's brother-in-law, Dr. Schmidt, treated him with some kind of unknown medicine. Jerry said his sister Rosie was also sent to Cleveland and treated by Dr. Schmidt. She returned complaining of stomach pains and a dry throat and mouth, and died a few months later. Jerry said Billik had given medicine to other family members, and several died not long afterward. When asked about his mother's death, Jerry said that Billik had made every effort to be alone with his mother the morning she swallowed poison. Shippy, who had seen his share of bizarre cases, called it "one of the most weird and remarkable stories ever told in a Chicago courtroom."[69]

Hoffman, however, saved the most important evidence for last: statements from the doctors who conducted the autopsies, beginning with that of Professor Haines. He read aloud: "This is to certify that I have examined the bodies of Ella, Ros[ie], and Mary Vrzal. They all contain arsenic in poisonous quantities and sufficient to indicate that it was the cause of death."[70] He followed that with statements verifying that no arsenic was used in the embalming process.

Hoffman asked the jury if they had heard enough to determine the causes of death for the three girls. They met for just a few minutes, then told the coroner that they were ready. For Mary, Rosie, and Ella Vrzal, the verdicts were the same: "[Each girl] came to her death . . . from arsenical poisoning." They further declared, "[S]aid arsenic was administered to said deceased directly or indirectly by one Herman Billik . . . with intent to kill."[71]

"The case will be turned over to State's Attorney Healy immediately,"[72] announced Hoffman. Mary Billik was freed, and the inquest continued, to await the autopsy results on Martin, Rose, and their daughter Tillie.

Over the following days, the gravity of the situation started to sink in. Billik became visibly nervous in sharp contrast to his stoic demeanor of the previous weeks. He started talking more openly with police, conceding more and more elements of their allegations, but Billik would always stop just short of a confession to murder. He acknowledged getting medicine from Dr. Schmidt. He said his nephew, Ben Parkison, mailed it to him from Cleveland; but as far as he knew, it really was some kind of medicine. If not, Billik claimed, Dr. Schmidt was the one who should be investigated, not him.

Billik also admitted to obtaining money from the widow of Standish York in Cleveland, but denied knowing anything about Mr. York's death. Then, police were stunned when Billik told them he had accepted money numerous times to provide people with poison. "In all my clairvoyance and witchcraft," he explained, "I was often called upon by men and women, mostly women, who wanted me to poison relatives. I often agreed to furnish them poison for a consideration."[73] But he claimed that he never really gave them any. "I would agree to anything for a sufficient price," he said, "but carrying out that agreement was a different thing. The worst I ever gave any of my poison-seeking clients was whiskey and saltpeter. They thought they were getting poison and paid well for it. I got the money and that's all I cared for."[74] Shippy sensed they were getting closer, but it still wasn't quite the complete confession he was looking for.

7

Professor Haines

JANUARY 1907

A full month after the inquest was convened, tests on Rose Vrzal's body still had not concluded. But Professor Haines was quite busy. The white-haired chemist had to analyze not only the internal organs of a half-dozen human bodies, but also pickled mushrooms, dead chickens, and who knows what else. And that was just from the Vrzal case—his lab was also trying desperately to keep up with a so-called "epidemic of wife murders"[75] in Chicago. Police records indicated that nineteen men were being held on charges of murdering their wives, and there was a long backlog in the court system, which State's Attorney Healy was struggling to remedy.*

As Healy and his staff prepared the evidence against Billik for the grand jury, one of the alleged wife-murderers, South Side contractor Knute Knudson, was brought before the court. Johanna Knudson had been diagnosed with gastritis when she died, but her

---

* Contrary to some sensational accounts, a person in Chicago was actually much less likely to be the victim of a homicide in the early 1900s than today. There were 145 murders reported in Chicago in 1906, and 144 in 1907 (*Chicago Police Department Homicide Record Index*). That comes to about 8.5 murders per 100,000 residents. In 2008 there were 513 murders (*Chicago Police Department Annual Report 2009*), or 17.7 per 100,000 people; and in the peak year of 1992 there were 943 (*Chicago Police Department Biennial Report 1999-2000*), roughly 34 homicides per 100,000 people.

sister went to police repeatedly, saying she suspected poisoning. Authorities eventually exhumed Mrs. Knudson's body and charged her husband with murder.

Assistant State's Attorney James Barbour admitted the evidence was scant. Because the undertaker used embalming fluid containing arsenic, when the coroner found a large amount of the poison in Mrs. Knudson's stomach it proved nothing. Prosecutors decried Knute Knudson as a cold-blooded killer, but the absence of scientific evidence bothered them. In questioning prospective jurors, they found that the overwhelming majority said they could not recommend the death penalty in a case based solely on circumstantial evidence.[76]

Prosecutors elicited testimony from doctors who compared Mrs. Knudson's symptoms, which included stomach pains and numbness, to the symptoms of arsenic poisoning; however, the bulk of their case relied upon the testimony of in-laws, acquaintances, and neighbors, who portrayed Mr. Knudson as an unfaithful, uncaring husband, and a disreputable man. Unfortunately for prosecutors, none of that proved that his wife had been poisoned. In rebuttal, Knudson had scores of people testify on his behalf, saying that he was a good husband and father, and an honest, hard-working man. The climax of the trial came with the testimony of Knudson's children.

Spectators stood in the aisles for a chance to see eleven-year-old Gustav and ten-year-old Annie Knudson testify. Annie instantly charmed the large audience as she took her place on the witness stand. She answered the attorneys' questions slowly and deliberately, carefully considering each one. She described her father as a loving family man, who did the best he could to care for his ailing wife. When she was finished nearly an hour later, Annie ran up to her father, threw her arms around him and kissed him. "Come, come little girl. You mustn't do that,"[77] scolded the judge, trying to conceal a slight smile. Later, when court was adjourned for the day, the children jumped into their father's arms and kissed him over and over, as the judge tried in vain to clear the courtroom.

The trial concluded on January 18th. After only eight hours of deliberation, the jury returned with their verdict. As soon as the words "not guilty" were uttered, the courtroom broke into cheers. The judge slammed his gavel to try to restore order, to little avail. The first person to congratulate Mr. Knudson was the prosecutor, James Barbour, who reached out and offered his hand, telling him, "I'm glad for you and your children."[78] Young Gustav had a few words about Barbour, who had prosecuted his father mercilessly, but then congratulated him on the verdict. "He's a funny man to treat my papa so," the puzzled youngster said. "I wouldn't shake hands with him."[79]

While awaiting her father's return home, Annie Knudson went through a large bundle of letters sent to her during the trial. Most were similar, expressing confidence in her father's innocence, and offering prayers and encouragement. One of them was in a child's hand, with the return address, "613 Blue Island Avenue."* It read:

> I read about you every day. I am sorry for you. I hope that they will free your papa for your sake. My papa is where your papa is now. I hope they will free him because I love him dearly. I am only 9 years old and I know he is innocent. I am yours in sympathy.—Edna Billik[80]

It was from Herman Billik's young daughter. Another letter was from Vera Jones, of South Green St. She was the temporary guardian of the surviving Vrzal children, Jerry and Bertha. She told Annie that she believed in Mr. Knudson's innocence. But she also included pictures of the Vrzal children, and wrote that she hoped "the law will give Billik what is owing to him."[81] It seemed like a peculiar thing to say to a 10-year-old girl, but Mrs. Jones was really addressing a much larger audience. Both she and the Billik family wanted to have public sympathy on their side. It would set the tone for the events which were to follow.

Both the Knudson and Vrzal cases were cited that month when the Illinois State Legislature banned the use of arsenic in

---

* Pre-1910 address

embalming fluids.[82] Lawmakers also referred to the already infamous case of Johan Hoch. It was believed that Hoch concealed many of his murders because once his victims were embalmed it was impossible to prove they had been poisoned. It was even surmised that he used embalming fluid with a high arsenic content to kill some of them, perfectly masking his deeds. He was only convicted after his latest deceased wife, Marie Walcker-Hoch, was buried by undertakers in Chicago who used a new type of embalming fluid: one that contained no arsenic. When Professor Haines found the poison in her body, it proved that she had been murdered. Publicity of the Hoch case led many undertakers, including those of the Vrzal family, to switch to arsenic-free compounds. If they hadn't, the Vrzal murders might have never been discovered.

Prosecutors had been uneasy about their lack of evidence in the Knudson trial, and felt like they ended up looking a little foolish. They didn't want that to happen with Billik. Professor Haines was ill during most of January, and unable to work on the Vrzal case, but State's Attorney Healy and Coroner Hoffman insisted on waiting for him, rather than having another doctor do it. His expertise and reputation were unmatched.

Dr. Walter Stanley Haines had been a professor of chemistry and toxicology in medical schools for almost thirty-five years. His father was John C. Haines, one-time Mayor of Chicago. Dr. Haines was one of the most knowledgeable and respected people in the medical community. But he wasn't just a local expert. He was considered one of the leading toxicologists in the entire country, if not the world. He was also said to be one of the most honest and likable people you could ever meet. All of this, combined with his natural ability as a public speaker, made him a tremendous asset to any investigation.

February 7-18, 1907

Haines was back on his feet by the end of January. He finished his work and released his findings in the early part of February. According to Haines, there was enough arsenic in Martin Vrzal's internal organs to have killed him. Doctors also discovered arsenic in the ashes and dead chicken—a bit of a surprise to those who had assumed Mrs. Vrzal died from chloroform poisoning. Haines formally declared that Rose Vrzal also died from chronic arsenic poisoning. Coroner Hoffman expounded on the findings in a statement to the press: "The fact that Mrs. Vrzal's liver was saturated with arsenic shows that her illness was not sudden. It shows that she had been fed that poison steadily for some time previous to her death and we will be able to show that Billik was a constant visitor at her house."[83]

A few days later, Haines presented his sixth and final report to the coroner. Tillie Vrzal was 18 when she died just before Christmas in 1905. She, like her parents and three sisters, had been poisoned with arsenic. While Haines found only "traces"[84] in her internal organs, there was reportedly more than enough in Tillie's stomach to have caused her death.[85]

February 21-26, 1907

The coroner's inquest concluded on February 21st, 1907. There were no more witnesses called. Billik didn't speak, though Hoffman gave him a chance. "We have no defense to make at this time, Mr. Coroner,"[86] said Billik's attorney, Otto Kolar. Maybe he thought the verdict was a foregone conclusion, but earlier promises to present evidence that would clear his client never materialized.

It had been more than ten weeks since the inquest began. Thankfully for the jury, they only met once or twice a week and, unlike a criminal jury hearing a murder case, they were not sequestered. Coroner's jurors not only went home, they undoubtedly read newspaper accounts and, in the case of the Vrzal inquest, heard much discussion about the case while outside of the jury box. There was no television nor even radio in 1907. Chicago was, however, blessed with a wide variety of newspapers. They were published at varying times throughout the day and week, and catered to every taste, and virtually every language, imaginable. Reading and discussing the papers' reports of the day's events was the chief source of news and entertainment at the time; and the press, like most of Chicago, was already uniform in condemning the Bohemian magic man as a brutal killer.

The jury reviewed the autopsy reports and, just as with the three girls before, declared that Martin Vrzal, his wife Rose, and their daughter Tillie had all died of arsenic poisoning administered "directly or indirectly by one Herman Billik."[87] Five days later, a grand jury indicted Billik on six counts of murder.

The Vrzal home on 19th St., and Herman and Mary Billik, as portrayed by *The Sunday Record - Herald, Chicago,* July 28, 1907.

8

Shippy's On the Case

During the month of March 1907 Chicagoans focused on the upcoming election. In a city known for its love of sports, politics was the greatest game of all. Mayor Dunne, a Democrat, was being challenged by Republican Fred Busse, the local postmaster and former State Treasurer. Both tried to style themselves as "reformers," but in reality they were quite different. Dunne was concerned with social issues, such as better working conditions and public ownership of transportation and utilities. He had appointed such notables as social reformer Jane Addams to the school board, and Clarence Darrow as special traction counsel. Busse, on the other hand, was backed by Chicago's powerful business interests.

The city was divided into thirty-five Wards, each represented in the City Council by two Aldermen. Every Ward had its own political organizations, headed by unofficial "bosses" who doled out favors, including jobs, services, and municipal contracts, in exchange for votes and contributions (often blatant bribes). Busse was a political boss from the North Side. He did his talking behind the scenes with the other Ward bosses, both Republican and Democrat. That was the strength of his very low-profile campaign. One might say he ran a "no-profile" campaign. Shortly after announcing his candidacy, he received minor injuries in a train accident which, he claimed, prevented him from campaigning. He made virtually no appearances or speeches. It proved to be the perfect strategy for a rather uninspiring candidate. On April 2nd, 1907, Fred Busse was elected Mayor of Chicago, garnering 49% of the vote to Dunne's 45%.

One of the prominent issues of the campaign had been the city's beleaguered transportation system, which consisted of numerous electric streetcar and elevated train lines, all of which were privately owned. They provided an inefficient, often confusing system, with an absence of any coordination among schedules and stops. Each line had its own fares and tickets. Dunne's failure to gain public ownership of the system was but one of several legislative failures he suffered. Because he wasn't a part of the city's regular polit-ical organizations, he was unable to influence city council mem-bers from either party to side with him on important votes.[88] The council was notoriously corrupt, and wanted no part of Dunne's attempts at reform. One alderman himself famously declared that, among its 70 members, there were perhaps three not "able and willing to steal a red-hot stove."[89] Former Mayor Carter Harrison II described the body as "a low-browed, dull-witted, base-minded gang of plug-uglies with no outstanding characteristic beyond an unquenchable lust for money."[90]

While Dunne's failure to resolve the traction issue was often cited as the reason for his loss, he probably lost more votes when he took on saloon businesses by drastically raising their license fees. The final straw, by Dunne's own account, was his refusal to cut a last-minute deal with leaders from the city's vice districts, who wanted police to ease up on them.[91] They were themselves Democrats, but backed anyone willing to protect their interests. When Dunne refused, they turned on him, giving the win to Busse, who favored a "wide-open town,"[92] meaning lax enforcement of the city's alcohol and prostitution regulations.

Busse's victory solidified power into the hands of a single coali-tion of Cook County Republicans. Busse had joined forces with South Side boss Charles Deneen (the former Cook County State's Attorney, who was now Governor of Illinois) to take control of local Republican politics. Cook County State's Attorney Healy

and Coroner Hoffman had both gained office with the sponsor-
ship of Busse and Deneen. Soon another figure from the Billik case
would join their ranks. Upon becoming Mayor, Busse promptly
fired the Chief of Police and replaced him with a Republican, none
other than Inspector George M. Shippy. He was sworn in on April
15th, 1907.

May-June 1907

As Billik sat in his cell awaiting trial, prosecutors reviewed the
assortment of related investigations that had been opened. The
"poisoned" mushrooms brought in by Barbara Herr turned out
to contain nothing more sinister than vinegar. And, just as the
mushrooms had not been poisoned, neither were Simon nor Emilia
Kubera. They both appeared to have died from natural causes.
Billik may have taken their money, but not their lives. Shippy's men
traveled to central Indiana and located the mother of Mary Tonek,
who had died so suddenly years earlier. She said that her daughter
had been engaged to a dentist named Joseph "Bilek" at the time of
her death, and that the man bore no resemblance to the accused,
aside from a similar-sounding name.

In Cleveland, no evidence against Dr. Emil Schmidt on counts of
poisoning emerged. And the investigation into the death of Standish
York seemed to be at a dead end as well: Mrs. York's sister refused
to talk to anyone. Cleveland's coroner didn't see any evidence to
pursue the matter any further, and closed the books on the death
of Standish York—again. Additionally, Shippy learned that Billik's
mother-in-law, Mary Cermak, had also died of natural causes.

In addition to the various law enforcement agencies from Illinois
and Ohio, there was yet another group of investigators looking
into Herman Billik. Detectives from the Metropolitan Life Insurance Company had begun their own inquiry back in December,
when they stopped payment on the check for Ella Vrzal's life insurance policy. Operating under the theory that Billik might have had

a history of defrauding insurance companies, they looked for evidence of his involvement in previous claims. They found nothing. The trail of victims Shippy once anticipated did not seem to be materializing.

Billik had a new team of court-appointed lawyers for his trial.* The leaders of the team were: Ross Wade Davis, a lanky thirty-two-year-old from Hopkinsville, Kentucky, and Francis E. Hinckley, who was only twenty-four, and didn't look a day older. Hinckley was short, wore glasses, and parted his hair to the side. Though he still looked like a student, he had graduated from Cornell University and Northwestern University Law School. That part of his resume was quite impressive. But he had little courtroom experience. It's doubtful that he or Davis had ever handled a case even remotely as serious or complicated as this. Surely neither had ever defended someone charged with a half-dozen murders. They compensated for their lack of experience at least somewhat, though, with their earnestness and exuberance.

They knew they faced an uphill battle, but Billik was adamant about his innocence. The lab reports established fairly well that all the victims died of arsenic poisoning, most of them *slowly*, over a period of weeks. Normally, only an immediate family member would be able to poison someone repeatedly, perhaps regularly, so it seemed to suggest that Billik was an unlikely suspect; but prosecutors believed that he had conspired with Mrs. Vrzal. The letters he had from her hinted at this. Billik admitted that the letters were genuine, but they talked about poisoning Barbara Billik, Herman's mother. Billik said it was all part of his scheme to keep getting money from the Vrzals, who believed he would pay them

---

* It's not clear why the change was made. It was most likely simply a routine matter within the public defender's office, though it is possible that Billik's first attorney asked to be removed from the case (as he was a political hopeful himself and may have been afraid of negative publicity for defending Billik). It's also possible Billik requested the change, but there is no evidence to suggest that.

back from money he would inherit when his mother died. He said he never really intended to kill anyone.

Hinckley and Davis asked about the alleged attempt to kill the Vrzal girls by turning on the gas in their house. Billik said he knew absolutely nothing about it, and that he wasn't even in town when it was supposed to have happened. Hinckley pointed out that Billik's own son was the main witness against him in that incident. Billik said that the boy lied. Herman Jr. had even told Billik's previous attorney, Otto Kolar, that he had made the whole thing up, but Kolar hadn't been able to convey that at the inquest.

Hinckley read through the statement Herman Jr. had given the police, and his testimony from the inquest. It didn't take him long to realize there was something wrong with the story. The boy had stated repeatedly that he and his father left right after Mrs. Vrzal turned on the gas, and that his father bumped into Dr. Napieralski on the way out. That meant that in the time it took Billik to walk from the kitchen to the front door, the house filled with gas, the neighbor, Mrs. Lorenz, noticed it, went to the drugstore across the street and called for a doctor, and the doctor walked several blocks to the Vrzal's house, arriving just in time to pass Billik on his way out the door. Dr. Napieralski himself said it took him ten minutes to get there just from the time Mrs. Lorenz called him on the telephone. No one at the inquest had questioned the time frame, though it was obviously beyond logic.

Herman Jr. also said Mrs. Lorenz came down just as Mrs. Vrzal was turning on the gas. Yet the house was apparently already so filled that Ella was overcome, and Mrs. Lorenz felt it necessary to go for a doctor. Mrs. Lorenz told police she never saw Billik or his son that night, but according to Herman Jr., she walked right past them and even stood in the same room with them. Since Dr. Napieralski wasn't able to identify Billik, prosecutors needed someone to place him at the scene, or they couldn't use the story as evidence against him. Herman Jr.'s testimony not only placed Billik at the scene, but also explained who the unidentified "young fellow" was that the doctor saw leave from the side door that night. But Herman Jr. had seemed uncertain of even the most basic details, prefacing many of his answers by saying, "I guess."[93] He had no idea how long ago the incident occurred, and was not even sure how many girls were involved. Dr. Napieralski reported treating two girls, but Herman Jr. initially mentioned only Ella.[94] He never said anything about a second girl until Asst. Coroner Barrett followed up a statement the boy made about Ella by repeatedly using the term "girls" in the plural. It was only after that, that Herman Jr. also started referring to "girls," instead of just Ella.[95]

Why, though, would he give false testimony against his own father? Herman Jr. said that Inspector Shippy threatened him: that Shippy told him that people had seen him at the house that night, and if he didn't admit it he would be locked up. The child, whose parents were both being held in police custody at the time, said he was terrified of being arrested if he didn't tell Shippy something. He thought if he said that Mrs. Vrzal turned on the gas, his father wouldn't be in any trouble. Now, police were threatening to charge him with perjury if he changed his story. Hinckley convinced him to go to the state's attorney's office anyway. Assistant State's Attorney George M. Popham, a heavy-set former defense attorney, had been assigned to prosecute Billik. He took a statement from Herman Jr. on May 13th, 1907. When asked if any police officers had threatened him, the youngster replied, "Shippy did about a week before I was examined. He told me that I should tell him all about the gas. If I didn't he would lock me up, put me downstairs."[96] He was referring to the lock-up in the basement of the Hyde Park Station, where suspects were often detained for lengthy interrogations, or "sweated," as police called it. Herman Jr. said he had told Shippy that he had no idea what he was talking about, but the Inspector was insistent.

"Shippy got me excited and scared . . . he told me certain people saw me there."

"But you were seen there. Jerry saw you there."[97] said the portly prosecutor, unconvinced.

"Oh, I was not there . . . I am going to swear in court that I was not there the night the gas was turned on and I don't know anything about that."[98] He said he had never seen Dr. Napieralski before the inquest, and never even heard about the incident until Shippy talked to him about it.

Popham tried to trip him up one last time. "Suppose those other people did see you there, Napieralski, and Jerry?"

"I know I was not there and I will still swear to it,"[99] he said confidently.

Popham could see he was getting nowhere, and ended the interview. He was satisfied that he could still prove his case with the remaining witnesses, whom he was now prepping for the rapidly approaching trial.

Part II

The
Prosecution

9

The Tribunal

When the case was called, defense attorneys said they would admit that the Vrzals had been poisoned, but not by Herman Billik. Hinckley said they would prove that the crimes were committed by someone else. It started a buzz in the courtroom. When prodded to explain, Hinckley would only say that they would reveal the person's identity during the trial.

Judge Albert C. Barnes would preside. He had only been on the bench for two years but already had a reputation as a no-nonsense type of judge, mainly resulting from his eight years as a prosecutor. He too was closely tied to the Deneen political faction. When Deneen was elected Cook County State's Attorney in 1896, he hired Barnes as a prosecutor, and eventually appointed him First Assistant State's Attorney. When Deneen ran for governor in 1904, he had Barnes slated as a candidate for judge. Republicans then had to decide who should succeed Deneen as State's Attorney. It was the only office in dispute at the Republican caucus. After much debate they were deadlocked. Eventually, a committee consisting of Deneen, Busse, and two other Republican bosses chose John J. Healy.[100] They selected Peter Hoffman to run for Coroner. Barnes, along with Healy, Hoffman, and Deneen, won handily in an election year dominated by Republicans. All four would play prominent roles in the Vrzal murder case.

June 28-July 2, 1907

On Friday, June 28th, 1907, Herman Billik appeared in the Criminal Courts Building to answer to six counts of murder. Though it was supposed to be a day of formalities, the courtroom was packed. Everyone was eager for a glimpse of the big Bohemian "sorcerer" accused of bewitching and murdering almost an entire family. Prosecutors asked that each charge be heard separately. Since each murder carried a potential death sentence, Billik would have to win six trials, or die on the gallows. Ross Davis made a motion to grant his client an immediate trial on all six counts, arguing that the evidence for each case was virtually the same. Assistant State's Attorney Popham argued that it was physically impossible for a defendant to be in six courtrooms simultaneously, apparently ignoring the possibility of hearing all of the charges together in one trial. Judge Barnes sided with prosecutors. He ordered the trial to begin—*only* for the murder of Mary Vrzal. The other five counts would be heard at an unspecified date. It was a major victory for the prosecution.

As expected, Billik requested a jury trial, and the long and tedious selection process began. Judge Barnes had already gone on record with his opinion of defendants who requested jury trials (which of course is their constitutional right): A few months earlier, while giving an address at a banquet of the Industrial Club of Chicago, Barnes pronounced, "Lawyers who have got a good case are always willing to submit it to a judge, and lawyers who have got a weak one want to leave it to a jury. They want to have a chance with men who may be bamboozled, who may not understand some point, who are not qualified to judge . . ."[101] Barnes may have already made up his mind about the case, but Billik hoped he could find twelve men who had not.

Jury selection took up the next few days. Numerous men told Barnes they were sick and couldn't serve as jurors. After the fourth or fifth man was excused due to illness, observers started whispering.

Billik must have worked a spell on them. Was there a curse? Some spectators even claimed that the men who were ill had all gazed directly into the eyes of the mysterious hypnotist. Billik's attorneys, and even Assistant State's Attorney Popham, scoffed at the suggestions. People had been feigning sickness to avoid jury duty for many years before this trial. More fuel was added to the fire, though, when a man who had already been chosen for the jury appeared to have some sort of trouble in the jury box. He swayed, staggered, and had difficulty standing. Barnes held a brief conference with the attorneys, as observers in the courtroom tried to contain more speculation. After a discussion, attorneys agreed that they knew what the problem was, and it wasn't Billik. They tried to be delicate about it, but it appeared the man was simply drunk. He was excused, and deputies assisted him out of the courtroom. The court selected another man to replace him, and the jury was complete. The final panel was a good mix of average working-class men: clerks and salesmen, a fixture hanger, an insurance solicitor, and a house-moving contractor. Based on the relatively few challenges made, one can only assume that Billik's attorneys were pleased with the selection. *

After completing the jury, Barnes called the attorneys, as well as Herman and Mary Billik, up to the bench. The judge, like everyone else in Chicago, had followed the Knudson trial, and he wasn't happy about the way Knudson's children had played on the emotions of observers. He wasn't about to let that happen in his courtroom. "This trial is going to be conducted according to the forms of law and there won't be any dramatic or sensational episodes,"[102] he ordered. He seemed particularly concerned about the presence of Edna Billik, who had accompanied her mother to every court appearance. "If the prisoner's wife and child are in court they are not to sit near him, but are to remain at the back of the courtroom beyond the rail . . . I will not permit any effort to prey upon the sympathies of the jury during the trial in this case."[103]

---

* According to a *Chicago Daily Tribune* article of July 2, 1907, on the first day of jury selection, prosecutors made six preemptory challenges, while the defense made only one.

July 3, 1907: Trial, Day 1

On Wednesday, July 3rd, 1907, both the Chicago Cubs and White Sox were in first place in their respective leagues, just a year after facing off against one another in the World Series. Chicago, once again, had baseball fever. But the hottest ticket in town was for Judge Barnes' courtroom, where the trial of Herman Billik was getting underway. Men in neckties and bowler hats and ladies in floor-length dresses filled every seat in the room, and it would stay that way for the entire trial.

Assistant State's Attorney Popham gravely outlined the prosecution's theory: "This man Billik conceived the plan to get all the money and property—including the wife—of Martin Vrzal. He intended also to obtain the life insurance of the children . . . He entered into this plot with Mrs. Vrzal because he held the woman under his influence and had mastered her affections to the extent that he had borrowed all her money. The state will prove that this plot continued up to the time of the death of little Ella Vrzal."[104]

Ella was the last child to die, some sixteen months after Mary. In fact, most of what Popham discussed happened well after Mary Vrzal died in July of 1905. Popham went on. "The state will show opportunity on Billik's part to poison the members of the family . . . Jerry Vrzal will tell you of a conversation in which Billik said to Mrs. Vrzal, 'You know in a short time your husband will be dead, and then we will get the children out of the way. I will kill my wife and then we will put my mother out of the way. After we get her money we will go to Europe and spend it.'"[105] After arguing so vehemently for all the charges to be heard separately, Popham now took every opportunity to tell the jury that the entire family was systematically murdered. Listening to his opening statement, one would never know that this trial was only for the murder of Mary Vrzal. Even the press almost always referred to Billik as being on trial for "killing six." Newspapers reported that Billik seemed amused, grinning and tilting back in his chair easily.[106] He was portrayed as an evil, uncaring monster. "The accused man spent a good deal of time impaling judge and jurors with his 'evil eye,'" read the *Chicago Daily Tribune*, "but it didn't seem to have much effect."[107]

In the afternoon, Popham called a parade of witnesses. They made it painfully clear that six members of the family died in succession, and that all of the bodies had been exhumed and taken into the custody of the Cook County Coroner. Nearly a dozen men took the stand, including undertakers, policemen, cemetery officials, even the president of the Frigid Embalming Fluids Company, who stated that arsenic was never used in his preparations. It was impressive, if not a bit of overkill. Conspicuously out of place with the rest of the testimony was that of Miss Mary Flynn, a public stenographer who told the jury she typed numerous letters for Herman Billik addressed to "Mrs. Rosie Vrzal." They were all requests for money, and some referred to Billik carrying out "some work he was undertaking," saying that he needed "a certain amount of money to finish some job."[108] Miss Flynn was followed by the undertakers and gravediggers, clearly giving the impression that this "job" must have been killing the Vrzal family. There was little cross-examination. The defense didn't dispute any of the facts, only Popham's arguments and insinuations.

July 5-6, 1907: Trial, Days 2-3

The next phase of the trial centered on science. Professor Haines testified that Mary Vrzal's liver contained about two and one-third grains* of arsenic in total. Haines believed that to be "enough to kill two or three men."[109] Popham wanted Haines to explain how the other Vrzals died, but Judge Barnes said prosecutors would have to prove a conspiracy existed between Billik and Mrs. Vrzal before introducing such evidence.

---

* One grain = approximately 0.065 gram

Dr. Mark Delafontaine, another respected expert, said that he found seven grains of arsenic in Mary's stomach, more than three times the lethal dose. It indicated that she was likely poisoned shortly before her death, since arsenic normally remains in the stomach less than 48 hours. The arsenic Haines found in the liver, on the other hand, indicated chronic (slow, gradual) poisoning, as it takes some time for arsenic to build up in the internal organs. Mary had been slowly poisoned over a period of weeks, then given a large dose within a day or two of her death.

Later in the day Benjamin Parkison provided crucial evidence for prosecutors. One of the biggest difficulties they had was figuring out where Billik might have obtained arsenic. It was used in rat and roach poison, for dyeing fabric and wallpaper, and by doctors and druggists for treating a variety of ailments, but detectives never found any at Billik's home, nor any evidence of him purchasing any. Parkison solved that problem. "I saw Billik in the laboratory of Dr. Schmidt in Cleveland," he told the court. "There were two bottles of white arsenic there, and I saw Billik handling them."[110] He said Billik became nervous when people began suspecting that the Vrzals had been poisoned, even before his name became associated with the case. "Dec. 4, when Billik saw the first newspaper account of the investigation, he asked me for a revolver, saying that he would rather shoot himself than be mixed up in the mystery,"[111] Parkison said. He also claimed that the day Mrs. Vrzal took poison Billik told him about it around noon, several hours *before* it actually occurred. While it was damning testimony, Parkison contradicted himself repeatedly, clearly unsure of the exact dates of the incidents, the time line of events, and even whether Billik asked him for a revolver or not.[112]

When Ross Davis cross-examined Parkison it became apparent that his conversation with Billik about Mrs. Vrzal taking poison actually took place the day *after* she had done so.[113] But later, after having a private discussion with State's Attorney Popham, Parkison changed his story again, saying the discussion did happen before she took the poison. Davis pointed out that at the inquest Parkison claimed he never heard Billik say anything the least bit suspicious, and specifically said numerous times that the incident where Billik threatened to shoot himself happened several weeks before the whole Vrzal affair even came about, and was the result of a completely unrelated argument between Billik and his wife. Parkison's response was that Billik had asked for a revolver twice: first two weeks before Mrs. Vrzal died, and then again on the day she took the poison.[114]

Parkison admitted that the labels on the medicine bottles in Schmidt's lab were written in Latin, which he couldn't read or understand, so he really wasn't sure what he saw Billik handling.[115] Davis then asked the young man some personal questions. It turned out that Parkison's past was nearly as murky as his testimony. He admitted to having run away from home numerous times, and was out of work after losing four different jobs in the previous eight months. Davis even asked him about being expelled from school and spending time in a reformatory, but Judge Barnes didn't allow him to answer.[116]

Afterward, Maria Fencl, a longtime friend of the Vrzal family, recounted how Mary Vrzal, though too ill to speak, on her death bed virtually accused Billik of murdering her. "Mary gave me such an awful look as she lay dying, and there seemed to be an accusation in her eyes,"[117] she recalled. She never told anyone of her suspicion at the time, and it's not clear why she assumed that "accusation" was directed towards Billik.

10

The Brother

By the time the state called 17-year-old Jerry Vrzal to the stand, he was already being touted by the press as "the star witness."[118] He did not disappoint. His testimony took up the better part of three days, and was *exactly* what prosecutors needed to show there was a conspiracy between Billik and Rose Vrzal, and allow them to introduce evidence of the other murders. Jerry was neatly groomed and sharply dressed. He was, however, pale and looked nervous as he told how his mother must have been under some sort of trance that allowed Billik to control her, and how the fortune teller had taken the family's savings. Billik's aged mother looked on from her seat in the crowded courtroom, as Jerry explained "the job," in which Billik was to kill the old woman and use her life insurance to pay the Vrzals back the money he had borrowed.

Jerry described how Billik once worked a charm on his father, Martin Vrzal, who was sick and unable to sleep: "After he had visited our house one morning, Billik took a bottle from his pocket and spilled the contents on the sidewalk and broke the bottle. I asked him why he did that and he said to make the charm work. When we got back home father was asleep."[119] But that was hardly the end of Billik's magic. "Then he took a paper on which I had written my father's name and the amount of his

Jerry Vrzal. *Photo courtesy of the Chicago History Museum, DN-0004385.*

life insurance, and waved it over father's face talking in a strange voice."[120] Billik then told Jerry's mother, "You know in a few days your husband will be dead, and the other ones, we will get them out of the way also, and if the kid [Jerry] will stick to us and won't say anything we will take him with us also. If he says anything on me, I will fix him."[121]

Listening to the testimony, Billik could barely contain himself. When Jerry recounted how Billik said he could kill a person so that "no doctor could tell," Billik became so agitated that it looked like he might leap from his chair to confront him.[122] But Jerry was just getting started. He remembered seeing Billik handle bottles of arsenic in Dr. Schmidt's lab, and described medicine Billik brought for Martin and some of the girls: it sank to the bottom when added to a liquid, just as arsenic would. He specifically remembered watching his father and sisters take the medicine from a spoon and swallow it. He said Billik brought medicine for Mary before she died: a bottle of liquid with white sediment at the bottom. He also remembered Billik bringing some sort of meatloaf for Mary, which she took for her lunch just before she died. And if that wasn't suspicious enough, Jerry said he actually watched Billik secretly pour a white powder into Mary's coffee one afternoon when he was over for lunch.

After Mary died, he said, Billik suggested raising the amount of Tillie's life insurance. A few weeks later, he brought a container filled with packets of white powder for the girl, which caused her to have vomiting spells. Jerry said, "She would complain of feeling tired, of sharp pains in her stomach, her lips became parched, her eyes swelled out, and her skin took on a dark yellowish color."[123] All are symptoms of arsenic poisoning. He described identical symptoms for each family member who died. Jerry said that when he objected to his mother giving the fortune teller any more money, Billik took him to Cleveland where Dr. Schmidt began "treating" him with some kind of medicine for his heart. Jerry said he was so weak that Dr. Schmidt told him he wouldn't live for more than a few months.

Jerry vividly described the attempt to asphyxiate three of his sisters. He said Rosie, Ella, and Bertha were all asleep in a bed in the kitchen. He was upstairs, and awakened by Billik and his son, Herman Jr., coming in the back door. He listened at the top of the stairs and heard his mother talking with Billik. "One said 'No, you turn it on,' and the other said, 'No, you turn it on,'" he recalled.[124] He said he came downstairs a few minutes later to find the kitchen filled with gas. He said his mother seemed sort of dazed, so he got the upstairs neighbor, Mrs. Lorenz. They noticed the three girls were unconscious, so Mrs. Lorenz ran across the street to call for a doctor, and he went back to bed. When asked if it was customary to have the bed in the kitchen, he said it was not. "The bed was moved to the kitchen that day and was moved back into the bedroom the next day."[125]

He then recounted the mysterious events of his mother's last day. Jerry said Billik used various ruses to get him out of the house that morning. Prosecutors suggested that Billik used the opportunity to induce Rose to commit suicide. Jerry said he accompanied Billik to Pilsen on the streetcar to look for Herman Jr., and returned home alone a few hours later, after the two somehow got separated. "When I went home I saw a bottle near my mother's bed with a clear liquid in it," he told the court. "It had a strong smell. My mother started to take some and I tried to take the bottle away from her, but she held on to it and took some of the liquid and then drank water. She put the bottle in the stove and went back to bed and went to sleep. After the doctor came I took the bottle from the stove into the alley and broke it up with a stone."[126] He said Billik came by the house before doctors arrived, but when he saw Mrs. Vrzal unconscious he left in a hurry, and said not to tell anyone he had been there. In his most direct accusation, Jerry claimed that on her death bed, his mother told him that Billik killed the whole family. He also said she had once shown him a letter, and told him to give it to police in case of her death, telling him it would "fix" Billik. Jerry didn't know what became of the letter. He never read it, and figured his mother eventually destroyed it on Billik's orders.

It was quite a story, everything prosecutors needed. In fact, they couldn't have scripted it any better. Oddly though, many of the incidents had never been mentioned before. Jerry's story seemed to have changed dramatically. At the first day of the inquest, he repeatedly and specifically said that Billik never gave anyone in his family any medicine, with the lone exception being a cream for Mary's pimples.[127] A month later, when called at the end of the inquest, he remembered several powders and potions Billik had given his father. Now at the trial, he described in detail numerous other suspicious concoctions Billik brought for each of his sisters, which Jerry supposedly watched them consume as they slowly suffered and died.

At the inquest, Jerry said he knew nothing about Billik borrowing any money. Now, he recalled his father, on his deathbed, asking Billik to repay a $2,000 loan. Jerry had taken the stand three times at the inquest, and provided numerous interviews and affidavits to police, but never once mentioned watching Billik secretly pour a powder into Mary's coffee, or hearing Billik say he could kill a person without being detected. Nor did he ever discuss Billik bringing a meat dish prepared especially for Mary. He even specifically denied any knowledge of that incident when he was asked about it at the inquest.[128]

Until the trial, Jerry never told anyone that he heard Billik tell his mother that his father would soon be dead, and the children would follow, and that if he kept the secret he would be spared. He never talked about his mother declaring on her deathbed that Billik had murdered them all. Until now, he said the only thing his mother told him before she died was, "Take good care of Bertha and yourself."[129] His latest description of his mother's final day placed Billik alone with Rose, acting suspiciously both before and shortly after she took the poison. At the inquest, Jerry said that, far from suggesting suicide, Billik consoled Mrs. Vrzal, and told her that everything would turn out alright.[130]

One would have expected all of this to be brought to the jury's attention. Hinckley asked to introduce a transcript of the inquest for that purpose, but Judge Barnes would only allow defense attorneys to read passages in which Jerry directly contradicted himself. He wouldn't let them use it to show what Jerry did *not* say at the inquest, and therefore show that he was now adding to his story.

11

Friends and Physicians

When they were finally finished with Jerry, Mary Vrzal's co-worker, Josephine Riha, told her story. "Mary and I always shared our lunch," she said. "Some time before she died she brought some chopped meat and I ate some of it. Two days later I was taken sick and I never have felt quite the same since. It caused me to vomit and I experienced a burning sensation in the throat."[131] She seemed pretty certain it was the meat that made her sick, but at the inquest Riha hadn't been quite so sure. "I never thought about the meat at that time," she had told the coroner's jury.[132] In fact, she said that she never really thought about that particular meal making her ill until the stories about the deaths in the Vrzal family began appearing in the news, a year and a half later. The two shared many meals, including one or two in between the suspicious meatloaf and when she threw up several days later. The state's own expert, Dr. Moyer, said that arsenic would not cause vomiting more than about twelve to sixteen hours after ingesting it.[133]

Mary Lorenz, who rented the apartment upstairs from the Vrzals on 19th St., testified about the family's illnesses which, as she described them, closely resembled arsenic poisoning. She also briefly described the gas incident. She said Jerry came to her door one night saying Bertha was dying from gas. She went downstairs and found Mrs. Vrzal trying desperately to revive the girl, and saw the two other girls lying in bed. She smelled gas, and ran across the street to the drugstore to phone the doctor, then came right back and waited for him with Mrs. Vrzal. She contradicted Herman Jr.'s story that she had come down to get milk, and said she never saw the boy or his father there. She also said she never saw Jerry again that night after he knocked on her door, and had no idea where he went. Assistant State's Attorney Popham wanted to call Herman Jr. to the stand in order to introduce the version of the incident he had given at the inquest, but Judge Barnes found his story too questionable, and refused.

July 10, 1907: Trial, Day 6

On Wednesday, July 10th, prosecutors brought more friends and neighbors in to testify. Mrs. Rose Benes had known the Vrzal family for eighteen years. She said she visited them often around the time Mary was ill. "About a week before Mary died, Billik was in the kitchen," she recalled. "Bottles of medicine were on the table. Mary was complaining of pains and a burning sensation in her throat. 'Throw away that stuff,' Billik said, indicating the bottles on the table. 'I can give you a little medicine that will cure you.'"[134] Benes thought Mary seemed suspicious of Billik, and reportedly quoted her as telling him, "I won't take any of your medicines. They might put me where they put my father."[135]* That story, however, contradicted other witnesses, like Josephine Riha, who had claimed that in the time leading up to her death Mary considered Billik "a great friend," and that Mary and the entire Vrzal family "thought very much of him."[136]

---

* The *Abstract of Record* (pp 242–243) indicates that Benes said Mary told Billik "she would not take any of *those* medicines," leaving some question as to whether she was actually referring to Billik's remedy or the prescription bottles from Dr. Novak that were on the table. Benes said she couldn't tell which medicines Mary was referring to.

Benes's testimony raised other questions. Since Mary was already sick and taking medication when Billik allegedly offered her his remedy, it could not have caused her illness, particularly if she refused to take it. And if Mary was openly suspicious of Billik, and practically accused him of murdering her father, why did Benes wait two years to tell the authorities?

Frank Zeman was a photographer who lived next door to the Vrzals on 19th St. The elevated train tracks ran right between the two houses, which were about thirty feet apart. Billik frequently used the side entrance to the Vrzal home, which he would approach by walking underneath the elevated tracks from 18th St., so that no one would see him making his rendezvous with Mrs. Vrzal. He was probably not aware that the window of Zeman's photography room looked right down into the side window of the Vrzal's house. Through a translator, Zeman told of watching Billik fondle and kiss Mrs. Vrzal, both before and after Martin Vrzal died. He said it was a bit of an open secret in the neighborhood that the two were romantically involved. Zeman said that about three weeks before Mr. Vrzal died, he watched Billik hand what he believed was some sort of medicine bottle to Mrs. Vrzal, then tear the label off of the bottle as the two discussed it. He said he heard Mrs. Vrzal say something like, "Do you think they will ever know it?" to which Billik allegedly replied, "No, they will never know it."[137]

Kate Engelthaler talked about the conversation she had with Billik at Dr. Caldwell's office the morning Rose Vrzal died. She said Billik told her that people in Pilsen were saying that he killed the Vrzal children, but he didn't understand why, because he loved them.[138] Prosecutors suggested that Billik brought up the subject of the deaths in the Vrzal family to see if he was under any suspicion, but, Mrs. Engelthaler was very clear about the fact that *she* brought up the subject with Billik, as she was reading a story from the newspaper about the deaths while they were waiting to see the doctor.[139]

Her testimony was followed by that of several stenographers who had prepared letters for Billik addressed to Mrs. Vrzal. Some were dated from Cleveland, though he was really in Chicago. Most of the letters were requests for money. Billik had admitted to pretending to be out of town as part of his scams to get money from Mrs. Vrzal. He paid young African American men to deliver the messages, and the Vrzals believed them to be Pullman Porters, carrying the letters from distant cities. Billik would find his messengers from among the newsboys and pool hall rabble he knew in the city's notorious vice district known as "The Levee." It was just a half-mile or so east of Pilsen, an area of roughly sixteen square blocks of segregated sin. Saloons, gambling halls, peep shows, houses of prostitution, and drug dens filled the section between 18th and 22nd Streets, from Wabash to Clark. Some, such as The Opium Joint, made obvious what was to be found within, while others, like the Why Not?, or the ominously named Bucket of Blood, made one wonder.

The Levee's selection of brothels was unparalleled, with options for every taste and every budget and ranging from the highest of high class—the Everleigh Club, a 50-room mansion lavishly decorated with oriental carpets, perfumed fountains, and even a gold-leafed piano—to the stretch of sleaze aptly known as Bed Bug Row. Chicagoans tolerated vice, seeing it as an unavoidable evil that was best kept to one area, away from residential neighborhoods. Though most of the activities were illegal, raids were infrequent, and usually targeted those who failed to meet the schedule of payoffs to police and politicians. Billik was known to frequent the Levee, though the nature of his business there is not clear.

JULY 11, 1907: TRIAL, DAY 7

On July 11th, prosecutors began by calling Dr. Charles Caldwell to the stand. Caldwell had never treated Mary Vrzal, so defense attorneys objected loudly, eventually gaining a scolding from Judge Barnes. He allowed the testimony, believing it might shed light on the alleged conspiracy between Billik and Mrs. Vrzal. Caldwell said that he first saw Mrs. Vrzal around noon the day she died, and saw no indication that she had taken poison. A little before two o'clock, he received the call that she was unconscious. Caldwell told how he asked Rose on her deathbed whether she had taken any poison, or had poisoned the children. "She shook her head, held up her hand as if to swear and said, 'Nay, nay,'" he recalled.[140] Ironically, the doctor's testimony did more to disprove a conspiracy between Billik and Rose Vrzal than to prove one. Since Mrs. Vrzal denied taking poison, or giving it to her children, then someone else must have murdered everyone, including her.

Marie Dundel lived upstairs from the Engelthalers, and was there when Dr. Caldwell first examined Rose that morning. She testified that Caldwell wrote out a prescription, and left around noon. When Jerry came home at about one o'clock, Dundel went to the druggist to get the prescription filled. She returned at one-thirty and Mrs. Vrzal was unconscious.

Dr. Napieralski then gave evidence about the "gas incident" (which happened a year after Mary died), and talked about the "heavy-set"[141] man he saw leaving the house as he arrived. Though he still couldn't identify Billik as the man, Jerry's claim to have heard Billik in the house that night made it seem likely that he was the mysterious visitor.

12

Sisters

In the afternoon, prosecutors called up Bertha Vrzal, the youngest survivor of the family who had just turned 8. After their mother died, she and Jerry were taken in by a kindly couple named Vera and H.B. Jones, who had written to the orphaned children and offered to give them a home. It seemed peculiar that they went to live with strangers rather than their own sister, Emma, who now owned the house that they all grew up in. In early April, Bertha did move in with Emma, and had now been living with her for three months. Jerry had chosen to stay with the Jones family.

Bertha had an angelic look, with a tiny round face, brown, shoulder-length curls, and a long, plain white dress. The courtroom was hushed as she took her place on the stand. Judge Barnes asked her if she knew what it meant to tell a lie. She did, and she knew she could be punished for telling one. For most of her testimony she spoke loud and clear, but some questions she answered in a whisper, barely audible. Judge Barnes repeated those answers loud enough for the court to hear. Popham questioned her slowly and very deliberately. She was only five when her father died, but remembered Billik bringing medicine for him, and for her sisters. "I saw Mr. Billik bring a white powder and some white pills to our house before Papa died. He gave Papa some powder."

"How did he give it to your papa?" asked Popham.

"In a teaspoon,"[142] she said. Bertha then stepped from the witness stand to the jury box to show them just exactly the amount—about a quarter of an inch on the tip of a teaspoon. "He brought more medicine when Mary was sick. This time it was in a black box."[143] She said he brought still more when Rosie was sick, but that her mother took that outside and spilled it under the bedroom window,[144] apparently trying to work some sort of magic charm.

"Did Billik seem like a good friend to your mama?"[145] asked Popham, trying delicately to discuss their relationship.

"Yes sir. He seemed to love her much. One time I saw him put his arms around her and hug her. They always sat close together when he was there." The hint of an affair between two married people created a stir in the courtroom. Bertha said that after her father died, Billik told her that he would be her papa, and that she should love him as she did her own father. "But," she quickly added, "I didn't."[146] She said she saw her mother give Billik money many times.

"How about the day before your mother died?"[147] asked Popham.

"Mr. Billik came there and sat with her close to her bed," she said. "He held Mama's hand and whispered something to her. She gave him some paper money but I don't know how much."[148] Bertha was a most sympathetic little girl. Not surprisingly, defense attorneys chose not to cross-examine her. When she left the stand, the state called Emma Vrzal Niemann.

The *Chicago Daily Tribune* called Emma "the backbone of the prosecution,"[149] saying her testimony was regarded as the most significant. Emma told how Billik worked magic, and provided potions and pills to the family over the course of several years, telling their fortunes, and taking a fortune from them in the process. She described her father as a strong man, who loaded and unloaded ten thirty-two-quart milk cans by himself every morning. She said he had never been ill before Billik came into their lives. When he did become sick, Billik brought him medicine. She said it was a brown liquid with heavy white sediment, and that her father would throw up after each dose. Eventually, his lips, throat, and tongue were so raw that he couldn't eat. His eyes became so red and swollen he could barely see. His face was yellowish, and at times black spots appeared on his skin. They were classic symptoms of arsenic poisoning. Billik looked nervous. He repeatedly wiped sweat from his brow and looked around the courtroom. He tried to remain calm, but he could hardly sit still as Emma told her story.

Two weeks before Martin died, the Vrzals sent for Billik, who was in Cleveland at the time. He asked for money to get to Chicago, stayed a short time, then asked for more money so he could return to Cleveland. Emma said that four days after he went back to Cleveland, her mother received a note from him which read, "Dear Mother, Do with this as I have told you."[150] Enclosed, she said, was a small black bag. Emma's curiosity got the better of her, and she opened it. "It contained a white powder. I sewed the bag up and put it back in the letter. I didn't want my mother to know what I had done."[151] Her father grew steadily worse, and died soon after.

Emma talked about how her parents once hired Billik to work a love charm on a man named Albert Rus,* whom she had previously dated. Though the charm was for her benefit, Emma said it was all her parents' idea. "I didn't care about it," she said, "but my mother did, and she paid him fifty dollars for it. Then Billik went to San Francisco and from there he telegraphed he was working on the charm, but that he would have to have $100 more. My father didn't want to send it to him, but my mother said we could not afford to fall out with Billik; he might do us some harm. So they gave me seventy-five dollars and I sent it to him by telegraph."[152] She wired the money, though she claimed she warned her parents not to send it. "A few weeks later he telegraphed again for $100, saying he was sick. My father again objected to sending the money but mother insisted, and this time I telegraphed him fifty dollars. When he came back he got fifty dollars more to go to Syracuse, New York to get some special herbs for the charm."[153] Despite giving

---

* Though his name is usually spelled "Rost" or "Russ" in transcripts, it was actually "Rus."

Billik hundreds of dollars over the course of several months, Rus married another girl.

July 12-13, 1907: Trial, Days 8-9

Emma's second day on the stand was long and dramatic. In the morning, she broke down repeatedly and fainted several times as she told the disturbing details of her sister Mary's last days. She described the agonizing, often gruesome, effects of slow arsenic poisoning. Her sister lay in bed for days, unable to eat even a bite, her mouth and throat parched and raw. She complained of terrible pains, especially in her hands and feet. "She screamed if one touched her hand lightly,"[154] Emma recalled. Observers, including jurors, were visibly affected by the testimony. Some women wept. Friends of the Vrzal family, who were seated near the front, became boisterous. "Isn't it awful,"[155] one cried. "Wretch!"[156] exclaimed another, before the bailiff brought the room to order.

Mary Billik sat near the back, some rows behind her husband. He occasionally glanced back at her, and she offered a reassuring smile. But Emma's testimony continued to make them both anxious. The Billiks' young daughter, Edna, stayed out of the courtroom on Barnes' orders, but she lingered just beyond the door in the back, sometimes turning an ear and straining to hear the testimony. Emma told how Mary, nearing death, began suspecting Billik of causing her torturous demise. Billik tried to look as if he was unaffected, but he was pale and sweating. He mopped his face with a handkerchief, moved his hands and feet constantly, and fidgeted in his chair. The calm and confident defendant that started the trial was no more.

"On the morning she died," Emma continued, "Mary told me she was not going to live. 'This is my dying morning,' she said, 'and I know who to thank for it. I shouldn't have taken that medicine that Herman Billik gave me.' She died a little while later."[157] Emma wept and struggled to catch her breath. Eventually, she went on with her remarkable tale. "Just before Mary died, while she was suffering greatly, she rose in her bed and screamed, 'Oh, I know whose work this is. Herman Billik has killed me.'"[158] Emma could barely continue as she relived watching her sister die right before her eyes.

"After she died I fainted. Billik came over to pick me up. I came to just as he stooped over me. 'Don't touch me,' I screamed. 'Keep your hands off me.'" As she said this she rose and made a gesture of repulsion, acting out the scene for the court.[159] With that, Emma collapsed. She dropped from the witness chair and onto the floor. Barnes called for a recess, as bailiffs rushed to lift Emma back into her chair. At the inquest, and in her early interviews with police, Emma never mentioned any of the dramatic moments that she now recalled so vividly—not even her sister directly accusing Billik of murdering her. Her story also contradicted witnesses who said Mary was too ill to sit up or even speak on her deathbed. During the recess Billik turned to the press table and smiled. "That's [just] good acting," he told reporters. "I'm not afraid."[160]

When she finally regained her composure, Emma told of taking the train to Riverside to see Billik a week before Mary died. The Billiks often spent the warm summer months there, living in a small, two-room tent in which he told fortunes for visitors to the idyllic little town. Billik told Emma's fortune with cards. Popham produced a handful of the cards and held them out before her. "There is the sign of death,"[161] she said, pointing to one of them. Popham held it up as Emma continued, "Billik pointed at that card and told me, 'That shows that you will be in mourning soon.' A week later, Mary died."[162] Popham showed the card to the jury, and told them it played a prominent role whenever Billik told the Vrzals' fortunes. Then, very dramatically, he introduced into evidence "the card of death."

Emma said that she and Mary were each insured for $800. She claimed that Billik tried to kill her first, just a few weeks after her father died. "Yes, Billik gave me medicine," she affirmed. "He brought some pills and white powders. The first I took made me sick, so I threw the rest away."[163] At the inquest she said that she was so suspicious that she only pretended to take the medicine. Now she described swallowing a half-dozen pills, and even drinking from the bottle Billik brought for her father, all of which made her vomit.

The attorney asked her about Jerry's claim to have seen Billik pour a white powder into Mary's coffee. Emma said that on that particular afternoon, as she went to sit down beside Billik at the table, he made her move so that Mary could take the seat. She then watched her sister drink the entire cup that was at that place. It seemed incredible that anyone would remember the details of an incident as insignificant as being asked to switch seats while having a cup of coffee two years earlier, particularly since she didn't see Billik pour the powder and Jerry hadn't told her anything about it at the time.

She said that the day after Mary died, Billik convinced her mother to increase the life insurance on the other girls. Emma estimated that Billik took about $6,000 from her family, though at the inquest she said she knew of only $3,000. She said he promised to pay them back, as he was due to inherit a lot of money when his mother died, but Emma now doubted that his mother had any money. "Mother and I visited Cleveland one time," she said. "His mother lived in poverty. She didn't even have carpets on the floor of her house."[164]

Emma's testimony, like Jerry's, was filled with stories she had never told anyone before. She even had her own "gas incident" to report. She claimed it happened a few weeks before the attempt on her three sisters. She had already moved out of the house, but came back to visit and spent the night. She said twice during the night she awakened to the smell of gas. Someone apparently turned on the gas from the stove shortly after she went to bed, and then again after she got up and turned it off. She had no idea who might have done it.

Emma was asked about numerous contradictions between her testimony and previous interviews and sworn statements she had provided (such as recalling Billik being present at times she previously said he was not, and saying she saw Mary vomit dozens of times after originally saying that she never threw up at all). "You know when you are excited you will say most anything," she said,[165] explaining that at the inquest she was still upset over her mother's death. "I did not know what I was talking about half of the time." She said that she remembered a lot of things after she got stronger and "came to [her] right senses."[166]

Defense attorneys had learned that shortly after Martin Vrzal died in March of 1905, Emma had a terrible fight with her mother and her sister Mary, and moved out of the house. Ross Davis asked Emma if she and her mother were having trouble at that time. "Yes, we did," she replied.

"What was the cause?" asked Davis.

"That man there," she said sharply, extending her arm and pointing her finger at Billik.[167] It startled everyone. "I told mother his medicine had caused father's death. I left home because I didn't want to die. Mary had said she would leave home too. We declared we would not work any longer for Billik. We gave Mother most of our earnings and Billik got them."[168] It was the first time Emma had directly accused Billik of murder. Davis tried to take control of the situation. He asked about the will that Mrs. Vrzal made out just before her death, leaving $1,000 each to Jerry and Bertha, but only twenty-five dollars for Emma. Davis asked why she thought her mother would take away her inheritance just before she died. Again, Emma turned the subject back to Billik, saying her mother wrote her out of the will because of all the trouble that she made over her mother's attention to him. Emma claimed that after each murder she voiced suspicions about Billik, but her mother just wouldn't listen.

Emma was quite a challenge. No matter what question Davis put to her, the answer was invariably to accuse Billik. She even claimed that her own father grew to hate her after Billik began coming around.[169] Finally, Davis asked her about something she couldn't blame on Billik. At the inquest Emma had identified herself as "Mrs. William Niemann," and said she was married in June of 1906. But Davis and Hinckley had discovered that Emma was not actually married to Mr. Niemann when she made that statement.

She had an interesting explanation. She claimed they were married *twice*. "I was married in June 1906," she explained, "Well, I was not exactly married by a minister; still we were engaged; my husband made an agreement to live as husband and wife, like all Bohemians do."[170] Davis reminded her that Niemann was German, not Bohemian, but Emma was unfazed. William Niemann was born in the western suburb of Downer's Grove, where he lived on his family's dairy farm. He was a widower with two young sons. Emma moved in with them in 1905, right after Mary's death. The two were eventually married legally, but not until February 1907,[171] several months after she apparently lied about it at the inquest.

Davis finished his cross-examination the following morning. It was Emma's third day on the stand, and it had taken a toll on her. Fainting spells and breakdowns, and tough questioning from attorneys, left her visibly exhausted. She and her siblings had made a strong case against Billik. Yet, it was hard to believe anyone could be so certain of times and dates for so many events from years before. Even the prosecutor commented afterward. "The Vrzal children show remarkable memories," said Popham. "They all have made excellent witnesses because of their ability to remember dates."[172]

13

Conspiracy

As soon as Emma stepped from the stand, Assistant State's Attorney Popham re-called Dr. Haines. It immediately set off a clamor. Davis and Hinckley both jumped up and voiced objections. Judge Barnes called all of the attorneys up to his bench. Popham wanted to introduce testimony about finding arsenic in the other bodies. Hinckley argued vehemently against it. After a long time, Barnes decided prosecutors had proven there was a conspiracy between Billik and Mrs. Vrzal to murder the whole family, and let Popham proceed.

Professor Haines said that he found arsenic in all of the Vrzal's bodies. He gave some technical testimony about the symptoms of arsenic poisoning, how much was sufficient to kill, and how long it takes to eliminate it from the body. He found a considerable amount (more than two grains) in the stomachs and livers of Martin and little Rosie, and even more in those of Ella. They all died from chronic arsenic poisoning, as did Tillie, though she had much less in her system. As for the mother, Haines reported, "I find arsenic present in both of the organs of Mrs. Rosie Vrzal in large quantities. In the stomach and liver, especially in the liver."[173] Just like Mary, Mrs. Vrzal had been slowly poisoned for some time, before ingesting a final, fatal dose.

It should have been apparent at this point that Rose Vrzal did not commit suicide. Who would slowly poison themselves over the course of weeks or months, particularly if they knew just how agonizing a death it would be? Yet, the *Chicago Daily News* that afternoon still reported that Mrs. Vrzal took her own life, and most accounts would forever state that she committed suicide.*
Prosecutors theorized that, after suspicions were raised about the deaths in the family and the police began investigating, Billik either poisoned Mrs. Vrzal or induced her to take her own life. But even if she did intentionally take poison before she died, someone was already trying to kill her. Haines' discovery of arsenic accumulation in her liver meant someone had been poisoning her for some time—beginning before Ella died, before there was any investigation, or even accusations. Surely, before the police investigation began, Billik had no motive to kill her, particularly since she appeared to be his main source of income. It was also virtually impossible for Billik to have administered the dose that finally killed her. Defense attorneys did a poor job of spelling this out for the jury, but the evidence very clearly put the time of the fatal poisoning between one and one-thirty in the afternoon; and there was nothing to indicate that Billik was at the house between ten-thirty a.m. and some time in the afternoon, after Rose was already unconscious.

Mrs. Dundel went to the drugstore to get Rose's prescription filled at about one o'clock. Jerry was home at that time, and Mrs. Vrzal was awake. When Mrs. Dundel returned at about one-thirty, Mrs. Vrzal was unconscious. That should have raised some suspicion of Jerry, since Mrs. Vrzal swallowed the poison during that

---

* Whether it was lazy journalism or simply a desire to go along with the police theory of the crimes, reporters never really questioned this notion. They preferred to focus on the more fantastical elements of the story rather than to get bogged down by the facts of the case.

very short time that he was alone with her, right after Mrs. Dundel left and Albert Engelthaler had gone back to work. Jerry himself admitted to destroying crucial evidence (the bottle of poison) and lied about it to police and doctors, even when finding the bottle might have helped doctors save his mother's life. Initially, police thought Jerry had been covering for Billik. It now seemed that Jerry was covering for someone, but not Herman Billik.

Might Mrs. Vrzal have thought she was taking the chloroform compound she routinely used as a sedative and painkiller, unaware that someone had added arsenic to it? Could the struggle that Jerry described actually have involved someone knocking his mother out with chloroform, before poisoning her with arsenic? Either scenario made as much sense as the bizarre suicide story Jerry finally told. Interestingly, in his very first interview with police, when asked about the mysterious bottle, Jerry replied, "Emma knows about that bottle, she told me Mother had a bottle but I did not see it."[174] Emma had stopped by the house the night before her mother took poison, while Mrs. Vrzal was at the police station.[175] And when Jerry went to Pilsen to look for Herman Jr. the next day, he virtually walked right past Emma's house* before he returned home and watched his mother swallow the poison. The two certainly had ample opportunity to be involved in their own conspiracy.

July 15, 1907: Trial, Day 10

On the tenth day of the trial Police Chief Shippy talked about the interviews he conducted. He denied using any "sweatbox" techniques to obtain statements from Billik, who made many admissions to him. Shippy told the court how Billik told him that Mrs.

---

* Jerry took the Ashland Ave. streetcar to 19th or 20th St., and said he walked from there to 18th St. and Blue Island and back several times before returning home. Ashland is just a block east of the old Vrzal home on 19th St., where Emma lived.

Vrzal wanted him to kill his wife and mother by means of his magic (or "hoodoo," as Billik referred to it[176]), so they could then get married. He admitted working charms and magic, and casting spells; and even told him that he routinely cheated the Vrzals out of money, sometimes traveling to faraway cities on their dime.

Police Sgt. Murningham then described overhearing a conversation at the station between Billik and his wife concerning some evidence they had secreted away; and how officers then found the satchel with letters from Mrs. Vrzal hidden at Billik's home. He suspected that Mrs. Billik had found the letters in her husband's pocket and hidden them away to use against him, possibly in future divorce proceedings. Popham asked to submit one of the letters.

Hinckley objected. He was adamant that it was an illegal search and seizure. After police had taken Billik, his wife, and Herman Jr. into custody, they had entered their home without a search warrant, gone through all of their things, and taken the satchel and other items. Hinckley argued that the letter was inadmissible even if police had obtained a warrant, as the purported author was now deceased, it was undated, and did not actually name the person to whom it was addressed. Judge Barnes asked Emma to look over the letter. She said it was her mother's handwriting, and Barnes allowed it into evidence. A translation of the letter (which was written in Bohemian) was read aloud for the jury:

My dearest friend,
You write to me that I should be as frank as you are toward me. Who is more frank, me or you? You know that I am. Why? That old woman is not worth that money. Just as I write this letter I have received your telegram. What are you thinking of? I haven't got $10 in the whole house and on Wednesday I need $108. I expected that you would help me out with something. Now I am broke. What shall I do now? You may as well give that old woman poison, so that you may help yourself to something. At least send me those children home. I am sick and you are only misleading me. Anyhow, I cannot help liking you so much, no matter if you like me or not. If you love me you would have done it long ago.

What I must suffer from people. I greet you and the children times over and send one hundred million kisses.

Your good and sincere lady friend,
Rosie Vrzal

P.S. And don't write me any more for money. It is useless. I cannot send as much as $1, because I have not got it.[177]

With that, the prosecution abruptly closed its case.

14

The Sorcerer

The next morning, Tuesday, July 16th, the defense began. In the most highly anticipated moment of the trial, they called as their first witness Herman Billik. People craned their necks and jostled in their chairs for a view of the mysterious clairvoyant accused of a ghastly series of murders. People expected to see some sort of monster. Instead he wore a suit and tie and his hair was neatly slicked, making him look more like a salesman than a sorcerer. His attorneys asked him few questions, allowing the beleaguered Bohemian to give his account unabated. That was probably a mistake. Billik was excited. He spoke rapidly in a thick Bohemian accent that was hard for many to follow. He had to be asked several times to slow down and to repeat statements for court reporters. Otherwise, he told his long and eerie tale without interruption.

He provided seemingly sound alibis for the periods of time when several of the family were poisoned and died. He also made a surprisingly strong case that for each and every death, Emma Niemann had ample opportunity and motive to murder. Billik's testimony was a virtual attack on Emma. Even after she moved out, he noted, she visited the Vrzal home often, and was there regularly during the times that her sisters were ill. He connected her to each of the deaths, painting her as a calculating killer now trying to frame him for her crimes.

Herman Billik. *Photo courtesy of the Chicago History Museum,*
DN-0006608.

Billik looked anxiously from juror to juror as he spoke. The
Chicago Daily News described him as "glib-tongued" and "shifty-
eyed."[178] They did note, however, that at times he seemed to touch
the audience with his story. The *Chicago Daily Tribune* saw a side
of the defendant they hadn't expected: "Instead of a weird crea-
ture with an 'evil eye' of hypnotic power holding mastery over

supernatural realms, Billik appeared as a much excited man trying to extricate himself from an embarrassing position."[179]

Billik said that the Vrzal home was not always a happy one. The turmoil invariably revolved around Emma. He said she had horrible arguments with her mother and her sisters, to the point that she literally threatened to kill them.[180] Things got so bad that Emma was eventually thrown out of the house. Apparently, the trouble all started about the time that Emma began dating a man named Joe Cooney. Both Martin and Rose Vrzal denounced their relationship, as did Emma's sisters. Cooney was not only much older, but he was married and had children.

"A neighbor asked me why Emma went with this fellow," Billik said, "and told me he was a married man and was a bad fellow. I told Emma and she said, 'no,' that he was alright and made lots of money and that he was going to marry her. She said he would build a big house for her and they would be happy."[181] Billik said he tried to get Emma to go with him to Cooney's house to prove that he was married, but she refused. So Billik got one of the other children to follow Cooney home one day to find out where he lived and went there himself. He found Cooney's wife sitting on the steps. "I told her her husband was going with a girl who he promised to marry, and she cried and said she and her six children were starving."[182] Billik said that when he told Emma what he had discovered she was enraged. "She asked her mother for a gun so that she could kill the man, and I told her I would go with her to see him. But she went with her sister and came back and told me she had told him she would kill him for deceiving her."[183]

But Emma continued seeing Cooney, and eventually became pregnant.* Billik said, "Her mother said she had disgraced the family with that married man . . . [and] sent her away from the house. She came to my wife and asked to board with us, but my

---

* Emma denied that she had been pregnant, saying she was diagnosed with "dropsy of the stomach," so Barnes only allowed references to some undefined "illness," though it was a midwife who was called in to treat her.

wife said she had not the time for boarders. Emma cried and said what could she do. I said for her to go home and I would ask her mother to forgive her."[184] He said Emma told him she was in a "family way," and asked him, "Don't you know anything how I can get rid of it?"[185] Billik went to a druggist, who gave him some pills, but when he brought them to the house, Mrs. Vrzal told him, "You are a fool to bring her anything. She has plenty of powders and medicine from that pimp,"[186] referring to Cooney, who, Emma said, "knew what to give her."[187]

Billik said he was at the Vrzal house when a midwife came and tended to Emma when she lost the baby. He said the woman even made a comment to him about "the Irish baby."* Billik described seeing a whole package of powders that Emma had under her pillow. They were just like the ones Emma had claimed Billik had brought for little Rosie (and Jerry said that Billik had brought for Tillie).

Emma was eventually allowed back home, but Billik said shortly thereafter he saw Emma physically assault her sisters Mary and Tillie, and threaten to "kill them all."[188] That was about six to eight weeks before Mary died.[189] After Mary's death, Emma was again asked to leave the house. At times, Billik stared at Emma or Jerry while telling his story. Both quickly became uncomfortable and look away. Many observers, including the attorneys, found the behavior unnerving.

Billik offered a sharp rebuttal to Emma's lurid description of Mary's dying day, in which she said her sister dramatically accused him of causing her death. In fact, Billik said, Emma's entire story was made up. She wasn't even there. He said she didn't come back from work that day until Mary was already dead. If Mary did say anything, Emma wasn't around to hear it. "Little Mary died when Emma was not at the Vrzal home. Mary died in

---

* Judge Barnes did not allow the defense to question the midwife about the nature of Emma's illness, or the procedure she performed, but they clearly believed that the baby was lost either as a result of some "medicine" Emma had taken, or that the midwife had induced or performed an abortion, which was illegal at the time. [*Abstract of Record*, pp 474–476]

my arms. Emma was sent for and fainted when she saw the dead child."[190] He said he did not try to pick Emma up, as she had so dramatically acted out.

Tillie was the second girl to die, about five months after Mary. Billik said Mrs. Vrzal told him that she died from drinking well water. "She fell sick just after she got home from a visit to the Niemann home."[191] That was out in Downer's Grove, where Emma was living at the time, supposedly engaged to William Niemann. Billik said Mrs. Vrzal told him Tillie was perfectly healthy when Emma took her out to the farm, but she returned quite sick, complaining of stomach pains, and never recovered.[192] Tillie was buried on Christmas Day, 1905.

Billik was out of town when Rosie died, and stayed away from the Vrzal house entirely for a period of months, during which time Ella became ill and died. All of the talk from Jerry and Emma about him bringing powders for them was false, Billik said. He did occasionally work charms, but that involved spilling a potion onto the ground from his "magic box." He never asked anyone to swallow anything. He said he brought some face cream for Mary's acne one time, and he did bring several bottles of whiskey with saltpeter for Mr. Vrzal, but that was three or four months before Vrzal died.

Billik had been out of town for months preceding and during the time in which Martin Vrzal began showing symptoms of arsenic poisoning and slowly suffered. The Billiks had actually moved away from Chicago in January of 1905. At that time, Martin Vrzal suffered only from slight rheumatism. Several months later, in March, Billik got a telegram in Cleveland telling him that Mr. Vrzal was gravely ill and that the family wanted him to come back to Chicago, presumably to try to save him with some type of magic charm. He told the family he had no money, so they wired it to him and he came back only for a day and visited Martin, who was already very near death.

Billik said that Mrs. Vrzal did ask him to divorce his wife, and that he was aware that it had become the source of speculation among the Vrzal children, but that he never seriously considered it. He said that the letter from Mrs. Vrzal that police "discovered" was not hidden by his wife for divorce proceedings, as Shippy and Murningham claimed. Quite to the contrary, Billik said that he kept the letter himself, planning to use it to blackmail Mrs. Vrzal. He realized that it was incriminating—against *her*. "I saved it to threaten Mrs. Vrzal with," he said. "She always was threatening to make me trouble because of the money I owed her. In the letter she suggested poisoning my mother, and I intended to use it to frighten her with."[193] Billik said he told Shippy about the letter himself, and even told him exactly where to find it.

As for the alleged attempt to kill some of the girls by gas, Billik said he absolutely was not there for any such incident, and knew nothing about it. Prosecutors placed the date of that event as July 27th, 1906. Billik said he spent the whole month of July in French Lick Springs, a spa town in southern Indiana, seeking treatment for a kidney ailment.

Assistant State's Attorney Robert Holt cross-examined Billik. Holt was an imposing man. He was a former college athlete, and an experienced attorney, in practice for twelve years. He was also a local Republican political leader, and one of the principals of the Deneen faction of the party.[194] Holt fired questions at Billik, who barely hesitated when answering. The interrogation did not appear to trip him up in the least, and there were no major revelations. Billik acknowledged that he had previously been married in Germany, but that he had no children from that marriage and was divorced long ago. It may have been seen as somewhat scandalous when it became apparent that the Billiks had two children before they were actually married, but that was the worst thing that prosecutors unearthed from his past.

The supposed-sorcerer admitted that all of his spells and charms were just a sham to get money. He had no magical powers, and couldn't really hypnotize anyone. "You lied to the Vrzals to get money, didn't you?" asked Holt.

"Oh, I had to tell them something,"[195] Billik reasoned. He confirmed the stories of "charming" the rival milk dealer across the street from the Vrzals, and suitors for Emma, including Albert Rus and William Niemann.

Holt wanted to portray Billik as a lifelong con man who never held an honest job. He seemed surprised when Billik presented a litany of previous occupations when asked what he ever did besides telling fortunes. Before turning to the occult for a living, Billik was a tailor for six or seven years, he had worked as a butler, and even owned a saloon in Cleveland for a time. He turned to clairvoyance full time only when he and his family moved to Chicago around 1900.

Holt also tried to give jurors the impression that people around Billik were dropping like flies. He brought up Billik's mother-in-law who had passed away, and even Standish York. Neither had anything to do with the murder of Mary Vrzal, nor with any perceived conspiracy to kill the Vrzal family, yet in a bit of a blunder defense attorneys did not object. Holt asked Billik when he first met Mrs. York. Billik said that after Mr. York died, the insurance company withheld payment and his wife approached him to foretell whether she would receive the money or not. He said neighbors had told her to see him due to his alleged psychic abilities, but that he did no work for her, and received no money. Holt ignored his response, and tried to cast more suspicion saying, "Wasn't it before her husband died, you were able to do that service?"[196]

The question clearly implied that Billik may have been involved in Mr. York's death, but again no one objected. Billik repeated that he first met the woman *after* her husband had already died. Authorities in Cleveland never found any evidence of foul play, nor even a hint that Herman Billik was involved in the matter at all. Standish York died of natural causes, in another state, eight and half years before Mary Vrzal was murdered. It was beyond irrelevant. Holt knew that, but the jury did not. Holt finished by asking Billik why he tried to avoid talking to police after Rose Vrzal died. Billik said he just didn't want to be a witness in the case. He never imagined he would be accused of murder.

Billik did a commendable job defending himself, though he tended to ramble and lose focus at times. Davis and Hinckley wanted to show that they weren't afraid to let him speak freely and answer questions but, by letting him do all the talking, they placed the onus on Billik to remember and refute everything. They might have served him better by directing his testimony so that all of the evidence was debunked in a systematic way.

15

The Defense

The next witness was Billik's brother-in-law from Cleveland, Dr. Emil Schmidt. He said that he and Billik were not close, and that he didn't even see him or speak to him from mid-1904 up until mid to late 1905, well after Mary and Martin Vrzal were already dead. He said Billik had never even been to his house before that, and had not been back since February 1906. He denied that Billik could have obtained arsenic from his lab. He never allowed anyone inside unaccompanied, and the only arsenic he ever had was in bulk form, in large lumps like peanuts. It needed to be processed by a chemist, using the proper equipment and methods, before it could be used as a poison. He said anyone else would poison themselves with the dust created when it is crushed. He did admit that the lab was not always locked, and it was within the realm of possibility for someone to sneak in and steal something, but he said he had only one container of arsenic for the past eighteen years, had precisely measured it, and was absolutely positive that every bit of it was accounted for. He scoffed at Jerry and Ben Parkison's claims to have seen Billik casually picking it up and looking at it in the lab. The container was high on a shelf, more than eight feet off the ground, among many hundreds of compounds and chemicals. If Billik did somehow identify the bottle, he couldn't have even reached it without first getting a ladder.

One of Shippy's men claimed to have seen arsenic in Schmidt's lab that was partially pulverized, meaning it could be used as poison. Schmidt said he never had any powdered arsenic in his stock, and that the officer was terribly mistaken. He said that during the investigation the officer searched his shelves in vain looking for arsenic, finally selecting a bottle of white powder that he believed was it. Schmidt informed him that it was in fact baking soda, then handed him the bottle that actually did contain the arsenic.

The doctor then explained Jerry's mysterious tale of being taken to his house in Cleveland and left there for months. He said that Billik brought the boy to him and told him that Jerry was sick, as the other children had been, and asked him to examine him. He said Billik told him, with tears in his eyes, "Do everything you can for him."[197] Schmidt said that when he examined Jerry he observed weak lungs and what he termed "intermittent heart."[198] He did give him some pills, but felt that fresh oxygen was the best medicine for him, so he encouraged him to get out a lot while there. He said Jerry was quite ill when he arrived, but gained seventeen pounds, and was substantially stronger and healthier when he returned to Chicago. He said he did send some dyspepsia tablets to Chicago for Jerry after Mrs. Vrzal wrote to him saying that the boy began complaining of indigestion after returning home.

Much of the rest of Schmidt's testimony centered on his adopted son, Benjamin Parkison. The doctor said that Parkison was a troubled young man. He had left home numerous times, and was thrown out of school. He said repeatedly that the boy's reputation was such that nothing he said should, or could, be believed. Schmidt said that in the previous few years, he had "chased the boy out of the house," and even returned him to the Children's Home at one point because, as he put it, "He would do no good."[199]

July 17, 1907: Trial, Day 12

Undertaker Jan Zajicek testified as to the costs of the Vrzal funerals, which averaged about $300 each. He was paid $245 for Martin's funeral, $342 for Mary's, and $308 for Tillie's. He was paid only twenty-six dollars towards Rosie's, and received nothing for the funerals of Ella and Mrs. Rose Vrzal.[200] Early on, prosecutors had claimed that Mrs. Vrzal failed to pay the funeral expenses, and instead gave the money to Billik, but that clearly wasn't the case. She obviously didn't live long enough to pay for Ella's funeral, nor her own. That meant that Rosie's was the only one not paid in full, and several of the prosecution's own witnesses had explained that fact, recounting how Mrs. Vrzal, distraught and clearly not in her right mind following Rosie's death, accidentally threw a paper containing several hundred dollars she had put aside for the undertaker into the stove while cleaning house.[201]

Prosecutors and police always pointed to insurance money as the motive for the murders, but Mrs. Vrzal collected only $2,400 total from the insurance, and paid about $1,400 of that for the funerals and grave monument. That left $1,000 to pay for the rather large family cemetery plot, approximately seventy-five doctor's visits, and fifty prescriptions.* The last two girls to die, Rosie and Ella, carried only $255 in life insurance *combined*. And Bertha, one of the targets of the gas attempt, wasn't insured at all. If Billik or Mrs. Vrzal were killing for insurance money, why were the girls insured for such a pittance? The fact that the funerals cost an average of $300 each should have made it clear

---

* Mrs. Vrzal paid $921 to the undertaker and $475 for the gravestone. Doctors testified to 19-20 visits by Dr. Caldwell, 45-50 from Novak, 3-4 by Murphy, at least one from Dr. Weiskopf, and one from Dr. Napieralski, in addition to two specialists who examined Mr. Vrzal but did not testify.

that money was not the motive. Far from profiting, Mrs. Vrzal was only pushed further into debt as a result of their deaths.

After all the talk about insurance money, the fact remains that Mrs. Vrzal never actually received a single dollar from the insurance policies on Rosie or Ella.[202] Rosie died August 31st, 1906 and the insurance company was still reviewing the claim for her $150 policy when Ella became seriously ill in early October. At that point there was no reason for Billik or Mrs. Vrzal to think that they would get *any* money from the insurance company if another child died. In fact, another death was probably the last thing they would have wanted. It would only have invited more scrutiny, and risked having their alleged plot uncovered.

Even if Mrs. Vrzal had been paid for the policies, it never would have covered her expenses. Ella was insured for a paltry $105. If you add to the cost of her funeral, the cost of fifteen[203] separate visits from Dr. Caldwell, plus the three or four[204] from Dr. Murphy, Mrs. Vrzal undoubtedly lost hundreds of dollars as a result of Ella's illness and death. Even more extraordinary was the fact that Ella's sickness came during the time when Mrs. Vrzal sold the house and milk depot to Emma's "husband," William Niemann, for $1,900 cash. If Mrs. Vrzal had all that money, why would she or Billik need to kill her child for $105 more? It was actually in Billik's best interest for the girls to remain healthy. It meant less money for doctors and undertakers, and more for him.

In a surprise move, Dr. Caldwell was called as a witness for the defense. He said that it was actually Emma who brought Rosie to his office the first time, and that for some reason she used a fictitious address on the paperwork. Emma denied it, but Caldwell was certain. His written records verified it, and he specifically remembered her from that visit. He even identified her in the courtroom. He said that she also brought Ella for her first visit to his office, and that in each case he found it unusual that they came to see him at all, because there appeared to be scarcely anything

wrong with either child. Under cross exam, Caldwell maintained
that he was absolutely positive that it was Emma who brought
Rosie in. Emma was called back to the stand to address Caldwell's
accusations. She claimed that the doctor told her outside of court
that he might have been mistaken.[205] However, when Caldwell
resumed his testimony, he flatly denied having any such conversation. One of them was lying.

Caldwell also brought Jerry's credibility into question. He said
that on the day Mrs. Vrzal took poison, Jerry told him that he had
returned home and found his mother already unconscious and had
no idea what she might have taken.[206] When doctors found the
cork under her pillow and began searching the house for the bottle
of poison, Caldwell told Jerry to help look for it. The boy returned
with an old dirty pop bottle he found in the yard, saying it was all
he could find. Jerry had obviously lied to them, even as doctors
were scrambling to save his mother's life.

The defense also called two newspaper reporters who had interviewed Jerry shortly after his mother died. Both men said that
Jerry told them that he had no knowledge of Billik ever bringing
any medicine to the house. Milton Cubbon of the *Chicago Daily
News* recalled, "He stated to me at that time that Mrs. Niemann
was crazy to accuse Mr. Billik, that Mr. Billik was a good man and
never did harm to anyone."[207]

The most riveting witness for the defense, though, was Billik's
charming little 9-year-old daughter Edna, who was finally allowed
to step from the darkened hallway and into the courtroom. With
all the other witnesses already called, she was the fortune teller's
last hope. She wore a white dress trimmed in lace, her long blonde
hair pulled into a ponytail and tied with a big ribbon. She was an
engaging child, with a wide smile and a pretty face. By the time she
climbed into the large witness chair, her tiny feet dangling from the
edge, observers were captivated.

At first she seemed a bit bewildered. She sat far back in her
seat, almost lost in the oversized chair. She was clearly frightened.
Defense attorney Ross Davis did his best to put her at ease. He
leaned forward and spoke softly and gently, trying to reassure

the girl as he began his questioning. A thunderous objection from Assistant State's Attorney Holt brought the child to tears. She trembled as Davis continued with his first question. Slowly, she grew more comfortable. She leaned forward, and began using hand gestures and body motions to describe events. Her eyes sparkled,[208] as she regained her composure and began telling her story. Eventually she was vividly playing out scenes from the bizarre tragedy, holding the rapt attention of the entire courtroom.

Edna described the nomadic lifestyle of the Billiks, traveling and moving frequently from place to place in Chicago, Cleveland, and even, for a short time, California. She told of her family living in a tent in suburban Riverside one summer, and how they went to visit the Vrzals just a few days before Mary died. "Mary and Emma had an *awful* fight,"[209] Edna told Davis. She said that Mary called Emma a "whore" for being with a married man who had six children.[210] "They had been quarreling and Mary was sitting on a chair and Emma called her a dirty name and then Emma went up and grabbed her and threw her on the floor and took hold of her hair, and dragged her just like this,"[211] she said, pulling at her hair wildly with both hands on the sides of her head, and swaying back and forth in her chair to act out the scene. She imitated the way that Emma dragged her sister Mary around the kitchen, even using accompanying facial expressions. Hands and feet flailing, she continued: "Then Mrs. Vrzal took a horsewhip and said, 'Get out of here!' and Emma called her a name and said that she would get rid of them all."

"Who said that?" asked Davis, for clarification.

"Emma."[212]

Edna also told how Emma had suggested that her father do away with Mrs. Billik. Copping a sly grin, she turned and imitated the way that Emma whispered the idea. She then mimicked her father's anger as he adamantly refused to carry it out. Davis asked Edna about another incident, which happened while she sat with her father and Emma on a bench at Riverside one afternoon. "Emma asked if Papa wasn't going to get rid of Ma," she told Davis. "That

Mary Billik and daughter Edna. *Photo courtesy of the Chicago History Museum, DN-0005088.*

if there was no other way he was to poison her and Papa said that he had not the heart to do that, and I started out crying and she said that I belonged to my ma and that I could go with her, and I didn't belong to my pa, and that she was going with my pa."[213] She said Emma at one point even told her that she could, "Go to hell."[214] After Emma left, Edna talked with her father. "I cried," she said, "and my papa said it was all right and that he wasn't going any place."[215] It was an emotional, heartfelt story. It certainly cast a shadow on Emma's credibility, but was it enough to spare little Edna's father from the hangman? Prosecutors decided not to question Edna. Davis helped her down from the witness stand, and the defense rested their case.

16

The Verdict

On the final day of the trial, prosecutors called several witnesses to rebut Billik's testimony about being out of town on July 27th, 1906, when the much-discussed attempt to asphyxiate the Vrzal girls was allegedly made. Several witnesses verified that Billik was in French Lick Springs from July 4th to July 22nd. Another witness, Mrs. Frances Chomates, said that on July 23rd, Billik arrived at Riverside, and stayed at her rooming house for a week. She said Billik went away in the day time, but was there in Riverside every evening. That actually implied that he must have been in Riverside the night that the gas was turned on, and not at the Vrzal home, some ten miles away. Nonetheless, he appeared to have been in the Chicago area that night, contrary to his testimony.

Attorneys then made their closing arguments. Assistant State's Attorney Popham condemned Herman Billik as "foul" and "contemptible," and "one of the most damnable scoundrels who ever lived on this earth."[216] Holding absolutely nothing back, he told the courtroom, "The man who steals up behind you and shoots you in the back is a gentleman compared with Billik."[217] Popham denounced the supposed master of the black arts as a heartless killer, and *demanded* that Herman Billik be put to death. Edna Billik started to weep, and for the first time in the trial, Mary Billik broke down, and she too began to cry. Popham went on without hesitation, "Poison has become the frequent route for fiends to get rid of their wives, and wives of their husbands and for carrying out the vile plots of assassination. Don't let it be said in the future: 'Look at the Billik jury, a tenderhearted, sympathetic jury . . .'"[218]

Hinckley objected, and Popham withdrew the remark immediately, obviously aware that it was improper. But the jury already heard him loud and clear. The Knudson jury had been publicly criticized for being too sympathetic. Many accused them of letting a murderer go free because they felt sorry for Knudson and his children. Popham's comment was a not-so-subtle reminder to the jury to avoid that same pitfall. He even told them, of little Edna, "She is here . . . to her shame . . . to arouse your pity if possible."[219]

Hinckley made the closing argument for the defense. He very directly accused Emma Vrzal Niemann of poisoning her family. For the motive, he pointed to the house and milk business, both of which were now owned by Emma and her husband. If anyone "profited" from the deaths, he declared, it was her.

Assistant State's Attorney Holt then made his own impassioned plea to impose the death penalty. When he was done, after much disagreement over the wording, Judge Barnes read instructions to the jury. They left to begin deliberations at twenty minutes past four. Barnes recessed court until eight p.m. He figured that would give the jury some time to get organized, and in the morning they could begin their work in earnest.

To everyone's surprise, just two and a half hours later, at around seven o'clock, jurors notified the bailiff that they had arrived at a verdict. Normally, such a quick decision in a complicated case bodes well for the defendant. The courtroom was packed. Everyone was anxious. The only one who seemed at ease was little Edna. She chatted with the lady seated next her and looked around the courtroom pointing out various people she recognized. As the court came to order, she carefully smoothed the folds in her pink dress, expecting her father would soon be coming home. The jury filed in. Billik was escorted into the room by two guards who stood at either side. After what must have felt like an eternity, the foreman verified that the jury had reached a decision. The clerk of the court stepped up and, with a booming voice, read, "We the jury . . . find the Defendant . . . Herman Billik . . . guilty of the charge of murder of Mary Vrzal . . . and sentence the defendant to die by hanging."[220]

Billik was quite literally staggered. He reached out and grabbed at a pillar to catch himself. He managed to recover, and stood up straight, but had a look of complete shock. He stared blankly into the eyes of his young daughter. "They have deaded my papa!"[221] Edna wailed. She began sobbing uncontrollably. Mary Billik gasped, and then collapsed. Her sons Herman Jr. and fifteen-year-old Frank (who lived in Cleveland) clutched her arms, trying desperately to hold her up as they wept. Billik's mother, and even the Vrzal children, cried loudly.

Judge Barnes, speaking loud enough to be heard over the clamor that now enveloped the courtroom, polled the jury and thanked them. Jurors said they agreed from the very start of their deliberations that Billik was guilty. It then took them only two ballots to determine that he should pay for the crime with his life. The evidence suggesting that there were other victims was key to their decision to give him the death penalty. Barnes excused the jury and ordered the prisoner to be removed. Billik was still in shock as deputies escorted him from the courtroom.

Billik spent a sleepless night in his cell, repeatedly denying that he harmed anyone, crying out to anyone who would listen. Early in the morning his family arrived. His mother Barbara, the focus of so much discussion during the trial, was there, as was his wife Mary, and sons Frank, Herman Jr., and eleven-year-old Emil. The only one missing was little Edna. She was so overcome by grief that she suffered a breakdown and Mrs. Billik had a neighbor watch her while the rest of family went back down to the jail.

Guards allowed them to meet along the bridge that connected the jail to the courthouse. Aside from being a passageway to take prisoners to their court hearings, it was used as an office by one of the jail guards. It afforded the family a modicum of privacy. There were a few chairs and desks, with locked steel doors at either end of the corridor that linked the two buildings.

It was a miserable scene. The family sobbed, and clung to the condemned man and one another for comfort. Billik tried to remain hopeful. "Don't you think I will get a new trial? I think so," he said, doing his best to smile through his tears. "But if I don't, we will take my case to the Supreme Court. What about the Supreme Court? Don't you think there they may spare my life?"[222] His mother and wife reassured him. They held him and whispered gently. The children wept as their father tightly clutched a handkerchief and wiped his own tears. "It is hard," he said, "to be convicted of murder when you didn't do it."[223] The clang of metal doors and screams of prisoners echoed in the background, but the family barely noticed.

Part III

Questions

17

Hope

Hinckley promised to do everything possible to secure a new trial. Billik tried to stay optimistic. His family visited regularly, helping to cheer him up from nights in a dismal cell. Edna turned ten just a few days after the verdict, but was still too distraught to see her papa. When Emil turned twelve a few weeks later, the whole family spent the day together. They tried their best to enjoy themselves, though they had little to celebrate. They hoped to get some good news from court. That afternoon, Billik's defense team appeared before Judge Barnes to argue for a new trial. They attacked the testimony of both Emma and Jerry, who claimed to have known of the murders of their father and sisters, yet said nothing until long after they were all in their graves.

Barnes said he would do nothing unless there was some startling new evidence. Hinckley then told him that he had located two new witnesses who would connect Emma to the murders. He presented Judge Barnes with an affidavit from a man named Gilbert Sellers, who worked at the railroad station in Galesburg. Sellers claimed that he and another man saw a woman they believed to be Emma Niemann in the station one night scraping the label from a bottle of poison. He said the bottle contained a white powder that looked like arsenic. Barnes wasn't impressed. He said it wasn't nearly enough to warrant a new trial, and that Emma had no conceivable motive to murder her family.

Hinckley again pointed to the Vrzal home and milk business, which Emma and her husband now owned. When they purchased the property, Mrs. Vrzal moved out, taking Jerry and Bertha to live with relatives. The house was big enough for all of them. Why did Mrs. Vrzal see it necessary to leave and move in with her cousin, who had a husband and four children of her own? Why were Emma and little Bertha the only family members who had not been poisoned? Had Jerry not recovered, Emma would likely have been made Bertha's guardian and controlled the entire inheritance. That, combined with her anger over being practically disowned by her parents and thrown out of the house, was motive enough. Hinckley suggested that part of Emma's plan was to implicate Billik in the deaths. She said several times during her testimony that she hated him, even before anyone in her family died. She also said of her own mother, "She didn't like me. Everybody knew it."[224] Why then would her mother (or Billik) poison everyone except her? And why would Mrs. Vrzal slowly poison herself with arsenic?

Judge Barnes, however, said that the evidence against Billik was entirely conclusive. He promptly denied the motion for a new trial and righteously declared that no man had ever received a fairer trial.[225] He set the date of October 11th, 1907 for Herman Billik to hang. The following day, Barnes gave a copy of Gilbert Sellers' affidavit to Police Chief Shippy. Officers picked up Sellers, and brought him to Emma's house. According to police accounts, Mr. Sellers immediately declared that she was not the same woman he had seen at the station, and they drafted an affidavit for him to sign. It was a major blow to Billik's fading hope.

Billik was moved to the "murderer's row" section of the jail. Life in Cook County Jail was not pleasant. Aside from being overcrowded, dark, and dirty, prisoners were barely fed. Billik was given three meals a day, two of which consisted of a tin of black coffee and a single slice of bread. The other meal was, invariably, a portion of very poor quality beef, vegetable, and another slice of bread.[226] Cook County Sheriff Christopher Strassheim, like his predecessors, made a sizable profit by pocketing the difference between the amount of money budgeted to feed prisoners, and how much he actually spent. He increased his take by purchasing half of all the jail's food supplies from Shepard, Strassheim, & Company, his own wholesale grocery business. He made no apologies, but refused to say exactly how much profit it brought him.

Subsequent investigations showed that Strassheim spent less than seven cents per day to feed each prisoner, while the budget was about twenty-one cents for every one of the 500–600 men held at the jail. It netted him a clean $30,000 a year, in addition to his $6,000 salary as sheriff, and the profits from his food contracts. On top of all that, Strassheim made an unknown fortune from the jail's "store," where he gave inmates a chance to purchase sweets and quality bread made in the prison bakery. He, of course, kept all the money. He maximized sales at his store by underfeeding the prisoners and denying them "luxuries," such as sugar, cocoa, and syrup, which they were then forced to purchase from him.

Strassheim, another close ally of Mayor Busse, didn't see anything wrong with it. "Where's the use in a public official having a business training if he can't turn his knowledge to account?"[227] said the sheriff-turned-wholesale-grocer. Strassheim couldn't understand what the big deal was. About the only thing he denied was the charge that the prison store was run by his nephew. The man was merely his niece's husband, he clarified, trusting that that should put an end to the scandal. The County Board did finally shut down the jail store, but Strassheim continued pilfering the prisoners' food money for several more years. It was hard to get the public outraged when prisoners were the victims of the injustice. That's what Herman Billik was learning.

Billik hoped to file an appeal, but the clock was ticking. It was not unheard of for men to be executed before they could come up with the staggering $1,500 in fees and bond money necessary. That was money Billik didn't have. He could act the part of a well-to-do aristocrat, but it was all a façade. Herman Jr. once said his father liked to tell people he was rich.[228] But all the talk of high living, fine furnishings, and carriages were wild exaggerations. In fact, the Billiks were quite poor. If they were going to finance an appeal, they would have to find some way to raise the money.

Billik had been so vilified that there wasn't much sympathy for him. Very few were willing to contribute anything to save his neck. The fact that he was a Bohemian immigrant didn't help. There was a lot of prejudice against Bohemians and other recent immigrants, who were often poor, uneducated, and generally looked down upon by more established Chicagoans. Ironically, the Bohemian community, which was particularly close-knit, wasn't going to get behind any big effort for Billik either. They had been cast in a very negative light by the whole affair: all the talk of magic and superstition, murder, and indecent relationships. It was all so scandalous. Most Bohemians just wanted to put the tragedy behind them.

From his cell, Billik wasn't able to do much to help his own cause. He could only pray that someone would step forward and put up the money to help save him. He was Catholic, but admittedly didn't go to church very often. Still, he enjoyed visits from the prison chaplain, and the various church workers that would come to the jail. Sister Rose was one of them. She was a Catholic nun from the Sisters of the Sacred Heart. She spent a lot of time visiting with prisoners, and came to know Billik well. He told her his family was now destitute. His children were practically starving and no one would have anything to do with them. Sister Rose introduced the Billiks to a woman involved in charity work at St. Mary's Church at 9th St. and Wabash. The lady offered to take in Mary and the children, and the church fed the desperate family.

Over the course of his visits with Sister Rose, Billik shared the details of his case. She became convinced that an innocent man was about to be executed. She said she would talk to the only person she could think of that might be able to help: Father O'Callaghan, the Pastor of St. Mary's.

18

The Priest and the Reporter

Rev. Peter J. ("P.J.") O'Callaghan had been head of St. Mary's for almost four years. He was short and slight, but a veritable lion on the pulpit. A witty and persuasive orator, the young Paulist priest was already one of the most prominent leaders of the growing temperance movement. His enthusiasm was contagious, his leadership undeniable. When he believed in something, he was likened to a locomotive running downhill: completely unstoppable.

He was born to Irish immigrants, and grew up in a large family in Salem, Massachusetts—ironically, the site of the infamous Salem Witch Trials. He had three brothers who became lawyers, and had planned to follow in their footsteps. He graduated from Harvard University in 1888, before recognizing his true calling. O'Callaghan then began theological study at the College of St. Thomas Aquinas, the novitiate of the Paulist Fathers at Catholic University in Washington, D.C. The Paulist Fathers stressed spreading the Gospel in innovative and exciting ways to get people interested in the message of the church. It was a perfect match for the charismatic young priest. He was ordained in 1893.

O'Callaghan was first assigned to a parish in New York City, preaching in missions. He quickly earned a reputation as an outstanding public speaker, and as a vigorous proponent of total abstinence from alcohol. After ten years in New York, O'Callaghan

Rev. Peter J. O'Callaghan. *Photo courtesy of the Chicago History Museum, DN-0052761.*

was sent to Chicago to take charge of St. Mary's. The neighborhood around the church had become somewhat of a run-down warehouse district, and Chicago's Archbishop Quigley invited the Paulist Fathers to re-energize the parish.[229] The dynamic and articulate O'Callaghan was chosen to lead the effort.

Sister Rose had first approached O'Callaghan during Billik's trial. She told him she had reservations about his guilt, but O'Callaghan paid her little mind. He regularly visited prisoners himself, and knew just how many said they were innocent. He didn't have the time to become absorbed in every case where a man claimed he was wrongly accused. He told Sister Rose at the time that if Billik was innocent, the court would determine so, and release him. But it didn't work out that way, and now he was condemned to die. Sister Rose begged O'Callaghan to at least talk to Billik to hear his story. Then he could judge for himself. O'Callaghan, rather reluctantly, agreed.

A few days later, he paid a visit to Billik at the County Jail. He was skeptical at the start, but soon got a sense that he was talking with someone who simply could not have committed the crimes. The pastor was pretty good at sizing people up. He had visited plenty of men behind bars, including a good number of murderers. He got no sense that Herman Billik was a killer. On the contrary, O'Callaghan found him sincere, and his story surprisingly believable. After a while he started thinking an injustice may have been done. Billik feared that his lawyers had deserted him. He had heard little about his appeal, and was now just weeks away from execution. He pleaded with the priest to help him. O'Callaghan said he'd meet with Francis Hinckley, the only lawyer still on the case, who by this point was working on his own time for free.

Though he worked tirelessly, Hinckley was having little success raising money for an appeal, and he was running out of people to ask. If it wasn't hard enough already, on September 15th, the *New York World* ran a story about Billik that was carried nationally by the *Washington Post*. It detailed the dastardly murders of the Vrzals, and called Billik "the meanest murderer on earth," who ruthlessly murdered small children for as little as $100. Less than a month before Billik's execution, things did not look good. Hinckley had plenty of issues to bring up on appeal, but he feared that, even if they did somehow find the money, the paperwork might not get done in time. It was a monster of a job. Between preparing legal arguments and raising funds, he had completely exhausted himself. He lost twenty pounds in the weeks after the trial.

When Father O'Callaghan came to see him, Hinckley told him that, aside from Jerry and Emma's testimony, most all of the evidence was remarkably consistent with Billik's version of events, and that the most damning allegations (such as Billik poisoning Mary's coffee and openly discussing his intention to murder the family) were never mentioned in the first several months of the investigation. Hinckley said the new stories almost miraculously filled in the gaps in the prosecution's case. Whenever they needed to prove some part of their theory, Jerry or Emma suddenly remembered it, right down to the date and time of virtually every incident. O'Callaghan knew a few attorneys he might convince to give a hand, and said he would personally help to raise the money. Hinckley could focus on the legal issues.

O'Callaghan then went to see Leonard "L.G." Edwardson, the editor of the *Chicago Examiner*, and convinced him to delve a little deeper into the case. He also spoke out on Billik's behalf from the pulpit of St. Mary's Church. He told his congregation that they should ignore their prejudices and preconceived ideas. There were many questions and, at the absolute minimum, Herman Billik deserved a chance to appeal his case. A man's life was as stake, he told them, and asked people to contribute what they could. At first, only a few responded, but word started getting around that it just might be possible that Billik was innocent. As more people talked, the cause attracted more attention, and more contributions began to appear.

OCTOBER-NOVEMBER 1907

On October 4th, exactly one week before Billik was to be hanged, Hinckley went to Judge Barnes to apply for a stay of execution. He said he needed time to prepare the voluminous appeal document, and announced that an anonymous benefactor had come forward to finance much of the appeal bond. Barnes granted the stay. He gave Hinckley thirty days to come up with the rest of the money and prepare the record for the Illinois Supreme Court. He rescheduled Billik's execution to November 8th. "Now I will get off," the suddenly hopeful prisoner told reporters. "They will see that Herman Billik did not know what killed the Vrzals. They may find out now about Emma Niemann."[230]

During the week, L.G. Edwardson came to see Father O'Callaghan. He told him that several days after the priest had spoken about Billik to his congregation, they received an interesting letter at the offices of the *Examiner*. It was several pages long. The anonymous author said he knew that Herman Billik did not kill the Vrzals; there were other people involved. At first, it sounded like it might be some kind of a crank letter. But the author clearly knew an awful lot about the case. There were many details; some had never been made public.

The letter mentioned Joe Cooney several times. It said that he hung out at a saloon called the Gerald, at the corner of 12th St. and Blue Island Ave. Apparently the Billik case was a frequent topic of conversation at the bar, and a lot of people there thought Emma was responsible for the murders. They knew Cooney had gotten her pregnant, and talked about how the Vrzal family felt disgraced and threw her out of the house, and how Emma vowed to kill the whole family as revenge. The letter went on to say that the arsenic was purchased from a druggist named P. Coffey, of 1543 W. 12th St.,* and even gave the names of several people from the neighborhood around the Gerald who knew about it.

O'Callaghan was excited. They now had some solid leads to follow up on. Edwardson published a story about the letter in the *Examiner*, and asked for the author, or anyone else with information, to step forward. He forwarded the letter to State's Attorney Healy, assuming it would be thoroughly investigated.

Edwardson did some digging of his own and found out a little more about Emma's old beau. It turned out that Joe "Tip" Cooney was well known on the West Side as a pretty rough character. He had been arrested numerous times, including a charge of manslaughter resulting from the death of a man in a barroom brawl a few years earlier. Cooney was married and had six young children. He was also dating Emma during the period of time that both

---

* Pre-1910 Address

her father and her sister Mary became sick and died. Edwardson learned that Emma would entertain Cooney at all hours of the night, even as her father Martin lie in bed dying.[231] He also discovered that Cooney was a rather large man, built quite similar to Billik. Edwardson believed he was the one Dr. Napieralski saw leaving the Vrzal home when he came to treat the girls for the gas incident. Interestingly, Cooney once listed his occupation as a "gas fitter."[232]

Edwardson even did a bit of undercover investigating, going to the Gerald himself. He said that while there, he overheard a conversation that verified many of the claims made in the letter. He had no hard evidence that he could bring to court, but he told Father O'Callaghan that a lot of people at the Gerald seemed to think Billik was an innocent dupe, and talked as if it was almost common knowledge that Cooney was somehow involved. They felt they were definitely on the right track.

There was an oddly familiar trial beginning around this time. In a bit of déjà vu, Assistant State's Attorney Popham was prosecuting the case against a Bohemian woman accused of poisoning her family with arsenic. Twenty-two-year-old Mary Sladek was accused of murdering her parents and causing her three brothers to become ill when they ate a cake laced with a heavy dose of rat poison. Police later discovered arsenic in the salt and sugar containers, as well as in flour and oatmeal in the house. The trial was yet another morbid spectacle for the citizens of Chicago.

Sounding a familiar note, Popham claimed that insurance money was the motive for the killings. Just as in the Billik trial, Popham attempted to bring in a parade of witnesses to verify that the insurance money had been paid. Seasoned defense attorney Joseph Burres objected, and the judge agreed that the testimony was overkill, and unnecessary. But Popham insisted, "That was the accepted method in the Billik case, and I can further show . . ."[233]

"I object to any reference to the Billik case," shouted Burres, who jumped up and began waiving his arms wildly. "I don't think the attorney has any right to bring up the Billik case," he exclaimed.[234] The judge agreed. "I don't care what is the adopted method in other courts. I might not decide to rule as they do," he told Popham sternly. "The Billik case has no bearing on this one."[235]

Mary and Edna Billik came down to the jail every day to visit Herman, so they were right next door to the courthouse when the Sladek trial was going on. The next morning, they couldn't help but go over and sit in on the proceedings. They took a seat in the back of the courtroom. As they waited for court to be called to order, a bailiff recognized them and told Edna that there was another little girl there to watch the trial too, just about the same age as her. In a short time he came back and introduced Edna to a little girl named Annie—Annie Knudson. Her father introduced himself to Mrs. Billik. His name was Knute Knudson. He was there to speak with Mrs. Sladek's attorney, Joseph Burres, who had also represented him.

The group recognized one another immediately, and began chatting. The two girls had exchanged letters, but never met. They became fast friends. They sat side by side in the same chair as the trial got underway. The testimony that morning focused on the dry scientific facts of arsenic poisoning, with which both children were all too familiar. Finally, the girls were allowed into the anteroom adjoining the main courtroom. They tiptoed inside where they were allowed to peer over the shoulder of a prison matron holding a tiny baby in her arms. Mary Sladek had been pregnant at the time of her arrest. Her daughter, Helen, was born while she was in jail awaiting trial, and was now just six weeks old. Prison workers nicknamed her "Liberty." Edna and Annie peeked in at the infant, who looked up at them and smiled. It was a heartwarming and remarkable scene. The three girls' lives were eerily linked in a web of mystery and circumstance. And each would take their turn at center stage to try to save a parent accused of murder.

Buoyed by the information from Edwardson, Father O'Callaghan continued his campaign with fervor. He hoped to get more people to come forward with information, and donations. He contacted the press, and even spoke out in the Bohemian language newspaper. The effort was gaining momentum. He decided to try to talk to Jerry Vrzal, who, he was sure, knew something more about the case. By that time, Jerry had started college and was away at school. Near the end of October, just a week before Billik was to be executed, O'Callaghan headed to Valparaiso University, just south of Chicago, in Indiana. He brought Edwardson along, and the two met with Jerry in his dorm room on campus. O'Callaghan did most of the talking. He told Jerry that they had been looking into the case, and he was now certain that Billik was innocent.

Jerry didn't say much, but did verify that Emma had been dating Joe Cooney when the deaths in the family started, and that his parents were not at all happy about their relationship. That's why they wanted so badly to see Emma marry her old boyfriend, Albert Rus, and asked Billik to "charm" him back for her. O'Callaghan sensed that Jerry was holding something back. Before leaving, he told him that if he was ever asked to testify again, he should simply tell the truth. It was not too late to do the right thing.

At about this same time, Emma wrote a bizarre letter to Jerry at Valparaiso. It read in part:

Jerry last week on[e] day I got a letter from a woman and it is the dirt[iest] letter you ever heard. It . . . said that Billik want[s] the priest to help him out—that the priest wants Billik to get him some nice girls like [he] used to—that they both would have a good time like they always had together.[236]

Apparently, Emma thought she could use it against Father O'Callaghan and his efforts to save Billik. She continued,

I will keep that letter—for I want to get the priest in trouble for he has put in the Bohemian paper that I am the murder[er] and in case Billik gets the rope that I would be arrest[ed] for a different crime.[237]

O'Callaghan considered Emma's story a feeble attempt to discredit him. He suspected that she concocted the letter herself, and thought it pointed to her guilt much more than it harmed his reputation.

The day after O'Callaghan's visit, Jerry took the train back to Chicago and went down to City Hall. He met with Assistant State's Attorney Popham, and told him about his meeting with the priest. Popham told him not to worry about O'Callaghan, and that he need not speak to him if he came to see him again. Jerry also went to see his sister to tell her. Emma said that the priest had been saying a lot of things about her, and that she was going to sue him.

Undeterred, O'Callaghan pressed on. "There is much prejudice against Billik,"[238] the priest noted. However, he left no question about his own feelings. "There is no doubt in my mind of his innocence," he told reporters. "Everything that I discover makes me ever more sure that he is not guilty."[239]

19

A New Mystery

On Monday, November 4th, just four days before Billik was scheduled to be executed, came absolutely shocking news. Emma's thirty-nine-year-old husband, William Niemann, was dead. He had died suddenly at their home on 19th St., in the early afternoon. Emma said he suffered from rheumatism, but that she had no idea how bad off he was. His condition had recently deteriorated, though no doctor had seen him for at least three days. "We did not think he was dangerously ill until he suddenly gasped for breath and expired in his brother's arms,"[240] she explained. But in her letter to Jerry, which she had written just a few weeks earlier, in mid-October, Emma had mentioned that "Neamann"* (as she always referred to her husband) was not well, and that she had a doctor coming to see him *daily*. It seemed odd to have a doctor visiting so regularly, then quit calling him right as her husband became gravely ill and died.

He evidently was in poor enough health that his brother Fred, who lived in Downer's Grove, saw it necessary to come and stay at the house for several weeks leading up to William's death. Fred

---

* The name was originally "Niemann," but Emma and William spelled it "Neamann."

Niemann described his brother's final minutes: "William had just taken up his long pipe to smoke and was seated in the rocking chair. Without any words he began gasping for breath, and before we could get a doctor he was dead."[241] Emma called Dr. Max Weiskopf, who had been treating her husband for his rheumatism. Dr. Weiskopf thought it looked suspicious. He refused to sign the death certificate. Instead, he notified Coroner Hoffman and suggested he open an investigation.

News of William Niemann's death spread fast. Public sentiment was shifting in Billik's favor. If it turned out that Niemann had been poisoned, it would raise enormous doubts about Billik's conviction, and possibly spare him from the gallows. Prosecutors and police knew that as well as anyone. Speculation about the cause of the dairyman's death was rampant. While Emma ascribed it to rheumatism, Fred Niemann had his own theory; though he wasn't convinced there was any foul play at hand, either. "I don't see any evidence of poison," the farmer declared. "He drank heavily of late, and that may have affected his heart."[242]

Coroner Hoffman, along with coroner's physician Dr. Henry G.W. Reinhardt, and Dr. Harold Moyer, went to the home that evening to conduct a postmortem examination. Moyer and Reinhardt refused to comment on their initial findings, but Hoffman announced, "We were not able to arrive at any conclusion as to the cause of death. We removed the stomach, intestines, liver, and kidneys, and placed them in jars. [Doctors] will make a microscopical analysis and, if necessary, a chemical analysis will be made later."[243] Billik's attorneys were careful of what they said, though they clearly had their suspicions. "It might result in a revelation that will show up this awful affair in the right light,"[244] said Hinckley.

NOVEMBER 5, 1907

The next morning, a coroner's inquest was begun. Little evidence was accepted, the only two witnesses being Emma and Fred Niemann. Their testimony centered on William Niemann's last hours, and seemed to leave the impression that there were probably not a lot of similarities between his symptoms and those of the Vrzals. Just as she had at the Vrzal inquest, and at Billik's trial, Emma created a commotion by weeping dramatically and fainting while discussing the death of her husband. She said he had actually been sick for about nine weeks. "He had been complaining for some time, but it was not until Oct. 4th that we sent for Dr. Russell, and then we found out that his complaint was rheumatism,"[245] she explained. Dr. Russell gave him some pills and a liniment to apply.

It's not clear why, but Emma subsequently called Dr. Weiskopf to examine her husband. He had treated Martin Vrzal several years back, and had diagnosed him with rheumatism before he died. He attributed Niemann's illness to rheumatism as well, and prescribed more medication. Emma said she didn't call a doctor in the days before her husband's death because he was sitting up in bed smoking a pipe, claiming to be free of pain, though he was unable to even stand up by that point. Fred Niemann testified that he sat at his brother's bedside all night the night before he died. During that time, he said, William breathed heavily, and appeared to be in intense pain.[246]

Emma said she didn't even know her husband was dead until she tried to take the pipe from his mouth. "Myself and my brother [-in-law] Fred carried him from his bed and placed him in a rocking chair in the basement, near the dairy, where we could watch him. He smoked part of the day and about eleven o'clock we carried him to his bed."[247] She claimed William said he was able to walk, but he quite obviously could not. He was no longer able to even fill his pipe with tobacco. Emma continued, "From that time on I filled his pipe several times and he sat smoking until the room was filled with smoke. When I went to fill his pipe at three o'clock I found him dead. My brother [-in-law] was in the room at the time and it was then that we called one of the neighbors to bring in a doctor so that we might be sure."[248]

Coroner Hoffman adjourned the proceeding until the next afternoon. Very little was learned, mainly because the people coming forward with information were not asked to testify. One neighbor reportedly told police that since the Vrzal deaths, William Niemann had feared being poisoned, and even canceled his life insurance policy.[249] The witness was never brought before the coroner's jury, but Emma herself verified that her husband canceled his life insurance in the months leading up to his death. "My husband carried no insurance because we no longer believe in life insurance,"[250] she told police.

If that didn't raise any red flags with investigators, one would think they'd listen to Niemann's own doctors. Not only did Dr. Weiskopf refuse to sign the death certificate and report the death to the coroner as suspicious, but he even suggested it may have been the result of poison. "I would not attempt to explain the cause of Niemann's death," he said. "It was a mysterious case. There were symptoms that might be attributed to slow poisoning."[251] Yet, in spite of all this, Dr. Weiskopf was not asked to testify at the inquest. Neither was Dr. Russell, who also treated Niemann in his final months.

Hinckley assumed that the police would jump into action. Clues were brought forward, but only some were investigated. Others would be "later,"[252] they promised, expressing no real sense of urgency. The case didn't seem to be a much of a priority. Hinckley wanted to know why detectives were dragging their feet. He was astonished when he was told that police were not actively investigating the matter. "Coroner Hoffman suggested we need not do further work until the result of the postmortem be known," said the lieutenant in charge of the case.[253]

NOVEMBER 6, 1907

On Wednesday, November 6th, Dr. Reinhardt and Dr. Moyer reported the results of their examination to Hoffman and Chief Shippy. After a long conference, Hoffman announced that the inquest would not resume until November 18th, which was *after* Billik's scheduled execution. He said that the test results would not yet be made public, though he claimed doctors had failed to find any trace of poison. Hoffman said that everything mysterious about Niemann's death would be explained. "Indications are that the man died from natural causes, hastened by his excessive drinking,"[254] he concluded.

Hinckley was beside himself. It had taken weeks to determine that the Vrzals had been poisoned. How could Hoffman (who had no formal medical training), in just one day, be so sure how William Niemann died? If no arsenic was found in Niemann's stomach, that didn't prove he wasn't poisoned. It only meant that he probably didn't swallow arsenic within a day or two of his death. Hoffman told Hinckley detectives would remain assigned to the case, but that didn't matter if they weren't actually going to investigate it. "The police didn't even make a search of the house for poison or poisoned food," said the flustered attorney. "I don't know whether Niemann was poisoned or not, but if it can be proven that he was, Herman Billik would be a free man inside of six weeks."[255]

The more Hinckley learned, the more infuriated he was. Ludwig Alexa, the clerk at the drugstore across the street from the Vrzal-Niemann home on 19th St., told detectives that Emma came in early Monday morning to use the telephone. He said she told him that her husband was exceedingly sick and she feared he might die.[256] He didn't know who she called, but it wasn't a doctor. For some reason Emma didn't call for a doctor until William died some hours later. The clerk's story directly contradicted Emma's claim that she didn't think her husband was in any danger, but Mr. Alexa was another witness absent from the inquest.

An even more peculiar story was confirmed by none other than the Cook County State's Attorney's Office. It turned out that Emma had worried for some time about the possibility of her husband dying suddenly, and her being blamed. More than a month earlier, she had written a letter to Assistant State's Attorney Popham, in which she told him of those very fears. She then met with Popham around the middle of October, and he apparently reassured her that there would no suspicion directed against her.[257]

20

Opposition

Jerry read about his brother-in-law's death in the *Examiner*, and came back from Valparaiso for the funeral. He didn't stay with his newly-widowed sister, but with his guardians Mr. and Mrs. Jones. After the funeral, he went down to St. Mary's to talk to Father O'Callaghan. He was starting to have second thoughts about Billik's guilt himself. The priest told Jerry that he was confident Billik would get a new trial and, when he did, Jerry would have to tell the *whole* truth. Jerry was still apprehensive. He said he'd get back to him when he was ready to talk more.

Many thought Niemann's death might bring a quick conclusion to Herman Billiks' plight, but that wasn't the case. "The sudden death of Niemann has caused considerable doubt as to Billik's guilt, but has not had any legal influence on the proceedings against Billik,"[258] reported Hinckley, whose client was still scheduled to hang in a few days. They had raised the last of the necessary funds, and Hinckley finally completed the mass of paperwork laying out all of the issues he was contesting from the trial. He filed it, and obtained a "bill of exceptions," which documented all of the objections to be argued on appeal. He now needed only to submit the 2,000 page missive to the clerk of the Illinois Supreme Court in downstate Springfield to get a stay of execution. The only problem was that there was only one copy of it, and Cook County

State's Attorney Healy refused to allow it to be sent to the Supreme Court. Healy justified his decision by saying they had a deal worked out in which he would provide a copy of the bill to Billik's attorneys, who were to provide his office with a copy of the abstract of the trial testimony that they were preparing but hadn't given it to him. Hinckley said he did submit most of the abstract, but Assistant State's Attorney Popham made so many changes to it that the meaning of much of the testimony was altered, so he never sent them the rest. It sounded like Healy and Popham had gotten the better of the young attorney.

Hinckley went before Judge Barnes and asked him to order Healy to turn the documents over for the appeal, something he thought would be a simple formality. He couldn't believe it when Barnes refused. He accused both Barnes and Healy of trying to rush Billik to the gallows, and charged the State's Attorney's Office with using underhanded tactics to prevent the appeal from being heard. He decided to go directly to Judge Orrin Carter of the Illinois Supreme Court to let him know what was going on. Justice Carter ordered Healy to hand over the bill of exceptions immediately, and ordered that Billik could not be hanged until the court was finished hearing his appeal. It was a close call.

Seeing little progress in the Niemann investigation, Father O'Callaghan went to Judge Barnes. He suggested that the milk dealer's last days sounded hauntingly similar to the deaths of Martin Vrzal and his children: Niemann's painful "rheumatism," and the way he gradually weakened, eventually becoming unable to walk, or even stand, as he neared death. O'Callaghan was an ardent critic of alcohol consumption, but even he doubted that it could be responsible for the effects that Niemann suffered.

Accompanying O'Callaghan to his meeting with Barnes was Dr. J. Sanderson Christison, a well known criminologist who was among those now helping with the effort to save Billik. Christison was outspoken on the subject of wrongful convictions, and had involved himself in several high-profile cases over the years. Need-less to say, he was not a favorite among Chicago's law enforcement officials. Only a few weeks earlier, Christison had started a ruckus at the inaugural meeting of the Chicago Criminological Society when he gave a speech in which he railed against Chicago police over the conviction and hanging of men without solid evidence. Christison was a medical doctor who had authored several books, including one called *Drink and Disease*. He told Barnes that he too found it unlikely that alcohol had caused Niemann's death. Barnes said there was nothing he could do. It was up to the police and the state's attorney to determine if a crime had been committed. O'Callaghan and Christison left disappointed.

Looking at some of his more controversial ideas, it's tempting today to dismiss Dr. Christison as somewhat of a crackpot. How-ever, most of his beliefs were fairly widespread at the time, in-cluding the notion that you could judge one's mental state (and propensity to commit crime) by the shape of their face. The Chi-cago police expert on the psychology of criminals, Dr. Harold Moyer, held similar beliefs. Moyer was the chief "alienist" for the county. He provided opinions on the mental state of defendants and witnesses appearing before the court. He was quite respected in the field, and held what would be considered mainstream ideas for the time. Among them was his belief that he could determine if a man was mentally ill just by looking at his photograph. "One of the characteristic signs of a degenerate is a want of symmetry between the two sides of the head and face," Moyer wrote. "As a rule, the insane may be classified by a study of their pictures."[259]

Moyer didn't agree with Christison on everything, though. Where Christison believed in reforming criminals, Moyer pro-posed increasing executions as a means of controlling crime. He noted that in the past the English had more than a hundred crimes that were punishable by death. "A dead criminal won't commit any more crimes," said the grim doctor. "I believe the hanging method would reduce crimes."[260] This was the same Dr. Moyer who worked on the Vrzal investigation and, more recently, the au-topsy of William Niemann.

A few days before the Niemann inquest resumed, the trial of Mary Sladek was wrapping up. Prosecutors felt they had a much better case than they had against Billik, mainly because a druggist identified Sladek as having purchased rat poison from him the day the family was poisoned. Sladek's attorney, Joseph Burres, pointed out that at the time of the murders the druggist hadn't really been able to identify her, but now, months later, he was suddenly all but certain that she was the woman. Burres also vigorously cross-examined doctors to whom Mrs. Sladek had herself complained of symptoms of arsenic poisoning. They could offer no explanation as to why they now said they did not believe her.

Mrs. Sladek's baby disrupted the proceedings numerous times. Mary cradled her in her arms until she quieted and fell asleep. Both mother and child were sick during the trial, and Mary got so little rest caring for her newborn that she actually fell asleep right in the middle of the courtroom at one point. Burres explained the situation, and in the process showed everyone what a loving, caring mother his client was. In his closing statement, Burres made an impassioned speech, telling the jury, "If you send her tottering to the gallows as you have the power to do, I say the last word she utters before she dies is, 'God care for my baby, oh my baby.'"[261]

Assistant State's Attorney Popham recognized that the jury was not likely to vote to hang a young mother. He said the state was not asking for the death penalty, and told jurors, "I, like the judge here . . . do not believe in capital punishment, although as sworn officers of the law we might be required to enforce it."[262] Then Popham made a proclamation that Herman Billik must have found more than a little ironic: "I believe that when the voice of God on Mt. Sinai thundered down the words, 'Thou shalt not kill,' the state was meant as much as the individual."[263] Father O'Callaghan could not have put it so well.

The jury found Mary Sladek "not guilty." Throughout the trial, it had been insinuated that Mrs. Sladek's husband feared his wife, and believed her to be guilty. He stayed silent during the proceedings, but afterward Mr. Sladek said he would welcome her home. "I would have come forward to help my wife had I been permitted,"[264] he told reporters somewhat cryptically, without elaborating.

One wonders if the outcome of Billik's trial might have been different had he been able to afford a top-notch defense attorney like Burres, who successfully defended both Sladek and Knute Knudson. There is no way to know, of course, but it's fairly certain that Judge Barnes would not have presided over the case, as Burres had once punched him in the face in the middle of a courtroom years earlier when Barnes was an assistant state's attorney prosecuting one of Burres' clients.[265]

21

Natural Causes

When William Niemann's inquest concluded on November 18th, it was a bit anticlimactic. His doctors never testified, nor did the neighbors who reported their suspicions to police. There was no "team" of medical experts to issue reports. Professor Haines, the eminent toxicologist, was *not* asked to do a chemical analysis; nor was Professor Delafontaine, though the two routinely handled such cases. Their absence was conspicuous. As expected, Dr. Reinhardt reported that he found no arsenic. He presented instead a long list of medical conditions to explain the thirty-nine-year-old's death. The jury accepted his findings, and Hoffman signed the death certificate with the following causes of death: "Cerebral and pulmonary edema, fatty degeneration of heart, chronic nephritis, alcoholic cirrhosis of liver, and gastritis."[266]

Each of those symptoms, as well as Niemann's severe pain, gradual weakening, and eventual paralysis, is perfectly consistent with arsenic poisoning. The *Handbook of Poisoning*[267] by Stanford Professor Robert Driesbach identifies the following symptoms of chronic arsenic poisoning: gastrointestinal tract problems, cirrhosis of the liver, chronic nephritis, dependent and localized edema, and cardiac failure. It sounds similar to Niemann's death certificate. The book further states that a "variable paralysis may progress over a period of several weeks."[268]

Among the most common symptoms of arsenic poisoning are stomach problems, or gastritis, a general term for inflammation of the lining of the stomach, an ailment from which Niemann suffered. While normally it is swallowed, one can also be poisoned by inhaling arsenic. Since Niemann smoked a pipe regularly, someone could have put traces in his tobacco (as well as his food) over a period of time and produced similar symptoms. Arsenic* is largely odorless and tasteless, and studies have shown that one can be poisoned by smoking arsenic-laced tobacco.[269] The Handbook of Poisoning indicates that one of the effects seen from inhaling arsenic particles is "pulmonary edema" (fluid on the lungs), another cause of Niemann's death given by the coroner's physician.

Arsenic is carried by the blood to the liver, then on to other organs and tissue. It therefore affects nearly all organ systems in the body. This is why arsenic poisoning can simulate so many different ailments, and can so easily be misdiagnosed. Arsenic interferes with metabolic enzymes, causing cells to die, and organ systems—particularly the kidneys, liver, and heart—to fail. William Niemann's death certificate indicates his heart, liver, and kidneys were all failing. Such multi-system disease is standard in fatal cases of chronic arsenic poisoning.

The liver filters toxins from blood. The more toxins, the longer the process takes, and the more damage results. Damaged liver tissue is replaced with scar tissue that eventually interferes with the normal processing of blood. This condition is "cirrhosis of the liver." Cirrhosis is commonly associated with alcohol abuse, but is caused by all toxins, including arsenic, which is very caustic, and does considerable damage to the liver. Cirrhosis is quite consistent with chronic arsenic poisoning. Kidney damage is also normally seen in victims who live at least a day or two beyond the initial poisoning, long enough for the arsenic to travel throughout their body. Arsenic directly damages the heart muscle, which weakens. Blood vessels widen, causing a drop in blood pressure and insufficient

---

* Arsenic trioxide (As_2O_3), the white crystalline powder form of Arsenic made famous as a murder weapon in mystery books and movies.

circulation (the victim's actual death is usually brought about by circulatory failure). Blood cells break up, and fluid (plasma) from the blood vessels leaks. This fluid can build up, creating a condition known as "edema." This normally occurs in the ankles, as well as in the face, around the eye sockets. This could explain the "cerebral edema" (fluid around the brain) found in Niemann's autopsy. As discussed earlier, edema can also occur in the lungs, particularly in cases of arsenic inhalation. The heart, like other organs, gradually deteriorates. Arsenic will cause a widespread fatty degeneration in organs and muscles, particularly when it is administered in small, repeated doses. This is most common in the heart and liver.[270] The fatty degeneration of the heart found in William Niemann, again, would fit in perfectly if he were the victim of slow, chronic arsenic poisoning.

The most unique symptoms of chronic arsenic poisoning present themselves anywhere from two to eight weeks after initial exposure. Victims begin displaying neurological effects, as well as unusual skin problems, such as a patchy dark pigmentation. These are generally considered the hallmarks of arsenic poisoning. We don't know whether Niemann did or did not have skin problems, but we do know that he suffered for weeks from severe pain in his extremities and that he gradually grew weaker until eventually he couldn't stand or even fill his pipe. The neurological effects of arsenic can be very slow and insidious. They start with a slight tingling or weakness in the hands and feet, and can progress to tenderness, numbness, and pain. In severe, long-term cases, in which the patient lives long enough, symptoms will progress to extreme weakness, possibly muscular atrophy, and eventually paralysis and quadriplegia. Coma is the final stage before death by chronic arsenic poisoning. Niemann's demise very much mirrored the neuropathic symptoms of severe, long-term poisoning.

It is true that alcoholism *can* bring about the symptoms that killed William Niemann. Alcohol abuse will cause cirrhosis of the liver, which can lead to kidney problems. It also can cause stomach and throat inflammation. Beyond that, the symptoms that Niemann displayed, in combination, would have been extraordinary for alcohol abuse, in particular the severe pain and weakness in the limbs, and gradual paralysis. However, the group of symptoms is exactly what one would expect to see in someone who has been slowly poisoned with arsenic.

If Niemann was poisoned, however, that meant that the Cook County Coroner's Office either botched the autopsy or intentionally altered its findings to cover up a murder. Either is a serious accusation. Had Professor Haines conducted his usual meticulous and exhaustive analysis and said there was no arsenic, the matter would have been put to rest. Unfortunately, the most knowledgeable and experienced expert was not assigned to the case. Instead, Coroner Hoffman chose Dr. Henry G.W. Reinhardt to inspect the tissue samples. Reinhardt had been with the Coroner's Office less than three years, was not a toxicologist, and was in fact only two years old when Walter Haines first became a professor of chemistry.

In addition to his relative inexperience, Reinhardt was not exactly impartial. He owed his job to Coroner Hoffman and the Republican cabal that ruled local government. On Hoffman's first day as coroner (after a conference with Busse and Deneen) he had appointed Reinhardt to be an assistant coroner's physician.[271] And Hoffman clearly did not want poison to be discovered. It would have cast an enormous cloud over Billik's conviction and suggested that the he, State's Attorney Healy, Police Chief Shippy, and Judge Barnes had condemned an innocent man. All of them had been very outspoken against Billik, and worked hard to convict him. There was little incentive for Reinhardt to search very hard for poison when its discovery would only create problems for him and the rest of his own political organization.

It could never be proven that Dr. Reinhardt didn't really try to find arsenic, but it can be suggested that, for whatever reason, he may have missed it. He could have made only a brief and superficial exam under the microscope, said he was unable to find poison, and still been telling the truth. But was it really likely that he conducted a sloppy, erroneous, or even fraudulent examination? Would he—could he—have intentionally covered up a murder to save the reputations of his boss and political allies?

What about Coroner Hoffman? It's well established that he was a political hack, but would he cover up a murder, or assign an incompetent doctor to a case, maybe even tell him to *not* find arsenic, to make sure Billik's conviction stuck? The answers are surprising.

Years after the Niemann inquest, Hoffman and Reinhardt were at the heart of a scandal so serious that it nearly resulted in legislature abolishing the office of Cook County Coroner altogether. It first came to light in 1916 when Reinhardt testified in a lawsuit brought against the Traveler's Insurance Company. A man died after taking a fall on an icy sidewalk, but the company denied his claim because Dr. Reinhardt determined that he died of natural causes: a heart attack, complicated by Bright's disease and sclerosis of the liver. Three prominent experts later testified that the man had *no* heart trouble, *no* sclerosis of the liver, and *no* Bright's disease.[272] They also discovered that the man's brain somehow disappeared while the body was in Reinhardt's custody, making it impossible to prove he had suffered a concussion from his fall.[273] Reinhardt eventually admitted that he had been paid by the insurance company to testify on their behalf. Coroner Hoffman warned him that the practice had to stop.[274] Unfortunately, that was far from the end of the matter.

A year and a half later, a man named Henry Hulke was struck in the head by a heavy piece of steel at the factory where he worked. He suffered serious injuries and died several days later. His widow filed a claim with the insurance company which, to her dismay, was denied. Dr. Reinhardt had determined that Hulke did not die from his injuries, but from cyanide poisoning. Coroner Hoffman tried to convince Mrs. Hulke to blame the doctor, Dr. Loeser, telling her that was the only way she would "get any money" out of the case.[275] She was incensed. She refused to go after Loeser, or to believe that her husband was poisoned.

Still, Hoffman openly accused the doctor of murder. Loeser had a hunch what was really behind the allegation. "I have been fighting the insurance ring for sixteen years," he explained, "and of course they are trying to discredit me . . . If cyanide was found in Hulke's stomach, then Reinhardt is the only one who knows anything about it."[276] Hoffman responded by scouring his records to identify patients that died under Loeser's care, implying that he murdered them too.

When the Hulke case went before the Illinois Industrial Board, two other doctors denied seeing any evidence of cyanide poisoning. Reinhardt admitted to receiving regular checks from various companies for treating workers injured in industrial accidents. If they died, Reinhardt would conduct the autopsy in his official capacity with the coroner's office, then testify as a paid expert on behalf of the company. It was an almost unbelievable conflict of interest. The board ruled that Hulke died from head injuries, not cyanide poisoning. They cleared Dr. Loeser of any wrongdoing and launched an investigation to determine if physicians were conspiring with insurance and industrial companies to deny compensation for injuries. They uncovered a mountain of suspicious cases. The *Chicago Daily Tribune* reported, "According to the transcripts in the new cases . . . Dr. Reinhardt . . . was a good right hand for the employers and insurance companies."[277]

When a man fell from a moving streetcar, Reinhardt claimed he died of pneumonia.[278] When a factory worker had a pot of molten metal spilled over him, Reinhardt decided it was really tuberculosis that killed him.[279] He even ruled that a worker at the Western Electric Co. who was electrocuted in front of coworkers died from heart problems induced by a large meal he had just eaten.[280] It was astounding. A veteran employee of the industrial commission commented, "It's a remarkable fact, that we never have yet found a really healthy man in any case as far as the physicians' testimony indicates."[281]

Reinhardt also helped clear two attendants from Dunning State Mental Hospital who were charged with manslaughter when a patient died following a severe beating. Nurses said the man was covered in bruises and was bleeding profusely. Reinhardt said he died of arteriosclerosis, not even bothering to mention his obvious injuries.[282] Coroner Hoffman finally fired Reinhardt, angrily declaring that he would never work for his office again.[283]

Getting rid of Reinhardt, however, did not end Hoffman's headaches. Accusations flooded in. Hoffman was accused of failing to call important witnesses at inquests, even fixing juries. It was discovered that scores of "repeat jurors" served at Hoffman's behest; one man served fourteen times in ten days. The most serious of the alleged improprieties, however, was from a North Carolina woman who claimed Hoffman and his doctors were paid by a bank to falsely declare that her sister had been murdered, even though a coroner's jury in her state had ruled the death accidental.[284]

Things came to a boil when it was announced that the upcoming State Constitutional Convention would vote on abolishing the office of Cook County Coroner, and having state medical examiners investigate suspicious deaths instead.[285] Hoffman could read the writing on the wall. He said his term as coroner would be his last, and named a panel of respected professionals to recommend changes to the office. Public attention died down, though. Hoffman quietly allowed Dr. Reinhardt to resume his position in the coroner's office, and forgot his promise not to run for office again.

Hoffman did eventually leave the coroner's office to become sheriff in 1922. His most notable achievement in that position was to become the first sheriff of Cook County to be incarcerated in his own jail. That happened after two notorious Prohibition gangsters confessed to bribing officials to be allowed to come and go from the jail practically at will. Hoffman was sentenced to a month in jail for allowing the scheme. He was tried on a more serious charge of conspiracy, but was found not guilty. Two deputy marshals later admitted to attempting to fix the jury in that case[286] and the scandal effectively ended Hoffman's public career.

Former Judge John H. Lyle, who spent his career fighting organized crime in Chicago, later wrote that Hoffman took orders (and generous campaign contributions) from infamous mob boss Johnny Torrio,[287] who was eventually succeeded by his protégé, a young hood named Al Capone. These damning examples certainly resolve any remaining uncertainty about the scruples of Hoffman and Reinhardt.

22

Truth

After William Niemann bought the Vrzal home on 19th St., he never put Emma's name on the title, even after they were finally married legally. Had he done so, she would have become the sole owner when he died. Instead, with the title in his name alone, ownership passed to his estate, and (eventually) to his two young sons from his previous marriage,[288] but only after a prolonged court battle over custody of the children between Emma and Niemann's family in DuPage. William Niemann's younger son was named Willie. He was nine. The older boy was thirteen-year-old Henry. Their mother was William's first wife, Louise, who died in 1903. It was her parents who were eventually granted custody, and became their legal guardians, and not their stepmother Emma.

For some reason Emma only fought for custody of the older boy, Henry.[289] He was almost fourteen at the time, and already working, so he probably wasn't much bother for Emma. Willie, on the other hand, was five years younger and didn't seem to care too much for his stepmother. Just a few weeks before William's death, Emma told her brother Jerry that she had her hands full with the child. "Willie, he don't [listen to] me," she wrote, "and he does the dirtys [sic] things he can do to me."[290] William Niemann died on little Willie's ninth birthday.

Young Henry grew up to have a daughter named Doris. She said that her father told her that the family did not want him and his brother to stay with Emma. When asked if they suspected that Emma had killed William, Doris answered without hesitation: "Yes, I believe they did."[291]

Arsenic stays in the body virtually indefinitely. It can be detected in hair and fingernail samples literally hundreds of years after one ingests it, and there is no statute of limitations for murder charges. Unfortunately, William Niemann's remains rest in an unmarked grave, in a large open area of the Oakridge Cemetery reserved for indigent people who are buried and, all too often, forgotten. It's doubtful that one could ever be certain enough that a particular grave contained his body to have it exhumed and tested for arsenic.

All the attention to Niemann's death brought not only sympathy for Billik, but also donations for his legal battle. Fr. O'Callaghan sent letters to literally thousands of people, including virtually every attorney in Chicago, asking for contributions. There was a lot of support among the legal community, many of whom who felt it was unfair that rich men were able to appeal their convictions while the poor were often denied that same opportunity.

JANUARY 1908

At the beginning of January of the new year, Jerry wrote to Father O'Callaghan. He had made up his mind, as he put it, "to do what is right."[292] He took the train back to Chicago, and went straight to St. Mary's. He told O'Callaghan that he had lied. He lied at the inquest . . . before the grand jury . . . at the trial; most all of his testimony against Billik was made up. He said he was pressured, and even threatened, by police and prosecutors to say most of the things. The stories of Billik bringing powders and potions for the family members were either greatly exaggerated, or completely fabricated.

He claimed that Emma had lied as well. He knew, because she told many of the same stories he did. He had been too frightened to say anything before, and was still afraid of getting into trouble. Before going back to school, he made O'Callaghan promise not to tell anyone what he had confided. It must have been almost impossible for the priest to contain himself.

A few weeks later, on January 17th, Jerry came back to Chicago. Determined to make up for the wrong he felt he had done to Billik, he sat down with Hinckley and O'Callaghan and pored over the testimony from the trial. The most damaging statement of all was Jerry's claim to have overheard his mother and Billik plotting to kill his father and sisters. It more or less proved a conspiracy, and opened the door to allow all of the testimony about the other murders. Jerry now said it never happened. The quote Popham repeated throughout the course of the trial, Billik saying, "You know in a short time your husband will be dead, and then we will get the children out of the way . . ." was made up. Jerry swore that no such conversation ever took place. And that was just the tip of the iceberg.

Billik did give his father whiskey and saltpeter when he was sick, but there was no white sediment that sank to the bottom. His father never took the medicine off of a spoon, like he and his little sister Bertha had described so specifically. He said that when Bertha was living with Mr. and Mrs. Jones, she said that she didn't remember anything, but after staying with Emma in the months leading up to the trial, she began "recalling" things, to which she then testified.

Jerry said Billik was called upon to work a charm to help his father sleep when he was sick, but the powders were spilled onto the sidewalk, which was how charms were supposed to work. They were never swallowed by Martin Vrzal or anyone else. Jerry never heard Billik discuss his father's, or anyone else's, life insurance. It was the insurance agent who suggested his mother raise Tillie's insurance. And virtually everything he said about Billik in regards to the gas affair was untrue. The gas was turned on one night, but Billik wasn't there, nor was Herman Jr.

The only medicine Billik ever brought for Mary was a face cream for her acne. Jerry's story of watching Billik pour a white powder into her coffee was an outright lie. He wasn't aware of Billik ever bringing any chopped meat to the house, either. He never heard Billik say he could kill someone so that it couldn't be detected, and never saw Billik handle arsenic, or any other bottles, in Dr. Schmidt's lab. Billik never threatened to "fix" Mary for telling her mother not to give him any more money, and he never threatened to "fix" Jerry if he told about their supposed plot to kill his father and sisters. And his mother made no accusation, nor even mention, of Billik on her deathbed.

When they were done going through the transcript, it seemed as if all of the most crucial evidence against Billik had been made up. The Illinois Supreme Court was still reviewing the appeal, so O'Callaghan went with Jerry to see Justice Carter. The judge said that, unfortunately, the court couldn't consider Jerry's claims. They'd have to wait for a decision on the appeal, and if Billik were denied a new trial, Jerry could then formally recant his testimony. It would be another month or so until the Court made their decision. All they could do for the time being was wait.

FEBRUARY 1908

The appeal, several thousand pages in all, was reviewed by the Illinois Supreme Court, who began hearing arguments in early February 1908. State's Attorney Healy, along with Popham and Robert Holt, appeared for the state. Billik's attorneys raised several issues, though only a few seemed to get any serious consideration. Hinckley only briefly alluded to the fact that the letter from Mrs. Vrzal had been obtained through what he considered an illegal search and seizure. Shippy had sent detectives to go through the Billiks' home and take evidence without a warrant; however, Billik had testified that he told Shippy about the letter himself, so it was hard to argue against allowing it to be submitted at the trial.

The court addressed Assistant State's Attorney Holt's mention of the deaths of Standish York and Billik's mother-in-law. Hinckley argued that Holt had tried to infer that there was something suspicious about the deaths, and that Billik was somehow involved. The court agreed that the discussion was improper, but noted that defense attorneys never objected to it during the trial. They decided the references were too brief and inconsequential to make much difference.

Hinckley did score one victory when the court determined that one of the instructions Barnes gave the jury was "not an accurate statement of the law,"[293] and gave prosecutors too much leeway to make improper arguments. However, they felt it was not serious enough to warrant a new trial. On February 20th, 1908, the court rendered its' decision: "The record shows no reversible error. . . . The clerk of this court is directed to enter an order . . . fixing the period between nine o'clock A.M. and five o'clock P.M. on the 24th day of April, A.D. 1908, as the time when the original sentence of death entered in the criminal court shall be executed . . . Judgment Affirmed."[294] Hinckley was devastated. After all his work, it still looked like Billik would die.

In their argument before the court, prosecutors had strongly defended Jerry as a credible witness, an indication of just how critical he was to their case. They defended Emma even more vigorously. They did admit that, aside from Billik and Mrs. Vrzal, she was the only other person that the evidence suggested could have committed the murders, but they piously pronounced, "No jury could be found in the bounds of Christendom that would give credence to even a possible inference to be drawn from the evidence in this case that Emma Neamann committed this crime."[295] For some reason, though, they still felt it necessary to argue her case repeatedly, portraying Emma as a devoted and loving daughter, with "not an earthly motive"[296] to commit the crimes. And, despite the fact that virtually everyone who knew the family testified that Mrs. Vrzal was a good and caring mother, they attacked her, saying, "There is sufficient evidence to believe that the mother was of a different character."[297] They depicted her as an immoral fiend, driven to kill her entire family to get money for an illicit lover. They still maintained that she had committed suicide by taking chloroform, and even devoted a whole section of their argument to the notion, entitled, "Mrs. Vrzal Takes Chloroform at 2:00 P.M. December 4." Prosecutors knew that Billik wasn't there when Mrs. Vrzal took the fatal dose of poison. They had to say she killed herself, or be faced with the fact that someone other than Herman Billik killed her. And if someone else killed her, it was likely that someone else killed the rest of the family as well.

Professor Haines found that Mrs. Vrzal had been slowly poisoned with arsenic for some time, since it was accumulated in her internal organs. She also swallowed arsenic shortly before she fell unconscious, as evidenced by the large amount found in her stomach. Dr. Caldwell repeatedly stated that she displayed symptoms of *arsenic* poisoning, though he allowed that she could have taken it in combination with chloroform. Even if she did take chloroform willingly, someone had already been poisoning her with arsenic, well before any stories appeared in the news, which prosecutors still claimed was the trigger to her supposed suicide. In their arguments, prosecutors ignored the doctors' findings, as well as the fact that on her deathbed Rose denied taking poison and wrote Emma out of her will.

Prosecutors made much of Rose Vrzal's indiscretions with Billik, but never mentioned Emma becoming pregnant by a married man who had once been charged with manslaughter. They knew that Emma regularly helped prepare the Vrzal meals,[298] but maintained that the fact that she was not living at home when most of the murders happened proved that she was innocent. They didn't tell the Supreme Court that Emma moved away because she had been thrown out of the house. Neither did they point out that, after she moved, she visited the family regularly, sometimes two or three times a week.[299] She cooked and brought food, such as canned goods and preserves.[300] The last three girls who were killed (Tillie,

Rosie, and Ella) all died over holiday weekends, when Emma was back home to visit.

All of the victims had arsenic in their stomachs when they died, meaning they all likely received their last dose of poison within a day or two of their deaths. It was well established that Billik was not around (and often out of town) during the days preceding many of the deaths, so he could not have personally administered those fatal doses. So, prosecutors reasoned, Mrs. Vrzal must have done so, in conspiracy with him. But Mrs. Vrzal didn't need to wait for the opportunity of a family gathering to kill her children. Emma did. And there was a definite pattern to the deaths that looked more like someone taking advantage of an opportunity or, in some cases, a killer trying to send a message, rather than one desperate for a few hundred dollars in insurance money.

Emma lived at home at the time her father was poisoned and slowly died. She was forced to leave the house shortly after Mary died.[301] After that, there were no deaths for the next five months. Then Tillie became ill while visiting Downer's Grove to celebrate Emma's birthday.[302] She died on December 22nd, 1905, the Friday before Christmas. Rosie died on August 31st, 1906. That was the Friday before Labor Day, which also happened to be Ella's twelfth birthday. Ella first complained of feeling ill right after Rosie's funeral[303] (which Billik did not attend[304]). She was fed her last dose of arsenic on Thanksgiving Day, 1906, and died early the next morning. Emma had ample opportunity to poison each of them.

In addition to the girls dying on holidays, Martin died on his daughter Rosie's thirteenth birthday, and William Niemann died on his son Willie's ninth birthday. The night someone tried to kill Bertha, Ella, and Rosie by turning on the gas in the Vrzal house was July 27th, 1906, exactly one year to the day from Mary's death. If prosecutors didn't notice a pattern, Emma and Jerry must have. As Popham noted during Billik's trial, "They . . . have made excellent witnesses because of their ability to remember dates."[305]

23

Threats and Fear

When Billik heard that he had lost his appeal, he said simply that he would die an innocent man. Hinckley wasn't quitting just yet, though. "I will petition for a new hearing," he said. "I intend to make every effort possible before I give up."[306] Father O'Callaghan had not given up yet, either. As soon as he got word of the court's decision, he contacted Jerry in Valparaiso. They would have to act quickly to have any chance of heading off Billik's execution. Jerry would have to step forward publicly with his story.

The next morning, Jerry boarded a train and headed for Chicago. He sat with Father O'Callaghan and Hinckley to prepare a formal affidavit. Jerry immediately began poking holes in the prosecution's theory that money was the motive for the killings. "A large and expensive funeral was provided for each member of the family who died,"[307] he said. When his father died, they erected an ornate monument, costing more than $450. Martin Vrzal was only insured for $1,100. If Mrs. Vrzal and Billik had killed him for insurance money, why would they spend so much of it on a monument for his grave? After paying for that, the funeral ($245), the cemetery plot, more than twenty doctor's visits, and at least eight different prescription medicines,[308] very little, if anything, would have been left.

Jerry admitted that his parents paid Billik for working his magic. He also said Billik borrowed money many times and never paid it back. Ironically, it was for that very reason that Jerry found it strange that Billik was charged with the murders. His living depended upon the money he got from the Vrzals. Besides, Jerry thought Billik was genuinely a good person. "He had always shown the utmost kindness to everyone that he knew and I never suspected him of doing any harm,"[309] he said.

Jerry claimed that Chief Shippy told him shortly after Billik was taken into custody that police had evidence that Billik poisoned the family. He didn't believe it at first, but he was brought into Shippy's private office where, over the course of several days, the Chief, Sgt. Murningham (who worked on much of the case), and another officer, "pounded it into [his] head that [Billik] had killed the family."[310] He said Shippy told him that if he didn't tell police what he knew about Billik, that *he* would be jailed and charged with the murders. Shippy even claimed that Billik had told them Jerry committed the crimes. "I was frightened almost to death," Jerry said, describing how he then started meeting with Shippy almost daily for weeks. "On almost every visit Shippy and the other officers threatened to arrest me for murder and said that Billik had told them a lot of things against me,"[311] he said.

He claimed that the officers had presented him with many lies that they said other witnesses had told them, and threatened to lock him up if he refused to corroborate them. He felt he had little choice. "For fear of punishment I made many statements at the coroner's inquest that were untrue."[312] After the inquest, Jerry said, he continued to see Shippy regularly until he testified before the grand jury. "He continually pounded these falsehoods into my head and told me if I didn't stick by them he would lock me up."[313]

Jerry repeated the stories to Assistant State's Attorney Holt, and later to Popham, whose job it was to prepare witnesses for trial. Jerry said he met with Popham as many as forty times before the trial began, sometimes for four or five hours. By that time, he had talked himself into believing Billik was guilty. After reviewing the case, Popham allegedly told Jerry that they needed to prove there was a conspiracy between his mother and Billik to kill everyone.

Jerry explained, "He outlined to me the facts that must be proved and I made up the falsehood . . . that I heard Billik say to my mother . . . that he and she would get rid of the whole family and take the insurance money and take me to Europe with them."[314] He now said that he never heard any such conversation.

Jerry said Popham then told him that they would have to show that Billik brought medicine to each family member who died. "He explained that arsenic sinks to the bottom when placed in water and that we must describe the medicine that Billik had brought there in such a way that it would appear to be arsenic."[315] Jerry said that that was when he made up various stories describing Billik bringing exactly just such a medicine to his father and sisters. He also made up some of the symptoms he said they suffered from to correspond to those that Popham told him usually follow arsenic poisoning.

"He told me that the state's attorney could punish the people he wanted to and let go the people he didn't want to punish."[316] For the most part, Jerry said, he went along with whatever Popham "required" of him during the trial. He said the only thing he refused, was to cry when Popham told him he should cry. He said the main features of his testimony, and nearly all of the details, were made up by the police, Popham, and himself. "The testimony I gave at Billik's trial is false in all particulars except such matters as were of a harmless nature . . ."[317]

Jerry enumerated the many stories he had told during Billik's trial that he now said were lies. He told Hinckley that before the trial began, Popham handed him about thirty pages, which were to be his testimony, and told him that he should take it home and read it over to refresh himself. He claimed that Popham told him not to tell anybody, and not to show the papers to anyone. He said that on two or three occasions he brought similar notes from Popham to Emma for her to go over. Jerry was certain that Emma and Bertha had also lied at the trial, and he suspected Benjamin Parkison had as well, since all of them repeated many of the same fabricated stories.

The group worked until almost midnight preparing the affidavit. Hinckley took the original to file with the Supreme Court, along with a motion for a new trial. The next morning L.G. Edwardson ran a summary of it in the *Examiner*.

Both Popham and Holt made light of the allegations. They said that Jerry, once touted as their star witness, wasn't really an integral part of the case, that Billik could have been convicted even without his testimony. Chief Shippy, who was personally accused in the affidavit of threatening and intimidating a witness, was unfazed. He made an even stronger dismissal of Jerry's statements, saying Billik could have been hanged without investigating the Vrzal case at all. "Why, I could have convicted Billik of killing a man named York at Cleveland, Ohio without going into any one of the six Vrzal deaths,"[318] boasted the big Chief. His claim was somewhat absurd. Shippy hadn't uncovered enough evidence to convince Ohio authorities that York was even murdered, let alone that Herman Billik was somehow responsible.

It is interesting that Shippy chose to bring up the York case in the context of Jerry's accusations of police intimidation. When Shippy's men were in Cleveland, newspapers reported on their attempts to locate Mrs. York through her sister, a woman named Cassie Chadwick. The *Newark [Ohio] Advocate* ran the following:

Columbus, O. December 18 [1906]—A request came from the Chicago Police that Cassie Chadwick should be asked the whereabouts of her sister, and that if she did not do so on request she should be forced to do so. No attempt was made by the officials to force the woman to tell but she was requested to do so.[319]

It sounded as if Chicago Police considered witness intimidation standard operating procedure. It also makes one wonder just what, exactly, they expected officials to do to "force" Chadwick to talk.

FEBRUARY 23-28, 1908

Before returning to school, Jerry attended Sunday mass at St. Mary's, then visited Billik at Cook County Jail. Jerry asked Billik to forgive him and promised to try to somehow make things right. After their meeting, Jerry spent some time with his old friend, Herman Jr., who, along with the rest of the Billik family, was still in the care of the mission workers from St. Mary's.

At that same time, a thousand miles away, a crazed gunman shot and killed a Catholic priest on the altar as he said mass in Denver, Colorado. The man claimed to be part of the Anarchist movement. The late 1800s and early 1900s were marked by a struggle between workers who felt exploited, and the business titans whom their labor made rich. Chicago, a capital of industry and commerce, was often at the center of that battle. Its enormous labor force included a multitude of immigrants with varying levels of skills. To protect themselves from the low wages, long hours, and unsafe conditions which were common, they formed labor unions and joined a variety of political movements. Among those, the Anarchist groups were the most radical. They favored a stateless society, without government or organized religion, to empower the masses. The rally that prompted the Haymarket incident had been organized by Anarchists, and it was a self-proclaimed Anarchist who assassinated President William McKinley in 1901—the danger they posed was considered very real.

During the week that followed the Denver murder, several priests in Chicago, including Father O'Callaghan, received letters threatening to kill them if they dared to speak out against Anarchism. Since Chicago was a hotbed of radical activism, the threats were taken seriously. The Chancellor of the Chicago Catholic Archdiocese said, "I am positive that anarchists . . . have prepared lists of priests and clergy to be killed, and am certain that some Chicago man has been marked."[320] Chief Shippy announced that Anarchist leader Emma Goldman, who had been scheduled to speak in Chicago that week, would not be allowed to talk in public on *any* subject. He warned that if she appeared in Chicago at all she would be arrested.

MARCH 1, 1908

The following Sunday, March 1st, Father O'Callaghan had two Chicago detectives guarding him as he took the altar at St. Mary's to begin mass. Chief Shippy had officers posted at numerous churches to head off potential attacks. O'Callaghan agreed to the precautions, but said he would not live his life in fear. "I am afraid of no one who writes threatening letters. It is the act of a coward, and I wouldn't be afraid to meet a dozen such creatures single handed."[321] It was a nerve-racking day. Chicagoans braced themselves, waiting for something to happen. Whether it was due to the diligence of police or not, priests in Chicago said mass without a hitch, and suffered no attacks. But the calm would be short-lived.

MARCH 2, 1908

The next morning, the city was jolted by news that an assassin had made an attempt on the life of Police Chief Shippy. Initial reports indicated that Shippy had shot and killed an armed intruder at his home early Monday, and that Shippy's son and driver were both wounded. Shippy himself was stabbed in the struggle, but his wounds were apparently not life-threatening. It was seen by many as retribution for the Chief's hard stand against Anarchists. There were also claims that Shippy's attacker, a nineteen-year-old immigrant named Jeremiah ("Lazarus") Averbuch,* was among a crowd that Shippy's men had dispersed with their

---

* His real name was "Jeremiah" or "Harry," but he was also known as "Lazarus," as history commonly remembers him.

billy clubs at a downtown demonstration a few months prior.

Tensions in Chicago could not have been higher. Chicago police, without warrants, stormed the homes of suspected Anarchists and rounded them up, along with their books, papers, and documents. They set up an "Anarchist Bureau" to compile lists of possible Anarchists, and begin deportation proceedings against any who had been in the country less than three years.[322] The whole city was on edge, wondering when or where the next attack might occur. Chicago's leader, Mayor Fred Busse, rather than putting on a brave face to try to calm fears, went out the next day and bought a gun.[323]

24

The Interview

In this atmosphere of near-panic, Jerry Vrzal was summoned to City Hall on Saturday, March 7th, for State's Attorney Healy and Judge Barnes to interview him about his affidavit. If he hoped they would simply accept his story and try to find out who the real killer was, Jerry was sadly mistaken. Judge Barnes fired questions at him right from the start. He seemed determined to find some hidden motive behind his claims. He asked who paid for his tuition, his clothes, his travel, even his train ticket to come meet with them that day. Was it O'Callaghan, or maybe Hinckley? They must have paid the boy, he thought. But nobody seemed to have given Jerry anything. The Cook County Guardian managed the money his mother had left for him when she died. From that, she paid his bills, and provided him a weekly stipend. The only other help Jerry received was from H.B. and Vera Jones, with whom he still lived when he wasn't at school.

Barnes couldn't seem to accept the possibility that Jerry had been pressured by nothing more than his own conscience. Jerry came to the meeting alone. He had no attorney or representative to object to any of the judge's questions or actions, which grew increasingly hostile. It was likely a tactic to try to get him upset, but Jerry kept his calm. Judge Barnes did not. He badgered the boy over the date and time of almost every movement he had made since the trial. At one point Barnes even took Jerry's personal date book from his hands and began thumbing through it, taking notes and asking for an explanation of virtually every mark made in the book.[324]

He grilled Jerry incessantly over his religious beliefs. Was he a Catholic? How often did he go to church? When did he last make a confession? He thought maybe Jerry had confessed to a role in the crimes, or perhaps that O'Callaghan had exerted some religious pressure to get him to change his story. Jerry said that all the priest ever told him was to "tell the truth."[325] Jerry was baptized a Catholic, but said he hadn't been a very good one. When he said that he hadn't been to confession in years, Barnes ridiculed him, asking mockingly, "Don't you pretend to be a Catholic?"[326]

Barnes himself was a Presbyterian. There's no evidence that he had a particular dislike for Catholics, but he did have a dislike for anyone (including churches) involving themselves in criminal cases, at least when it was on behalf of the accused. Years earlier, as an assistant state's attorney, Barnes actually suggested blowing up a church that had dared to take up money for the legal defense of a man that he was prosecuting. The defendant worked as a janitor at the Mayfair Methodist Church on Chicago's Northwest Side, and was accused of several assaults in the neighborhood. Convinced that the police had the wrong man, the church helped raise money to defend him. Barnes was livid. He went on a tirade against the church in court. He was even reported to have questioned the decency of the women of Mayfair, and then went so far as to suggest planting explosives in the church. "If the people of the Mayfair congregation were so desirous of lending their aid to a criminal of the lowest motives," declared Barnes, "what was needed in the basement of the church more than a janitor was a charge of dynamite."[327]

When the Mayfair Church presented a resolution to then-State's Attorney Deneen, asking for Barnes' removal, they didn't even get an apology. Barnes emphatically denied insulting the women of Mayfair. Amazingly, though, he not only admitted to endorsing blowing up the church, but he repeated the comment.

"I do not uphold lynching," said Barnes, "but the moral indignation that leads to it is more commendable than the maudlin sentiment evinced in this case by this church congregation. I stated that if that was the kind of morals inculcated in that congregation, then they need dynamite in the church basement more than a janitor."[328] Barnes didn't dare to make such comments about Father O'Callaghan, particularly following the Denver priest murder and threats on O'Callaghan's life. It's fair to say, though, that Barnes likely resented O'Callaghan's meddling in the Billik case in much the same way he did the Mayfair congregation years earlier.

Unable to uncover any ulterior motive for Jerry to change his story, Barnes tried to scare him a bit. He reiterated that anything he said could be used against him, and implied that they planned to follow through with perjury charges. He asked Jerry repeatedly if he was still willing to say that he lied. Each time, Jerry said that he understood he had perjured himself, and was prepared to accept his punishment. He knew he was finally doing the right thing. Barnes reminded him that Ben Parkison had corroborated some of his stories. Was he lying, too? Jerry said he'd never spoken to Parkison about it, but Father O'Callaghan was trying to track him down to find out.

Throughout the interview, Jerry made it clear that he was sure Billik hadn't killed anyone. He said he was also sure that his mother wasn't involved either. That prompted Barnes to ask if any "outsider" could have done it. "Well this fellow that used to go with my sister might have done it,"[329] Jerry replied. He was referring to Joe Cooney. Though he was at the Vrzal home often at the time of the first two murders, Cooney had quit seeing Emma before the last few girls died, so investigators never considered him a suspect. Barnes finally asked Jerry directly if he thought Emma committed the murders. "Why, if Billik didn't do it, she must have done it,"[330] he replied bluntly. He said in every case, Emma saw her sisters two or three weeks before they died, and, "always came back on the day they died."[331] Jerry said she wasn't around much, though, during their final, agonizing days, when they suffered so horribly. He said Emma's stories about watching her sisters languish in pain were outright lies. In fact, he said, Emma lied about "most of the things"[332] she testified to. Jerry said Emma sat in on most all of his meetings with Popham, listening carefully as he went over his testimony. He said they would even compare notes sometimes to make sure their stories matched. The story they both told at trial about Martin Vrzal being spoon-fed medicine is a perfect example of how prosecutors allegedly got them to corroborate the most important elements of their case.

According to Jerry, he originally told Popham that his father was already dying when Billik sent a powder to be used as a charm to cure him. Jerry said the family followed Billik's directions and spilled the powder out on the sidewalk in front of the house.[333] He said Popham told him that story wouldn't do him any good, and that it would weaken their case if he testified that way. Popham declared, "Now you know the powder wasn't sent as a charm from Cleveland. Your father had taken that."[334] When Jerry didn't change his story, Popham grew angry and told him, "You ought to freshen your memory and see if he did not take it out of the spoon."[335] Jerry said that the next time, he told Popham his father drank the medicine from a bottle. But, apparently that was still not quite what the prosecutor wanted to hear. "No," he told the boy sternly, "He took it out of a spoon, and you testify that way."[336] Jerry eventually changed his story, in front of Emma, saying his father was fed the powder from a spoon. Emma suddenly began telling the exact same story. Popham thought it was important enough that he highlighted the alleged incident in his opening remarks at the trial, describing to the jury how Martin Vrzal was "fed" Billik's medicine from a spoon.

Jerry said many other lies were eventually "corroborated" in this same way, with he and Emma simply repeating each other's stories. Some were partially based on truth, such as the letter that their mother told them to give to authorities in case she should die, to "fix Billik up."[337] During the trial, it was clearly implied that the letter referred to the deaths in the family. One would think Jerry and Emma would have been careful to preserve such an important clue, given the circumstances, but it was never found. Now Jerry explained that there really was such a letter, but it merely laid out the fact that Billik owed the family money. It made no suggestion that he had killed anyone.

Other things were completely made up, such as the claim that Billik brought chopped meat for Mary. "My sister Emma put me up to that,"[338] Jerry admitted. He said she repeated the story four or five times, asking him to testify to it, until he finally went along with her. And when Jerry told Popham he never heard Billik ask if his father was insured, Popham told him, "Now, Billik would be a fool if he didn't ask that," so Jerry added it to his story.[339]

Barnes asked Jerry about his claim that his mother, as she lay dying, told him that Billik had poisoned the whole family. Jerry said that the only thing his mother said on her deathbed was, "Take care of yourself and Bertha."[340] She didn't even mention Billik. Jerry said that the police badgered him for weeks, repeatedly telling him that his mother must have said something. Finally, he made up the statement implicating Billik, and they seemed happy. Jerry said the police were convinced Billik was guilty right from the start.

And what of incriminating statements Billik supposedly made when police first began investigating Mrs. Vrzal? Jerry said Billik told him, "Why don't they take the bodies out of the graves and see if there is any arsenic in them? That will show there is nothing [to] it. No use your mother worrying. Just let them take [the bodies] out, and they will see."[341] It sure didn't sound like the words of a murderer.

The judge didn't like what he was hearing, and grew ever more impatient. When Jerry said he planned on studying law some day, Barnes was incredulous. "Study law?"

"Yes, sir," replied Jerry.

"You think that you will make as good a lawyer as you have a liar, do you?"[342] growled the judge.

Perhaps hoping Jerry was now off-guard, Barnes asked him again if he believed that Emma had killed everyone. "I have my suspicions," Jerry maintained.

"You would rather believe your sister killed them, than that Billik killed them, now?"

"Yes, Sir."[343]

State's Attorney Healy seemed even more upset than Barnes when he began his portion of the interview. Rather than probing for more information about the murders, Healy's questions seemed designed to try to show that Emma couldn't have been responsible, though Jerry's answers didn't exactly support that notion. When Healy pointed out that Emma didn't even live with the family when the younger girls died, Jerry told him that she visited regularly, and that his sisters even visited Emma at Downer's Grove. "Tillie went out there once . . . and she came home sick, and she said she would never go back to that farm,"[344] Jerry said. When Healy asked what the problem was, Jerry said, "She came home sick, had pains in the stomach."[345]

Healy asked how Emma got along with the rest of the family, clearly assuming that Jerry would say they had a good relationship. Instead, he told Healy, "Well, none of them liked her."[346] In fact, he said, nobody seemed to like her. He said she was always angry, and there was *always* a fight when she was around. Healy shrugged it off. He seemed to think that if Emma didn't get the insurance money, she had no motive for murder. Jerry said money may not have been her motive, but if she had been able to kill the entire family, she stood to gain quite a bit. As it was, Emma had possession of the Vrzal home and milk business, while Billik and his family were completely destitute and Jerry lived only on the insurance money his mother left him.

Healy asked Jerry if he was home when his family took ill, implying that he too could be a suspect. "Yes," he replied, "and I got sick."[347] In fact, Jerry had likely been poisoned himself, according to Dr. Moyer. He had a heart lesion,[348] and had been in declining health until the Vrzal deaths became front page news. Emma and Bertha appear to have been the only family members who were not poisoned. Jerry said that Emma once told him that she had seen a fortune teller (other than Billik) who told her that the family was being poisoned, and that he too was going to die. Jerry said he didn't suspect Emma at the time, but that he did now. He believed that Emma had something to do with all of the deaths.[349]

Cook County State's Attorney John J. Healy. *Photo courtesy of the Chicago History Museum, DN-0081140.*

Healy wasn't listening. "So far as you know," he asked, "[Emma] treated her sisters affectionately and loved them as one sister would love another, didn't she?"

"No sir," Jerry shot back.

"Do you think she hated them?" asked Healy.

"Yes sir."

"Do you think she hated your mother and your father and you?"

"Yes sir," came the reply again.[350]

Emma had said herself that she believed neither of her parents liked her.[351] Prosecutors also knew that she had been thrown out of the house several times, and was written out of her mother's will. Nonetheless, they seemed fixed in their belief that Emma was a good daughter to a family that seemed to dislike her so much.

Healy then addressed Jerry's claims of police intimidation, and Jerry didn't back down from his accusations, even naming the officers he said were involved. "Nobody threatened you with violence?" Healy asked.

"They threatened me the very day my mother died, the next day,"[352] Jerry replied. He said he was told that if he didn't testify to certain things, he would be locked up and charged with the murders himself. He said Shippy told him that he needed to place Billik at the gas incident, and that other officers suggested the story about poisoning Mary's coffee.

When they were finally done, after four-and-a-half hours of intense, often hostile, questioning, there were virtually no inconsistencies in Jerry's story. The problem was that he was accusing the Chief of Police and the state's attorney's office of serious misconduct. He had placed Shippy and Healy squarely on the defensive.

25

Failure

Father O'Callaghan and the rest of Billik's growing group of supporters lobbied State's Attorney Healy for weeks, calling for a new
trial. They gave him all the information they had gathered, and
waited. And waited. They went down to City Hall, but Healy refused to meet with them. He seemed interested only in defending
the original prosecution. Frustrated, L.G. Edwardson wrote a letter
to Healy. He enclosed a copy of the anonymous letter received at
the *Examiner* back in November. "The letter which I enclose is the
solution to the entire affair," wrote Edwardson. "The men referred
to are all acquainted with Emma Nieman[n]'s guilt."[353]

He told Healy all about Joe Cooney, and even provided him
with a copy of his mug shot and criminal history. He said that
Cooney was the large, shadowy figure seen leaving the Vrzal house
the night of the gas incident, not Billik. He told of the conversa-
tions he overheard at the Gerald Saloon, noting that he had already provided him with the names of the men involved in one
such discussion. He told him where the arsenic was purchased,
even the name and address of the druggist. He also mentioned that
a "suspicious character" had been visiting Billik in his cell, asking
if "Tip" Cooney was somehow involved in the case. "This man
Cooney is mentioned quite often in the testimony of the trial," Edwardson continued, "and when I tell you he is in the know of the

whole affair I know that I am right."[354] Edwardson suggested that Healy try to find the author of the anonymous letter. There's no evidence that Healy ever made any public effort to do so, and it's not clear what, if anything, he did to follow up on the other clues given to him. He apparently did write a letter to Joe Cooney, asking if he was willing to discuss the case. Not surprisingly, Cooney wrote back that he knew nothing, and that was the end of the matter.

A few days later, O'Callaghan tried again to see Healy. This time, he brought Benjamin Parkison with him. Parkison was now saying that he too had been pressured by police to make accusations against Billik. At first, Healy was too busy to meet with them;[355] O'Callaghan was persistent, however, and Healy did finally agree to at least speak with Parkison, though he wasn't about to admit to any wrongdoing, particularly in an election year.

Meanwhile, Chief Shippy had plenty to worry about outside of the whole Vrzal mystery. An investigation was underway into allegations that Chicago police (including Shippy himself) were providing protection for gambling operations in parts of the city. People were also starting to raise questions about the shooting of his alleged attacker, Lazarus Averbuch, wondering if he might have killed the young man unnecessarily.

MARCH 24, 1908

On March 24th, 1908 an inquest was held over the death of Lazarus Averbuch. Shippy said that the young man appeared at his door early in the morning with an envelope in his hand addressed to him. He said the man looked suspicious, so instead of taking the letter, he grabbed him by the wrist. The youth pulled a knife from his coat and stabbed him. Shippy's adult son and his driver, James

Foley, came to his aid. After a short scuffle, Shippy and Foley managed to fire several rounds into Averbuch, killing him.

Some questioned how a man as large and powerful as Shippy
(with the aid of two other men) was unable to subdue the much
smaller nineteen-year-old without having to shoot him numerous
times. There were also questions about just how dedicated an
"anarchist" Averbuch really was. Speculation ranged from the
possibility that Shippy used excessive force, to the prospect that
Averbuch (who spoke little English) may have come for a letter of
recommendation and was murdered in cold blood when Shippy
mistook him for an assassin.[356] To no one's surprise, the coroner's
inquest determined that Shippy had acted properly, and he and
Foley were exonerated of any wrongdoing.

March 30, 1908

Emma and Jerry appeared before the Juvenile Court of Cook
County on March 30th, to battle over custody of their younger
sister Bertha and, potentially, control of her inheritance. Bertha
had been living with Emma for almost a year by this time, but
Jerry, who was now eighteen, filed a petition with the court asking
that she be taken away from her.

Emma was already in the middle of a custody battle over her
two stepsons with their mother's family. Now she had another
court fight on her hands. No sooner was the case called than Emma
fainted and collapsed in the middle of the courtroom.[357] She was
eventually victorious, and Bertha stayed with her in the family's
old home on 19th St.[358] Emma's stepsons, Henry and Willie, however, never returned to her.

April 9-13, 1908

On April 9th, two weeks before Billik's execution date, the Illinois Supreme Court announced that they would not hear his case again; they no longer had any jurisdiction over the matter, and could not even consider Jerry's retraction of his testimony. The decision was not entirely unexpected, but Hinckley was dumbfounded when he was informed that it was now technically too late to bring the matter before any lower court, either. It seemed that no one had any authority to grant Billik a new trial, even with the main witness against him now admitting to having perjured himself, and claiming other witnesses lied as well. Billik had only one chance to avoid his date with the hangman: he requested a clemency hearing before Governor Charles Deneen. If he failed to intervene, Billik would die on April 24th.

There was considerable optimism that Deneen would halt Billik's execution once he reviewed the case. Three witnesses (Jerry, Parkison, and Herman Jr.) now said they lied, and were raising serious doubts about the truthfulness of others. Listening to the state's attorney describe the case, however, one might have thought there was no controversy at all. "All the evidence that I have discovered so far points towards Billik's guilt," said Healy, "and I have no evidence that tends to involve anyone else." [359] It seemed somewhat disingenuous, since Jerry, the son and brother of the victims, had come right out and accused his own sister of committing the murders. Did Healy really believe Jerry would want to free the killer of his entire family and blame his innocent sister? Had Jerry said that he personally made up the lies he told at the trial, instead of blaming police and prosecutors, Healy may well have accepted it.

On Monday, April 13th, the Illinois Supreme Court issued its final order directing Sheriff Strassheim to execute Billik on April 24th. When Billik was notified, the reality that he might be about to die struck him. He collapsed. "Oh, will no one save me?" he cried. "I am innocent. I am innocent of these awful crimes." [360] The clemency hearing was scheduled for the end of the week. "We have demanded this hearing . . . not as mercy but as a right," Hinckley declared.[361] Father O'Callaghan recruited Stephen S. Gregory, a prominent attorney (who would eventually become president of the American Bar Association) to help with the plea. Gregory was no stranger to controversy. He assisted the defense in the Haymarket case and, along with famed jurist Clarence Darrow, had defended Patrick Prendergast, who assassinated Chicago Mayor Carter Harrison in 1893. They hoped Billik would fare better than Prendergast, who was eventually executed.

Part IV

The
Death March

26

The Pardon Board Convenes

On Saturday, April 18th, Governor Deneen and his two-man Board of Pardons, consisting of Charles Eckhart and Ethan A. Snively, came to Chicago to conduct the hearing. The board's job was simply to make a recommendation to the governor. The decision was completely up to Deneen. He had several options. He could grant Billik a full pardon and free him, he could commute his sentence to life in prison, or he could deny the petition and allow Billik to be hanged on Friday morning. As soon as the men walked through the door of the Criminal Courts Building, they were greeted by ten-year-old Edna Billik. She jumped from her seat and ran to the startled governor sobbing, "Oh Governor, Governor, save my—"[362] She was quickly grabbed up and moved to the side. Deneen and the men from downstate could see right away this was to be no routine pardon hearing. The *Chicago Tribune* called it "one of the most remarkable ever held in Cook County."[363]

Edna was joined in the waiting area by her brother Herman Jr., and their mother. Jerry Vrzal and little Bertha were there, as was Benjamin Parkison. One look at the group reminded one just how much of the case against Billik had been provided by children—children who now said they were pressured into giving false testimony. All of them wanted to speak at the hearing, particularly

Edna Billik in front of the courthouse before the start of the Pardon Board Hearing. *Photo courtesy of the Chicago History Museum, DN-0052710.*

Edna. She had accompanied O'Callaghan to fund raisers and had become quite a spokesman for her father. But time would only allow for Jerry and Parkison to testify. It was to be a *very* long day. Billik was prepared to appear before the board personally, but ended up nervously passing the hours in his cell, praying and wondering.

The hearing was held inside the grand jury room. The men sat around a large table, with Governor Deneen directing the proceedings. The state was represented by State's Attorney Healy, Judge Barnes, and former Assistant State's Attorney Holt (who was now an attorney for the City of Chicago). Assistant State's Attorney Popham was there as a witness, as was Police Chief Shippy, who brought along eight of his officers. It was certainly an intimidating group.

Deneen had enjoyed a long and close relationship with both Barnes and Healy. When he was the state's attorney, Barnes was his first-assistant. When Deneen ran for governor, he made sure Barnes was slated for judge, and designated Healy to succeed him as state's attorney. It would have been difficult to find a pair who held more influence with Governor Deneen. Additionally, Holt was a local political operative of Deneen's, and Shippy was a close confidante of Deneen ally Mayor Fred Busse. It looked like the deck might be stacked against Billik.

But Billik's new friends had assembled a pretty formidable team themselves. In addition to Stephen S. Gregory, who presented most of the legal arguments, Father O'Callaghan aroused the interest of another prominent Chicago attorney: former Mayor Edward F. Dunne. After losing the election to Busse, he was taking some time away from politics, but was still very much in the public eye. Dunne was one of the top Democratic politicians in Illinois, and Republican Governor Deneen was in the middle of a campaign for re-election. Deneen didn't want to cause any uproar by appearing to treat Dunne unfairly, or give the impression that he would let an innocent man hang. It put some pressure on him to pardon Billik, or at least commute his sentence to life in prison.

The first witness was Benjamin Parkison. He said that the most damaging parts of his testimony were *not* true. He had not seen bottles of arsenic on the shelves in Dr. Schmidt's lab, and he denied hearing Billik say that Mrs. Vrzal had been poisoned before she was actually poisoned. He said that during the investigation, Shippy called him down to his office. When he told the chief he had nothing to say about the case, Shippy had him locked in a cell downstairs. He said he was held for five or six hours. During that time, he was ordered to talk and threatened by Shippy and Sgt. Murningham, as well as Assistant State's Attorney Popham.[364]

State's Attorney Healy began his rather stern cross-examination, glaring at the young witness with Shippy and Murningham looking on. Parkison suddenly wasn't so sure what happened, or what he had testified to. "Were not you told on all occasions to tell the truth and nothing else?" asked Healy.

"Yes," replied the suddenly hesitant Parkison.

"And did not Mr. Popham say to you that if you did not tell the truth you could be punished?"

"Yes. That was what he said."[365] Of course, that's also what Jerry and Herman Jr. said. They said they would make a statement, then police or prosecutors would yell at them to tell the truth, until they eventually changed their story to something that was accepted.

Parkison was pretty definite at first that he didn't hear any talk about Mrs. Vrzal being poisoned until later in the afternoon of Dec. 4, but Healy badgered him, and he appeared confused about the exact timing of events, which were obviously not clear in his mind. Finally, Healy asked him if maybe his memory was better at the time of the trial. "Why I remembered more then that I do now, yes sir,"[366] he said. It had the effect of virtually nullifying the rest of his testimony before the board.

Dr. Caldwell was the next witness to testify on Billik's behalf. It quickly became apparent that prosecutors did not want the board to hear from him. They repeatedly interrupted him with objections. Healy and Holt said the doctor had nothing new to add and that they didn't want to waste the board's time, though they spent more time arguing against allowing Caldwell to speak than the doctor did testifying. Caldwell still insisted that he first treated little Rosie Vrzal on July 31st, 1906, when Emma brought her in to his office,[367] and that was a problem for prosecutors. That was just four days after the gas incident at the Vrzal home, but apparently no mention of it was made. It seemed peculiar that Emma would take her sister to the doctor, yet fail to mention a potentially life-threatening gas poisoning the girl suffered just a few days earlier.

Caldwell came to believe that the vague symptoms he first saw in Rosie were the result of three or four weeks of regular arsenic poisoning.[368] Prosecutors themselves had proven that Billik was out of town for most of that July; however, Emma had testified that she stayed at the Vrzal home overnight and that Rosie visited her at the Niemann farm in Downer's Grove, both in the early part of July,[369] right about the time someone presumably began poisoning the child. Then, in early August of that year, Rosie went to Dr. Schmidt's house in Cleveland. Emma had claimed her sister was healthy when she left, and returned a week later, sick and dying. However, the trip occurred after Dr. Caldwell began treating her; she clearly was not perfectly healthy, and Emma knew it, since she was the one who had taken her to the doctor. Rosie went to Cleveland *because* she was sick, and Mrs. Vrzal hoped Dr. Schmidt might be able to help her, as he did Jerry. Caldwell emphasized that Mrs. Vrzal seemed to be a very loving mother, eager to do everything possible to save her children. With that, he was abruptly dismissed.

27

Letters and Lies

Jerry was about to address the board, when Healy introduced a letter that Jerry had written to Father O'Callaghan back in October. He told the priest that he wanted to meet with him to convince him of Billik's guilt. Healy portrayed it as proof that Jerry really thought Billik was guilty, but O'Callaghan explained that he had actually given the letter to Healy as evidence against Emma. She had put Jerry up to writing it, and told him to save all of his correspondence with O'Callaghan to somehow use against him. Of course Jerry did eventually meet with O'Callaghan, but, rather than convincing him of Billik's guilt, they both became convinced of Billik's innocence.

Jerry then gave the board a letter that Emma had written, in which she said that she wanted to get O'Callaghan in trouble.[370] He also talked about another bit of correspondence he had received, which he said was what first made him think that he had done a terrible wrong. He said that shortly after the trial, one of the jurors wrote to him expressing concern about some of his testimony. But when Jerry said that he had thrown the letter away and no longer had it, he wasn't allowed to discuss it any further.

A great deal of the rest of the morning was spent with Gregory going over the bulky transcript of the trial with Jerry, line by line,

identifying all of his false testimony: he did *not* overhear a plot between his mother and Billik, *never* saw powder poured into Mary's
coffee . . . "What explanation do you desire to make to these
gentleman?" Gregory asked. After hesitating for a moment, Jerry
explained, "After my mother died I had no one to go to except
my aunt. Inspector Shippy sent for me and I told the story as I
knew it. Then the police kept pounding it in my head that Billik
had killed my folks and that he said that I was in it. They told
me that I was implicated and that they could charge me with the
murders. Then later they got me and little Herman Billik together
and told me that Herman said he and his father were there the
night the gas was turned on and that I was there."[371] He described
how police badgered him until he finally promised to testify about
it. He named more than a half-dozen officers, including Shippy
and Murningham, who he said were involved. "They said that they
would protect me," he continued. "They saw me at Des Plaines
St. Station every day for two months. They told me I had to come
down every day."[372]

Jerry told how Assistant State's Attorney Popham said they
would have to prove a conspiracy between his mother and Billik
to convict him, and how he eventually made up stories to go along
with it. He said that nobody specifically told him to lie but, "It
was pounded into me so much that I must give certain kinds of
testimony that I finally yielded."[373] He said Father O'Callaghan
was the first person to whom he told the truth. "The first time he
told me Billik was innocent I told him I did not believe it," Jerry
said. Eventually, though, he had a change of heart. "I saw [Father
O'Callaghan] because I was worried in my conscience because I
had told a lie on the witness stand and wanted advice."[374] Jerry
said that no one had pressured him or offered him anything to
change his testimony.

Holt then presented a letter written by Jerry's college roommate,
Earl Hall. It was sent to Assistant State's Attorney Popham right
after Father O'Callaghan, accompanied by L. G. Edwardson of the
Chicago Examiner, first went to talk to Jerry. It read, in part:

Jerry was this afternoon visited by a priest. With the priest was a man who gave his name as Edwardson . . . We are both convinced that the latter is either a lawyer or a detective. The two questioned Jerry for three hours concerning his evidence in the Billik murder case. It is their intention to try and prove that Niemann, the husband of Jerry's sister, is the murderer. I am studying law and advised Jerry that he write you of this at once.[375]

Holt was trying to impeach Jerry's claim that he hadn't been pressured to change his story, but the letter also suggested a motive for someone to kill William Niemann. It was postmarked from Valparaiso, October 29th, 1907, just six days before Niemann's death, and made clear that Jerry was, at that point, aware that Niemann and Emma were being investigated as suspects in the murders. The very next day, Jerry came all the way back to Chicago to see Emma, then went back to school. A few days later Niemann was dead. With Billik's execution (which was then set for Nov. 8th) just days away, might someone have feared that Niemann was going to talk, and killed him to keep him quiet? It was right after Niemann's death that Jerry's conscience got the better of him and he made up his mind to tell Father O'Callaghan that he lied at Billik's trial.

Jerry told the board that, at one time, he believed Billik was guilty, but not anymore. "I have had a long time to think of it now," he said, "and I know that he was innocent."

"You think he was a good man?" asked Holt.

"No, he did lots of wrong things," Jerry answered, "but he did not murder anyone."[376]

When Holt and Healy were finally done with Jerry, it was Francis Hinckley's turn to address the board. He presented to them a typed letter addressed to Governor Deneen. "This statement," he said, "is merely for the purpose of showing that the persons who passed upon the weight of the evidence regarded Jerry's testimony as worthy of some consideration, and that Jerry was not, as Mr. Holt has suggested, merely an unimportant witness."[377] Hinckley read the letter aloud:

I am one of the jurors who found Herman Billik guilty of the murder of Mary Vrzal and voted for the death penalty. I heard Jerry Vrzal testify and believed his testimony . . . that he had heard Mrs. Vrzal and Billik plotting the death of the family; I believed his testimony to the effect that Billik had brought bottles of medicine to the members of the family, which medicine answered to the description of arsenic; I believed his story to the effect that he had seen Billik put some white powder in Mary Vrzal's coffee. These statements confirmed my belief in Billik's guilt. If he had not testified to these matters, I should not have voted to hang Billik. If these statements, or any one of them, is false or is not based on fact I think Billik ought to have another trial.[378]

It was signed by *six* of the jurors.

Prosecutors called several witnesses to try to discredit Jerry. Maria Fencl said she had a conversation with him when he came to Chicago to tell Emma about O'Callaghan and Edwardson visiting him at school. She said he claimed to have told the men that he thought Billik was guilty, but they insisted that Emma committed the crimes, likely with Niemann's help. Jerry told Mrs. Fencl that he planned to tell investigators that his sister and her husband did commit the murders. She quoted Jerry several times as saying that that was "the truth," but also said he made comments to the effect, "If others can tell lies, I can tell lies." She said he wasn't specific about who the others were, or what lies had been, or would be, told.[379]

Apparently, Jerry had become convinced that Emma and Niemann really were the killers, but he had no hard evidence. Perhaps he planned to make up more stories, just as he and Emma had done to Billik. Mrs. Fencl's daughter Elsie (a close friends of Emma's), told Emma what Jerry had said, and Emma reported the conversation to police. When Jerry came back to Chicago several days later for Niemann's funeral, he and Emma were no longer on speaking terms.

Next, the state called Jerry's college roommate, Earl Hall. He was asked about an incident in which Jerry had supposedly asked Emma for ten dollars and she told him she didn't have it. Holt suggested that Jerry then decided to get back at her by pretending that she murdered their family. Hall said Jerry had been anxious about money at times, but seemed relaxed and even "elated"[380] after completing the affidavit saying that he lied at Billik's trial. Holt said that showed Jerry must have profited somehow, and was enjoying his new celebrity status, but Dunne pointed out that his behavior was also natural for someone who had just been relieved of a great burden. Hall was Healy's witness, but he actually backed up the most important part of Jerry's story: that he lied at Billik's trial. Hall said that after Jerry's statement was published in the *Examiner*, he asked him about it. He said Jerry told him, "Well, I didn't know all I told at trial."[381]

Assistant State's Attorney Popham was next. He denied ever discussing a conspiracy with Jerry, and said he never induced him to lie in any way. He admitted that when he first took the case, police told him that they thought Jerry was holding back information, and knew of a plot between his mother and Billik to murder the family. Popham acknowledged that at some point in their interviews, Jerry began describing just such a conspiracy, but denied pressuring him to provide the testimony. He also defended police officers. "In all my experience," declared Popham, "I never met a more honest set of officers than worked on this case with me."[382] He finished by telling the board that Jerry's testimony had been of only minor importance, anyway.

Police Chief Shippy had only recently returned to work, fresh from his exoneration in the killing of Lazarus Averbuch. As expected, he stoutly denied any part in pressuring or threatening witnesses. "Did you ever attempt to influence this boy [Jerry]'s testimony or threaten him in any way?" Healy asked. "Certainly not. I told him to tell the truth at all times,"[383] said Shippy, repeating a familiar phrase. He denied ever telling Jerry that Billik had implicated him in the deaths, or that he would lock him up if he didn't say certain things.

Then the chief was asked about Ben Parkison, who seemed to have suffered a sudden memory loss on the stand earlier. It turned out that Shippy and Sgt. Murningham, the two men Parkison directly named as having threatened him, seemed to have taken an unusual liking to him. For some reason, Chief Shippy arranged a job for Parkison at the Western Electric Company, and Sgt. Murningham presented his accuser with a gift of a new winter coat.[384] In addition to their extraordinary generosity, they had also reminded Parkison of the power they held. After he quit the job Shippy set up for him, Parkison went to see the chief, who had him locked in a cell. Shippy described the incident this way: "I asked him why he quit over there. He said he did not want to work and I said 'I will put you downstairs for a while. That will do you good.'"[385]

Parkison, like Billik's wife and children, had sought food and shelter from the mission at St. Mary's. While Healy tried to make an issue out of Parkison getting assistance from charity workers, he seemed to think it quite natural for the Chief of Police to arrange a job for a witness who had accused him of threatening him. Shippy had also arranged a job for Jerry shortly before Billik's trial began.[386]

Gregory then asked Shippy how Billik's name was brought into the case in the first place. Shippy said it was Emma who first mentioned him. She came to the station while her mother was being interviewed and told him, "You look for Herman Billik."[387]

28

Arguments

It was after six o'clock when Father O'Callaghan finally rose to speak. He explained his interest in Billik's case: how one of his parishioners brought Mary Billik and the children to the church mission, and he asked a few of his assistants to try to help raise money for an appeal. He said that when Hinckley told him about the "anonymous benefactor" coming forward just days before the execution, he relaxed, satisfied that he had done what he could, still uncertain whether Billik was actually guilty or not. When he finally went with Dr. Christison to meet Billik, he became convinced of his innocence by the prisoner's own story. Every fact he gathered from Billik and the family checked out. "The little children's story would corroborate, and Mrs. Billik's story would corroborate and a thousand-and-one things of that kind emphasized my first impression,"[388] he told the board. But it was Hinckley who truly brought him into the battle to save Billik. "I learned that the money that was supposed to be gathered for Billik's appeal was merely the savings of his lawyer who had put in his all that he might continue the fight; it was Mr. Hinckley. His heroism inspired me to make every effort."[389] O'Callaghan then decided to come out publicly. He spoke from his pulpit, went to the newspapers, reached out to his friends for help, and eventually got the truth from Jerry Vrzal.

O'Callaghan said everything he learned since then confirmed his conviction that Billik was innocent. He was particularly intrigued by the fact that so many animals owned by the Vrzals had died without explanation. He recalled a conversation he had with Judge Barnes: "I told him that I thought it was very suspicious that the dog died, and the chickens died and the pig died and all the animals that were fed with swill died, and the horse did not die with the oats and hay. I told him that the fact that during all the time the month[s] that elapsed from the time Emma left home until the last death of the children, that vegetables and preserved cherries and cheese were coming from [Niemann's] farm constantly, and that these were the vegetables out of which the swill was made for the feeding of those animals."390* He said Barnes responded that he would have been happier at the time of the trial if Billik's sentence had been life in prison instead of death.

O'Callaghan said he received many tips, and that they continued to come in. Only a few nights earlier, a saloon keeper from the West Side approached him, trembling, and told him a story about Joe Cooney and a girl he believed to be Emma Vrzal. O'Callaghan was confident that the real killer(s) had not yet been captured. He said he gave Healy the names of four men who knew about the case, but no one was ever contacted.

Amid the reams of documents in Billik's case file, is a single sheet of paper containing four handwritten names, with the word "accomplice" next to one. There is no other writing or explanation. It appears to be from the Pardon Board Hearing, likely written by one of the men of the board. The writing is hard to make out, but it looks like, "James Murphy," "[R____?] Susinger," and "Henry D[u?]ly" (with what appears to be "accomplice" written next to his name). The fourth is only a last name, possibly "Niemann." Did one of these men have the answer to the mystery, or even assist the "real" killer(s)? Unfortunately, there are no other references to any of them (with the obvious exception of Niemann, if that is what it says).

---

* The dog actually died before Emma moved to the farm.

Healy, presumably upset at being called out in front of the governor for his lax investigation, grilled the priest, though it seemed unnecessary and somewhat mean-spirited. Healy tried to discredit him, belittle his efforts, and make him look ill-informed. O'Callaghan admitted he did not attend the trial, and had not read each of the thousands of pages of evidence. "All I can say is I am a friend of criminals," said O'Callaghan, beginning to tire of the badgering. "I know of more holdups than most policemen. Probably I know of more murders than anybody else in this room. From my instinctive knowledge I believe this man is innocent of such a crime as murder."[391] The men then took a well deserved one-hour recess.

When they reconvened, it was Judge Barnes' turn. He measured his words very precisely. He said he had no reason to doubt Billik's "guilty complicity,"[392] but wasn't sure that he had personally poisoned anyone. "I realized that the case was largely one of circumstantial evidence,"[393] he said. Barnes was also bothered by the character of many of the witnesses, saying, "A large part of the testimony lie[s] with the ignorant and the superstitious."[394] He said he always felt that "somebody" knew more about the case than they told, and that misstatements were made. He singled out Jerry's claim to have overheard his mother and Billik discussing murdering the family, in particular, as "an improbable story."[395] Nonetheless, he said that he had no doubt of Billik's guilt. "I have found no reason for changing my views," he told the board. "As to whether his sentence should be changed is not a matter for my recommendation."[396] Barnes did say, however, that it was true that he would have been more satisfied with a punishment other than death.[397] It offered Billik a ray of hope.

Then State's Attorney Healy began. He was adamant that the verdict was solid, and that Billik should be put to death. "I believe, after a careful perusal of Jerry's testimony, that there was no mistake in the trial of this case"[398] he said. He fiercely defended his office's work, then spent the rest of his long speech talking about the "gas incident" at the Vrzal home, which he seemed almost obsessed with proving. Healy said that even though Jerry had retracted his statements about Billik being present when the gas was turned on, other witnesses placed Billik there. In truth, the *only* other witness who said Billik was there had been Herman Jr., who had recanted his testimony long ago, also saying he was threatened by Shippy. His story was so questionable that Judge Barnes had refused to even allow it into evidence at the trial. Now, the state's attorney was arguing that the already-discredited story was the "proof" that should seal Billik's fate.

Hinckley and Gregory objected, but Healy continued his diatribe. He seemed to take the whole matter quite personally. His reputation and political aspirations might crumble if it were proven that he had convicted an innocent man in such a high-profile crime. So he dug in his heels. He knew someone turned the gas on. He just couldn't seem to accept the fact that, without Jerry's testimony, there was virtually nothing to indicate that Herman Billik was there. Mrs. Lorenz didn't see him, though she clearly should have. Dr. Napieralski's vague description of a shadowy, heavy-set figure he could not identify was the only thing to remotely tie Billik to the incident. Napieralski described a second man he saw leaving the house that night as being "eighteen or nineteen years [old]"[399], and about five-foot-four.[400] Healy had decided that that must have been Herman Jr., who had just turned *thirteen* a few weeks before the incident and, according to Jerry, was "a little more than four feet tall at that time."[401]

There was also some question as to when it even occurred. Napieralski testified at the inquest that his records showed it happened on July 21st, 1905,[402] but at some point afterward, prosecutors started saying that the incident took place on July 27th, 1906. At the trial, Napieralski wasn't sure. He said he hadn't gone over his files, or brought them along, so he could only say it happened "some time in July 1906."[403] If it happened on July 21st, 1906 (assuming he misspoke at the inquest and just got the year wrong), Billik couldn't have been there, as prosecutors had shown he was in French Lick Springs until July 23rd. Prosecutors had been so meticulous in documenting their case, yet they had failed to verify the date of the incident, or even make sure that their witness looked over his records before testifying. Healy simply ignored the inconsistencies and urged the governor to let Billik's execution proceed.

When Healy finally finished, Dunne addressed the board. The former judge and mayor introduced himself by saying, "I am simply one in the community that have become so much interested in the apparent fact that in this case a man's life may be taken without his being guilty beyond a reasonable doubt."[404] Dunne felt that, at the very least, Billik should be tried on one of the other five counts of murder, which were still unresolved. "If they could find a jury to convict him without Jerry Vrzal's testimony," he said, "that ought to be done."[405] It seemed like a reasonable compromise between hanging and an all-out pardon.

A grave injustice would be done, he warned, by hanging Herman Billik. He said Healy had not been completely "candid" in his presentation,[406] and that the state's attorney was acting with the zeal of a prosecutor too long associated with a case to recognize its apparent flaws. He took Healy to task for his lengthy discussion of the gas affair, and for misleading the board. "[Mr. Healy] introduces and discusses before Your Honors evidence that was never in the record of this case; that never reached Judge Barnes and never reached those twelve men."[407]

As for the evidence that *was* introduced at the trial, Dunne said that every important fact came from either Emma, Jerry, or both of them. Their testimony coincided closely, with no direct contradictions between them. If Jerry's original story was false, he reasoned, then Emma's must have been also. Dunne reminded the board that even Healy and Barnes agreed that parts of the account were improbable, including the most incriminating evidence of the entire case: the conversation where Billik told Mrs. Vrzal that they would kill the whole the family. "If that is improbable and unnatural," Dunne asked, "what about the rest of the story?"[408]

Dunne said Jerry had no motive to come forward to free the murderer of his family. He was paid only his expenses to come to the hearing, and was put up at St. Mary's, but made no money. He had nothing to gain if he weren't now telling the truth. "Just think of it!" Dunne exclaimed. "Here is a boy that knows of the murder of his father and four of his sisters, one after the other. Before his mother died of course there would be some motive to protect her from punishment on the theory that [she and Billik] were acting together. But here months after the mother is dead, this boy without any earthly motive whatever tells a clergyman that calls upon him ... that the story he told at the trial . . . with regard to this scoundrel, if it were true, is wholly false."[409]

Dunne then turned to Popham, who, he said, was "decidedly in error"[410] in claiming that Jerry's testimony was insignificant. "The affidavit given by these six jurors," Dunne proclaimed, holding up a copy of their letter, "shows that Jerry Vrzal's testimony instead of being of minor importance was regarded by the jurors as of the utmost importance."[411] He concluded, "Six jurors tell this board that if [Jerry's] evidence was out of the case they would not have convicted this man of the crime with which he is charged, isn't there such a reasonable doubt in this case as to justify your Honors in preventing another miscarriage of justice in this county?"[412]

29

The Hearing Concludes

By now, it was after ten o'clock at night. Luckily, only two more men would address the board: Former State's Attorney Robert Holt and Stephen Gregory. Holt had supervised Billik's prosecution and cross-examined witnesses at the trial. He was remembered by many as the man who made Edna Billik cry on the stand. Holt told the board that *he* planned to make the final argument, though it had already been agreed that Gregory would go last. To Holt's dismay, Governor Deneen didn't go along with him. He *made* Holt go next, and so the fireworks began.

Holt implied that Jerry was only a marginal figure at the trial, and said his new testimony, "does not affect the case very much."[413] He said he always believed that Jerry was in on the conspiracy, and that he was changing his testimony because he was afraid Billik was going to "squeal"[414] on him, though Billik already had more than a year to "squeal" without doing so.

Jerry's other motive, said Holt, was revenge on his sister for refusing to give him money (apparently this referred to the ten dollars Emma denied him). The notion that Jerry would free the killer of his family and accuse his innocent sister over ten dollars was almost laughable, but Holt didn't draw many chuckles with his next accusation. "[Jerry] has been making easy money from these fellows who are fighting for Billik,"[415] he announced. "He has now found somebody else who supplies him on the money proposition, and he wants to stand by the fellow who is now furnishing the money."[416] He was all but directly accusing Father O'Callaghan of paying off the chief witness in a murder trial.

O'Callaghan had heard enough. "Did you address me as fellow?" he asked, rising and facing Holt. "I am not used to that, sir."

"I did not address you, Father," Holt replied, trying to dismiss the now riled priest.

"I have intelligence. I am not a fool," said O'Callaghan, "I think you did."[417] He was completely indignant. He stood and glared at the attorney, his bright blue eyes ablaze. Healy jumped in, and suggested that Holt's statement had been misinterpreted. Dunne and Gregory said they thought his meaning was pretty clear, but they agreed that Holt probably wished he hadn't said it in such a way. They managed to calm things, and O'Callaghan sat back down, but Holt made no apology. He continued, turning his attention back to Jerry. Maybe it was fame that was driving him to lie, Holt wondered. "He is a boy who thinks a whole lot of a little temporary notoriety,"[418] he told the board.

Holt's final insult was directed at the jury members who signed the affidavit saying they would not have voted to hang Billik if not for Jerry's testimony. Holt belittled them and their statement. "There are jurors who will sign a piece of paper for anyone who goes around and wants them to sign," he said. "I say it is nonsense and not worth that much consideration."[419] He ended his ten minute tirade with a bitter conclusion, "I cannot conceive of a case where a man . . . would more deserve to be hanged."[420] With that, he gathered his things and left.

More than thirteen hours after the hearing began, Stephen S. Gregory made the final plea for Billik's life. He said he regretted the short time he had, "But," he jested, "I take some satisfaction in following the eloquent, I had almost said the intemperate,

appeal of the learned counsel who has just addressed you."[421]
Gregory said Billik should be pardoned because there was not a
shred of evidence that had not been torn away by Jerry's admission. No one had been able to show any contradictions in Jerry's
testimony before the board, and he had absolutely nothing to
gain by coming forward.

Then Gregory addressed Holt's comments about Father
O'Callaghan. "I was surprised that he saw fit to refer to this noble
man who has interested himself in this case, and to whose interest
in it is due my participation . . . I was sorry that he saw fit to refer
to him as he did, and to intimate that he was the man who was
going to furnish money to this boy to get him to change his testimony."[422] Gregory said it was easy to see how a boy troubled by
his conscience could confide in a man like Father O'Callaghan,
"whose ingenious face and candor, and magnetic personality are
well-calculated to accomplish so much for humanity in his sacred
calling . . . I can conceive myself no warrant for the suggestion of
the learned former state's attorney."[423]

Prosecutors clearly wanted to marginalize O'Callaghan's influence. They portrayed him as a sort of soft-hearted cleric, who
perhaps was being taken advantage of, or didn't understand the
intricacies of such a complicated case. Ironically, on top of his considerable experience dealing with criminals, O'Callaghan was ar-
guably the most educated man in the room as a Harvard graduate
with years of post-graduate study. Healy defended Holt, saying he
had not directed his comments at O'Callaghan, but that just started
the whole clamor all over. "I am a man of intelligence, and I never
was charged with being a 'fellow,'"[424]* protested the priest. When
things settled down again, Gregory directed the Board's attention
to the subdued tone of Judge Barnes' testimony, which allowed
that he would be satisfied if Billik's punishment were reduced.

---

* The term "fellow" once had a very derogatory connotation. *Webster's New
Collegiate Dictionary* (Springfield, Massachusetts: G. & C. Merriam Co., 1979)
indicates the now obsolete meaning: "A person of one of the lower social classes;
a worthless man or boy."

Barnes wasn't shy. If he thought Billik should be put to death, he would have left no doubt.

Gregory said that in his first statements to police, Jerry never mentioned any of the stories that were most incriminating against Billik: the poisoning of Mary's coffee, the conversation between Billik and his mother, the bringing of medicines. "None of those things appear," he said. "They came afterward as a gradual evolution."[425] He agreed that Billik was guilty of being intimate with Mrs. Vrzal, but that nothing more had been proved. He said that beyond Jerry and Emma's testimony, the state had very little. There were suspicions, but no real evidence. Gregory held up the voluminous transcript of the trial, and declared, "There is absolutely nothing of weight that would justify the verdict that was rendered in this case that was not in all particulars corroborated by the testimony of this young man."[426] Jerry's testimony held the entire case together. "It is idle for counsel for the state to stand here and say, 'It matters not, it is of but little importance.'"[427]

Gregory displayed a copy of the prosecution's brief to the Illinois Supreme Court. He noted Holt's name on the cover as counsel, and then showed how prominently the testimony of Jerry Vrzal was featured in their argument. "And there italicizes and double leads the story of Jerry Vrzal, relies on the story of Jerry Vrzal." Gregory then read from the document, "'You know in a few days your husband will be dead.' And it appears in this record not once but four times, and there it is referred to and it was the vital and essential fact in this case. And why? Because of the question of punishment."[428] Gregory said everyone was aware that there was a reluctance to hang a man based strictly on circumstantial evidence. He pointed again to the same quote, featured so prominently in the state's argument. "There, and there only," said Gregory, "is to be found any direct evidence which could take this case out of the category of a case of circumstantial evidence. It does not establish the guilt of Billik that he sent medicine to the Vrzals. It is a circumstance, which may tend with the other evidence to establish guilt. But here you have the direct evidence of the boy who said he stood there and heard his mother and heard Billik say, talk over the conspiracy and heard Billik tell her, 'Yes, you know your husband will be dead in a few days. We will then get rid of the rest. If the boy is alright we will take him.' That was the direct evidence and the only direct evidence . . . that is found in this record."[429] Gregory said that the state's attorneys were well aware of that. "And that is why the learned counsel relied upon it and put it in the record four times and put it in their brief and italicized it and double leads it as the feature in this case."[430] Popham had even featured the quote in his opening remarks to the jury.

Lastly, Gregory had some words about the gas incident, upon which, as he put it, "the learned state's attorney dwelled for so long."[431] He pointed out that Bertha was not insured at all, so the *combined* life insurance on the three girls involved in the incident was $255, barely enough to cover the cost of one funeral, and certainly not the motive for a triple murder. If there was a two-year-long conspiracy to murder for money, as prosecutors claimed, it would have been easy enough for Mrs. Vrzal to fully insure the girls before killing them.

Gregory claimed the story, as told by Herman Jr., was preposterous, and patently unbelievable. He pointed out how ridiculous it would be for Billik to take his young son out late at night to watch him commit the cowardly murder of three young children. "The fact that the boy had no part in that crime, where the only effect of him being there would be to qualify him as a witness against his father, and render it possible by methods which are not unknown in this community to secure his testimony, that it would have been the last thing that this man would have done is certain."[432]

It was approaching eleven o'clock. Gregory reminded the men that Easter Sunday was just an hour away and asked the men to reflect on the divine attribute of mercy. Even if Billik hadn't proven his innocence, there were so many questions that he deserved their mercy. The meeting was adjourned, and the men went home to spend Easter with their families. Herman Billik's life was now in the hands of Governor Deneen.

APRIL 19, 1908, EASTER SUNDAY

Chicago's Easter of 1908 was picture-perfect: clear blue skies and a radiant sun. Churches were packed, and decorated throughout with vibrant floral displays. The real show, however, began when services concluded. Finely dressed worshipers spilled out to promenade home in a brilliant parade that illuminated the boulevards of every neighborhood: brightly colored gowns, and hats adorned with flowers, feathers, silks, and ribbons of every hue. Nowhere was the scene more picturesque (and pretentious) than along Lake Shore Drive. Observers came in large numbers to watch the procession of the city's wealthy society women stroll home from Holy Name Cathedral and St. James Episcopal Church, to their stately mansions overlooking Lake Michigan. It was a glorious day for most of Chicago.

Herman Billik spent his day in a cell, praying and visiting with his family and a reporter who came to interview him. Billik wore a small palm cross on his coat lapel. His eyes were red. He looked terribly depressed and nervous.[433] Some worried that he might collapse under the pressure, but he said he was strong. "I am confident that I am going to be squarely dealt with, and that means everything to me," he said. "Father O'Callaghan has done valiant Christian work in my behalf, and if I escape the gallows I owe my life to him alone of all human agencies."[434]

O'Callaghan was confident that if Billik was given a trial on one of the other charges, it would be a fair one. "Billik now has friends to look out for him,"[435] he said. But he was still unhappy with the police and the state's attorneys, and made no effort to hide it. "The guilty go free and the innocent are punished in Chicago over and over again to my certain knowledge," O'Callaghan proclaimed. "A prominent attorney told me that it is easier to free a guilty man than an innocent one in many cases. The guilty one knows the whole situation and is able to direct his attorneys. The innocent man doesn't know and acts confused, making a bad impression and furnishing a good opening for the prosecution."[436]

Then he startled reporters, saying there was a good chance that other people would eventually be charged with the murders. "The information I have received from three different sources points to four men and a woman as the murderers of the Vrzals," he said somewhat mysteriously. Then, even more mysteriously, he added, "The third corroboration of my suspicions came today and I believe that if Billik has more time we shall be able to get the evidence to prove it."[437]

On Monday morning, Francis Hinckley came racing in to the County Jail. He had good news: Governor Deneen announced that he was granting Billik a reprieve until June 12th so the board could review all of the testimony. Billik hugged Hinckley, who was almost as excited as he was. As they celebrated, others joined in. Billik had become quite popular at the jail, not only with other prisoners, but with his keepers as well. Dozens of guards came to congratulate him and wish him well.[438]

Hinckley thought the reprieve was an indication that the board was leaning towards granting a pardon. "I do not think Billik will hang," he affirmed. "It is all bosh for the state's attorney to say they could have convicted Billik without Jerry Vrzal's testimony. In the brief sent to the Supreme Court they based the whole strength of their case upon it."[439] Billik had plenty to be happy about after this, his third reprieve, but State's Attorney Healy put things in perspective: "This reprieve means only that the board has postponed its decision."[440]

30

Disturbing

APRIL 22, 1908

A few days later, Father O'Callaghan announced that he had received a disturbing letter. It was placed in the donation box at St. Mary's, tightly folded and wrapped in a black crepe cloth. On the outside fold was drawn a crude skull and crossbones. Next to that it read: "father O'Callaghan dam [priest?] of Mary church, death is near you."[441] This was not the work of an Anarchist, but from someone unhappy with his digging into the Vrzal murders. Inside was a chilling message in red ink, with thick spatters, giving it the appearance of having been written in blood: "death warrant to dam O'Callaghan of dam Mary church Wabash Ave.—we are going to dynamite Mary and her little lamb—also the dam attorney Hinckley who is nothing but a thief, raskel, murderer— there days are numbered—2 dirty son of a bich." On the reverse, it continued, "dam Mary . . . dynamite shall visit you."[442]

O'Callaghan notified the state's attorney's office, and even Governor Deneen. He suspected that he knew who was behind it but, with no proof, little was done. He decided to contact a handwriting expert to see if he could identify the author.

MAY 1908

In spite of the threats, Billik's friends continued investigating. If there was going to be another trial, they wanted to leave no doubt of his innocence. They followed every possible lead. Dr. Christison was even in the process of writing a book on why he believed Billik was innocent. Then, suddenly, things took another twist.

On May 9th, 1908 a bizarre story was reported in the *Chicago Daily Tribune*. It told of the fight over a corpse between two rival undertakers who each claimed the right to remove a body which the police had discovered in an apartment. Somewhat lost in the morbid tale was the identity of the man whose body they were arguing over. It was Dr. J. Sanderson Christison. He had been found dead in his room at 24 Walton Pl.* Neighbors heard him entering the room at about one o'clock in the morning. At eight a.m., the proprietor of the house smelled gas in the hall and opened his door. Christison was unconscious, with the gas turned on. They called for a doctor, but before he arrived, Dr. Christison was dead.

The coroner's office conducted an inquest that same day. They took testimony from a few people who lived in the building. The circumstances indicated that he was overcome by gas, though it doesn't appear that an autopsy was done to confirm it. The jury concluded that Christison died "from asphyxiation due to turning on and inhaling illuminating gas in his room," adding, "From the evidence presented we the jury are unable to determine whether said gas was turned on accidentally or otherwise."[443] The term "otherwise" implied suicide, but when it was learned that Christison had been seen in the company of two unidentified men only hours before he died, some wondered of there was something more sinister afoot. After the story was publicized, two men came forward. They said they found the doctor lying in the gutter at State St. and Maple at about eleven-forty p.m., apparently under the influence of some drug. They searched his pockets and found

---

* Pre-1910 address

a card with his address on it and took him home, just a few blocks away.[444]

There was no reason to suspect the men of foul play, but their story did raise questions. How did a prominent doctor end up lying in the gutter unconscious? Where was he coming from (or going to) so late, and in such a condition? What type of drug had he taken (or perhaps been given), and might it have actually caused or hastened his death? Since no autopsy or toxicology tests were done, the answers remain unknown. Lastly, if the men brought Christison home before midnight, who was heard entering (or leaving) the doctor's room at one o'clock? Maybe someone just got the time wrong. The inquest was not re-opened. The death was classified as an accident/possible suicide. Adding to the mystery within a mystery however, was the peculiar fact that, in addition to the book about Billik's innocence, Christison was in the early stages of another book: one discussing the difference between suicidal and murderous wounds.[445]

Meanwhile, O'Callaghan submitted the threatening letter to Warren A. Drake for analysis. Drake had over forty years of experience as a handwriting expert, handling every type of case from forgery to kidnapping, and even murder. Most importantly, though, Drake had worked on more than a hundred cases for the Cook County State's Attorney's Office.[446] Most recently, he helped Chief Shippy's cause at the inquest of Lazarus Averbuch by verifying that Averbuch had personally addressed the envelope he carried to Shippy's house.[447] O'Callaghan chose Drake because he knew prosecutors couldn't discredit his opinion.

Even when a person tries to disguise their handwriting, much of the style of their writing can remain surprisingly identifiable. Experts generally agree that the handwriting of an anonymous letter of any considerable length can usually be identified if a good sample of writing from the actual author is available for comparison.[448] In

this case, Drake was given a three-page letter written by Emma
Niemann to compare.

June 1, 1908

On June 1st, Drake issued a lengthy and detailed report, con-
cluding: "I hereby express it as my opinion and belief that the
aforesaid anonymous, threatening letter is in the same handwriting and was handwritten by the same person who wrote the
aforesaid standard."[449] In other words, Emma Niemann wrote the
letter threatening O'Callaghan and Hinckley. Drake was definite
in his opinion. He cited scores of similarities in the writings that
he considered "distinguishing" characteristics. One such feature he
termed "peculiar and distinctive," was an emphatic drop-stroke
ending many words, which he said occurred in the anonymous
letter "not fewer than forty or fifty times," and was repeated practically identically in Emma's letter "not fewer than sixty to eighty
times."[450] Allowing for the fact that the writer of the anonymous
letter changed the slant of their writing, Drake felt the peculiar
structure of certain letters and combinations were very strong
evidence, saying, "[They] present as precise identity as is usually
found in writings concededly executed by the same person."[451] It
was about as certain of an identification as could be established.

31

Despair

Billik's execution was set for Friday, June 12th. Governor Deneen spent much of May making campaign appearances, and there was no word about Billik's case. Finally, he announced that the Board of Pardons would meet on June 5th to go over the testimony, and that he would make a decision soon after. O'Callaghan wrote to tell him that his suspicions about Emma writing the threatening letter had been confirmed. He sent Drake's report, and even the original letter itself. The fact that she wrote anonymous letters didn't prove that Emma was involved in any murders, but O'Callaghan said it should raise questions about her reliability as a witness. "Assuredly her conduct in all of this is not that of an innocent woman giving testimony of what she knows, with no other interest than to see justice done," O'Callaghan wrote. "In the scales of justice the testimony of an accuser such as Emma Niemann against Herman Billik ought to weigh no more than the testimony of Herman Billik against Emma Niemann. No man should die upon the testimony of such an accuser as this woman, who does not scruple to threaten me with death."[452] He warned against taking a man's life based on false words; the original jury, and even the state Supreme Court, had based their decision upon fabricated evidence, and six jurors had declared they would not have convicted Billik if not for testimony that was now known to be false.

O'Callaghan seemed to think that in the end, Deneen would grant Billik a pardon to so he could get the fair trial he was entitled to. He closed by saying, "I have great confidence in your sense of justice. I believe that in the years to come I shall never be able to render you a larger service, in testimony of my gratitude for kindness shown me, than I do in making possible the abiding assurance, which events will make a certainty, that you have saved an innocent man from legal murder at the hands of the State of Illinois."[453]

June 5-6, 1908

On Friday, June 5th, the Board of Pardons met in Springfield. Unfortunately, Governor Deneen left after only a few hours to make a political speech in nearby Lincoln, Illinois.[454] When they met again on Saturday, they agreed that the portions of Jerry's testimony which he now said were untrue, should be taken out. They would then review what was left, and decide whether or not they thought Billik was guilty. They spent the entire day sifting through thousands of pages of testimony. When midnight came and went, it was apparent that they would have to come back on Monday to finish, and make their decision.

June 7, 1908

On Sunday, Mary Billik and all four children came to visit Herman at the jail. Even their oldest son Frank was there, having come from Cleveland. Despite the somber nature of the visit, Billik was upbeat. "I am confident the Lord will take care of me,"[455] he declared. He was grateful to his fellow prisoners, and even the guards, for making life bearable. "I have been made happy by the encouragement and help given me by other prisoners here," he said, "and all have prayed that I be not punished for a crime I did not commit."[456]

"I know Father O'Callaghan and others who have worked in my behalf have obtained evidence enough to cause the governor and the pardon board to save me from hanging,"[457] he said confidently. Yet he was also prepared for the worst, saying that in the end, if he must die, he would walk to the scaffold without fear and proclaim his innocence. "I have done many things during my life which may not have been right," Billik told a reporter, "but I have repented and have asked forgiveness."[458]

The family spent several hours together. When they very reluctantly began to say goodbye, Edna, who was kneeling beside her father, held out her arms and began to pray. "O God, please save my papa,"[459] she pleaded. As she did, a most amazing thing happened. Word began filtering through the jail, from one tier to the next, one ward to another. Within minutes, the shouts and laughter that had filled the cavernous building quieted, and one-by-one prisoners joined in prayer with the little girl. Eventually nearly the entire prison, some 650 inmates, were praying for Herman Billik's life to be spared. Even the most hardened criminals reportedly dropped to their knees and offered a prayer.[460] Billik was overcome by emotion. It was a spontaneous and moving display, unprecedented in the history of the jail, and so remarkable that it was reported across the country. Even the *New York Times* told its readers, "The Cook County Jail was transformed into a house of worship for several minutes yesterday . . ."[461]

June 8, 1908

On Monday morning, the Board of Pardons announced their decision in Springfield. Gov. Deneen was not even present as Ethan Snively read a prepared statement. "We have examined the record," said the Chairman, "and excluding that testimony that Jerry Vrzal says is false, we find left ample proof on which to convict."[462]

Snively noted that the decision was supported by State's Attorney Healy and Judge Barnes. Healy had been adamant that the governor not give in. He, like Deneen, was running for re-election. If Billik's life were spared, it would be tantamount to admitting that his prosecutors tampered with witnesses or, at the very least, botched a major murder trial. He couldn't afford such a scandal just eight weeks before the election. Herman Billik would hang as scheduled on Friday morning.

Hinckley couldn't believe it. "I don't see how it is possible for the Board of Pardons to come to such a decision." he said. "The evidence as I view it was conclusive that Herman Billik should not hang. I am much surprised. I thought at least the sentence would be commuted and an opportunity for another trial given."[463] It appeared all but over. But the young lawyer still wasn't ready to quit. "I will not give up the fight until the last minute,"[464] he proclaimed.

Jailer Will T. Davies gave Billik the news. When he learned that his last real hope was gone, tears rolled down his cheeks. He tried to say something, but choked up. When he was able to talk, he could only tell Davies that he worried what a blow it would be to his family. "Well, if they are going to hang me let them go ahead," he said, drying his eyes. "I've always been unlucky. I don't care so much for myself, but I do care for the sake of my wife and children."[465] After a while he calmed down and tried to be positive. "I still have hope because I am innocent," he said. "If the officials insist on committing judicial murder, I can face death bravely. I shall be ready when the time comes," he said with newfound bravado. "An innocent man has nothing to fear."[466]

That brave façade quickly melted, however, when his family came to see him. "Herman, God has forsaken us!" Mary cried, "Do they really intend to kill you?"[467]

"Oh, God only knows what will happen." he replied. Then he bent down and reached his arms around little Edna, and began weeping. He took each of the children in his arms, and kissed them. Observers said he told them "to be good and try to remove the stain which even the hanging of an innocent man had placed upon their names."[468] When the family finally parted, Jailer Davies came by to offer some words of encouragement. Billik was again hopeful. "I wonder what Father O'Callaghan will do?" he asked.

"I haven't heard from him," replied Davies.

"Well, he'll do something yet," Billik assured him. "I have not given up hope."[469]

Father O'Callaghan was, in fact, already at work. That evening, he issued an appeal that was published in newspapers across the state:

> *To the People of Chicago and Illinois: Believing that Herman Billik is not guilty of the murder of the Vrzal family, and desiring to have his death sentence commuted, I appeal to all persons to aid me in his behalf. I desire signatures on a request on the governor that Billik be spared from hanging . . . mail to: Father P.J. O'Callaghan, 490 Wabash Ave., Chicago.*[470]

Billik would not die without every possible fight having been made.

JUNE 9, 1908

The next morning, O'Callaghan sent a personal letter to Governor Deneen. He begged him, "in the name of human justice," to intervene. "As the laws are written, you may not be able to provide Herman Billik with a new trial, or the means to secure it," he wrote, "But at least it lies within your power, and your power alone, to prevent a disgrace to justice which, without your action or the assistance of God, is set to occur in the Cook County Jail on Friday, June 12."[471]

Edna Billik also wrote a letter asking that the governor show mercy and spare her father's life. She, however, sent her plea to Frances Deneen, the chief executive's young daughter. "Dear Little

Friend," Edna wrote, "Won't you please ask your papa to save my poor dear papa? I love my papa just as you love your papa—and he is to die on Friday. Please help my papa and I will pray for you and your papa."[472] It was an unabashed play to the emotions of Deneen and the public, but if there was any hope of saving her father, she would have to attract all the attention and sympathy she could.

Billik was moved from his cell to the "death chamber," a secured area in the small prison library. It was much more spacious and comfortable, but provided a disquieting notice that his execution was now very close at hand. Prisoners circulated a petition asking the governor to commute Billik's sentence. The mood within the complex was somber, the silence noticeable. Then, prisoners began hearing the sounds of workmen—just a little at first—then steady, unmistakable sounds: hammers pounding, wood creaking. One by one, the men realized that work had begun on the scaffold upon which their fellow prisoner would soon be executed. It was a dreadful, inescapable reminder.

The wooden planks and beams that made up the gallows were normally kept in storage, and only brought out and assembled a few days before executions. Hangings were no longer conducted in public in Cook County, but they were carried out in plain view of a good number of prisoners,[473] right inside the jail. The long corridors of Cook County Jail had multiple tiers of cells, with a catwalk running along the outside of the upper tiers. The gallows was constructed at the very end of the corridor, the platform level with the catwalk. The prisoner would be led down the catwalk and onto the platform, where he stood on the trap-door (or "drop") facing down the long hallway. The jailer secured the noose hanging from the cross-beam above around his neck and gave a signal to the hangman, who stood obscured from view behind the prisoner. The hangman then cut a rope that held the trap-door, dropping the floor out from beneath the prisoner.

It must have been an awful sight, particularly if the prisoner didn't die instantly. The Haymarket "martyrs" (as they were eventually remembered by many) suffered horribly, writhing for some six minutes before finally choking to death in front of horrified witnesses.[474] All of this would be visible to the entire wing of inmates. Even those in other parts of the jail, unable to see what was happening, could not escape the violent thud of the "drop," which was said to be audible even from the street outside. Morbid curiosity-seekers would congregate outside the prison on execution days, listening for the sound. The prisoners didn't want that "thud" to be the last sound Herman Billik would ever hear, and they were determined to do what little they could to help their desperate friend. Several men asked if they could hold a special prayer service for Billik at the jail. Jailer Davies contacted Father O'Callaghan.

That evening, the small chapel inside the jail was filled to capacity. O'Callaghan presided over the unusual service, in which criminals of every variety, including robbers and murderers, raised their hands and voices to the heavens, asking for Herman Billik to receive justice. In the middle of the ragtag congregation sat Herman and Mary Billik with their children. Mary could barely lift her head. She held her husband's hand and wept quietly. Prayers and song filled the air for nearly two hours, with several men getting up to address the crowd.

Father O'Callaghan, never at a loss for words, was himself so moved that he could barely speak. "There is none more Christ like than he who, innocent of any wrong, is led to the scaffold to death," he said finally. "This man here with us—our brother—we feel is innocent. God forbid that he be sacrificed."[475] He paused for a minute to try to collect himself, but could say no more. As he returned to his seat, one of the inmates, David Anderson, grasped O'Callaghan's hand in thanks. Anderson, who was himself sentenced to death for the murder of a policeman, had helped organize the service.

Prisoner Peter Muchowski then stood. Holding Billik's hand, the confessed burglar turned to the crowd. "Boys, we all know this fellow too well to think he would murder anybody," he said. "We've all had our troubles. We know how it goes with a man that's down and we can sympathize with the fellow who is getting the hard knocks. It's all the harder though when you know you're getting a raw deal."[476]

"They're doing a good man wrong here," Muchowski declared, "and we must help him out if there is anything we can do. Let's all pray that our friend Herman won't—that they won't use that platform that they are building out there."[477] The mere reference to the scaffold made the prisoners uneasy. Billik's children cried uncontrollably. Will Davies, who was responsible for overseeing construction of the gallows, offered his own prayer for Billik.[478] The prisoners seemed genuinely touched that their jailer took part in the service, and thanked him profusely when he was done.

The prisoners then called for little Edna to address them. Billik hoisted the tiny girl up on to a table, where she stood so the men could see her. "They're not going to kill my papa," she cried. "They shan't . . ."[479] She choked up, and tears streamed down her cheeks.

"I guess it's time for the little girl to go to bed,"[480] Billik said, trying to muster a smile. He lifted her up off of the table and back onto the ground. With that, the service came to an emotional end. The prisoners filed out of the chapel slowly. Each offered his hand to Billik and his family, and then returned to their individual cells.

32

Every Effort

<u>JUNE 10, 1908</u>

While the prayer service had been going on Tuesday night, Hinckley was on his way down to Springfield. Wednesday morning he appeared before the Illinois Supreme Court to once again ask them to set aside Billik's conviction. It was a long shot at best, since they had already refused to even consider it. Meanwhile, in Chicago, Stephen Gregory was filing a very different motion in federal court. He was asking for a writ of habeas corpus,* arguing that Billik had been denied his constitutional right to due process because Judge Barnes never gave him a chance to say anything before he was sentenced. "The points raised in the petition are inconsequential,"[481] said State's Attorney Healy, giving the motion little chance. Judge Kenesaw Landis agreed to hear arguments from both sides the following morning.

Billik heard about the efforts being made, and for a moment celebrated the fact that there was still a scrap of hope that he might be saved. His children apparently misunderstood and thought he had been set free. "Can't you come home with us now?" asked Edna, who grasped her arms around her father's neck, and kissed him repeatedly.[482]

---

* An order to bring a detained person into court, usually for a decision on whether the detention is lawful.

"No, I must stay here a little while before I can go,"[483] he answered.

After the initial excitement wore off, Billik once again fell into despair. "Mr. Hinckley and Mr. Gregory are fine men and I know they are going to fight for me to the end," he said, "But I guess I am doomed . . . I don't suppose the points raised will be given much consideration."[484] Even though he feared his cause was lost, Billik wanted everyone to know that he appreciated those who stepped forward to help him. "I am thankful for what everyone has done for me," he said. "I never knew there were so many kind people in the world. Especially am I grateful to Father O'Callaghan."[485]

Billik may not have known it, but just like Hinckley and Gregory Father O'Callaghan still had a few tricks up his sleeve too. The day after his plea to the public was published, thousands of letters of support for Billik poured in from all over Illinois. Some were hastily scrawled notes on scraps of paper, others lengthy and thoughtful letters. More than a few were from prominent citizens, typed on impressive letterheads. They were from doctors, lawyers, businessmen, bankers, even a Chicago police matron and a suburban mayor.[486] O'Callaghan seemed to have awakened all of Chicago. People circulated petitions everywhere. They posted them on the walls at their work, and in public places like barbershops and railroad offices.

O'Callaghan was busy making arrangements for what he called "the whirlwind finish of a campaign for justice for an innocent man."[487] He planned a series of mass meetings all over the city the following day. He wanted to put as much pressure as possible on Governor Deneen. He had thousands of fliers printed up advertising the meetings, and volunteers handed them out throughout Chicago. Just in case their efforts to save Billik fell short, O'Callaghan also made arrangements to say a special mass after his execution to pray for the deliverance of his soul.

June 11, 1908

On Thursday morning, the day before the execution, the news was not good. The Illinois Supreme Court wasted no time announcing that they were denying Hinckley's motion:

> *There is no power or jurisdiction in this court to set aside the judgment on account of what this young man [Jerry] says; if it should be regarded as true and if it were set aside for the purpose of further consideration the judgment could not be reversed. The court has no power to consider anything except matters contained in the record.*[488]

They cast doubt on Jerry's claim that the state's attorneys made him lie, saying, "It is questionable whether this man's words are true; he has demonstrated that he is unworthy of confidence."[489] Ironically, Billik was now about to be executed based on the words of that witness, who they deemed "unworthy of confidence." The court said only the governor could intercede, even if it were somehow *proven* that Billik was innocent. The only other hope lay in federal court, where Gregory was making his arguments before Judge Landis that morning.

Kenesaw Mountain Landis was only forty-one years old, but his head full of bright, silvery-white hair made him look much older. He was small in stature, with a fiery disposition and a sharp wit. Landis enjoyed a reputation as an honest, though unconventional judge, prone to making controversial decisions in high-profile cases. He would eventually gain fame as the first Commissioner of Major League Baseball after presiding over the 1919 Chicago "Black Sox" scandal (in which players intentionally lost the World Series in exchange for payoffs from gambling bosses). At this point, however, Landis was best known for the $29 million fine he levied against Standard Oil for an anti-trust violation, the highest ever assessed in a U.S. Court up to that time.

Landis listened to Gregory's argument, then told the assistant state's attorney that he needn't even make a statement. He saw no merit to Gregory's petition, and was denying the request. Gregory said he would then like to appeal Landis' decision to the U.S. Supreme Court, and asked for a stay of execution to do so. Judge Landis promptly dismissed the idea. He wouldn't interfere in Billik's execution in any way. Gregory continued his argument, however, and must have said something that got the judge's attention. Landis suddenly decided to at least allow Gregory to make a case for granting an appeal. He told the attorneys to come back the next morning to cite some legal precedents, and he would then make a decision by eleven o'clock.

There was only one problem with that: Billik was scheduled to be executed at *ten o'clock*. "The Sheriff may hang Billik early in the morning," Gregory quickly noted, "and in case there is a favorable decision in this case we may find the man dead."[490] Landis made the assistant state's attorney promise to move back the time of the execution until after his ruling. He made it clear, however, that he wasn't planning on granting any appeal, so it was only a one hour reprieve.

33

A Whirlwind

As soon as Landis adjourned court, Father O'Callaghan hurried off to begin the long day of rallies planned. The first was scheduled for noon at the Great Northern Theatre, a large playhouse downtown on Jackson Blvd., near Dearborn. O'Callaghan was running late, and didn't get there until almost twelve-thirty. When he arrived, the sight must have exceeded his wildest hopes. There were huge crowds on the street, pushing and jostling with police officers who stood around the entrance to prevent any more people from entering the already overflowing theater. Inside, several thousand downtown workers packed the seats and aisles, listening intently to former Mayor Dunne, who opened the program.

Dunne talked about Herman Billik's life and his family. The man he described was not at all the murderous monster people had read about, portrayed in almost mythic terms for the past year and a half. He was in fact a father and a husband, though admittedly no saint. Billik had his failings, Dunne assured the audience, but he never murdered anyone. Taking his life would be the ultimate injustice. Dunne called on Governor Deneen to grant a pardon, then yielded the stage to Father O'Callaghan.

O'Callaghan, who had practically just walked in the door, methodically went over the entire case, and the many facts that suggested Billik was not guilty. "I not only think this man is innocent;

Handbill advertising mass meetings in support of Herman Billik. Illinois State Archives, *Executive Clemency Files 1835-197, RS103.096.*

I know it,"[491] he told the crowd. Speaking with a rare passion, the cleric completely captivated them. If any among them had come merely as a curiosity, they were in very short order converted into believers that an innocent man was about to be executed. They wildly cheered his calls for justice, and joined him in prayer for the condemned father of four. O'Callaghan led up to the climax of his speech in dramatic fashion, finally declaring, "If he dies tomorrow it will be nothing but legal murder."[492] Many were brought to tears by the presentation, which would play out again and again throughout the day, all across the city. Even those who tried to contain their emotions wept openly when ten-year-old Edna Billik joined O'Callaghan on stage. The priest took her small hand as she begged the audience, "Please help me save my father; talk to the governor."[493] It was the most affecting part of an emotional hour.

O'Callaghan informed the large crowd that the news from federal court was not good. The legal avenues to save Billik were all but exhausted. Aside from the unlikely prospect that Judge Landis would allow an appeal of his own decision, the only hope was for the governor to intervene. O'Callaghan urged everyone to contact Deneen. Literally hundreds of people came forward to offer their help. They decided to form a committee from among them to go down to Springfield that evening to try to convince Governor Deneen to stop the execution. They selected a group of nine, including several prominent citizens. Francis Hinckley, who had just gotten back from Springfield after filing his motion with the Supreme Court, joined them.

While the newly formed committee planned the strategy for what looked to be Billik's last chance, the prisoner himself was preparing for the inevitable, completely unaware of the drama that was playing out beyond the walls of his cell. In the afternoon, Billik's mother phoned from Cleveland to say goodbye to her only son. Barbara Billik was now bedridden, and unable to travel to Chicago. "To hear your voice again makes me tremble," she told him. "I love you and believe you innocent . . . and it kills me not to be able to do anything to help you."[494] She was crying, and barely able to get the words out.

Billik tried to keep his composure the best he could. "Mama, I must say goodbye to you, tomorrow is my last," he said. "I wish that I could kiss you goodbye, but it will not be for long. We will see each other again up above."[495] He asked to have his body brought back home to Ohio to be buried. Mrs. Billik became hysterical at the thought of her son's impending execution, and cried out, "Oh, Herman, is there no means of saving you?"

"I am afraid not. It is too late now,"[496] he told her, resigned to his fate. He could no longer speak. Billik and his mother both sobbed uncontrollably, and he dropped the receiver.

Meanwhile, Father O'Callaghan's campaign for justice continued. Accompanied by Edna Billik and Jerry Vrzal, O'Callaghan spent the entire day going from one packed assembly hall to the next. Word spread across the city, and there were no less than seven mass meetings scattered about the farthest reaches of Chicago. From Our Lady of Lourdes School Hall at Leland and Ashland on the far North Side, to Holy Cross at 65th and Maryland [497] on the city's South Side; the stirring demonstrations seemed to be happening everywhere.

The *Chicago Daily Tribune* would declare, "The most remarkable series of efforts to save Billik from death ever known to criminal history has been made. And the climax of the long drawn out struggle came . . . in a series of perhaps the most intensely emotional mass meetings ever held in Chicago."[498] Large crowds attended every one. At times they roared in unison, at other times they prayed. The sight of Edna Billik brought nearly all of them to tears. Much of the city became so worked up, one observer called it "a pitch of almost hysterical fury."[499]

At five-thirty, one of the largest of the gatherings was held at Brand's Hall at Clark and Erie, on the near-North Side. The hall was filled with people who stopped on their way home from work. "We have gathered here in an effort to save an innocent man from death,"[500] O'Callaghan told them starkly. He explained the legal technicalities he had been grappling with, and the unusual quandary Billik was in: "If by perjured testimony a man secures a judgment against you for twenty dollars the law has provided that this money cannot be collected. When an innocent man is condemned to death because of perjured testimony, however, the law can do nothing. No means of saving the man from death has been provided by the courts."[501]

"What will the state gain by taking the life of Herman Billik?" he asked. "What of the official who has so little mercy in his heart that he cannot save this man, convicted at best on circumstantial evidence, from death?" O'Callaghan warned, "Woe be unto the man who when a human life is in the balance thinks of political considerations."[502]

Then Edna walked to the center of the stage with her twelve-year-old brother Emil. Heads bowed, they were a truly pitiful little pair. "Ladies and gentleman, are these the children of a murderer?"[503] asked O'Callaghan. Many in the crowd, both men and women, were already crying when Edna spoke. "Please help me save my papa. They—they're going to kill him," she told them, wiping tears from her swollen eyes. "God help you!" came a shout.[504] Young Emil put his arm around his little sister and walked with her back to the side of the stage and sat down. They covered their faces, quietly sobbing.

Jerry Vrzal took the stage next. He told the audience that the police pressured him, even threatened to hang him for the crimes, if he didn't say certain things. "I lied on the witness stand and now Billik is to be hung for this crime which he did not commit," he said. "I lied about these things and I hope to God that I can do something now to save Billik from this unjust punishment."[505] He even offered to change places with him, if he could. "I am ready to go on the scaffold and die if need be. I have worried about this until I scarcely can think. After I testified at the trial I went back to school, but I couldn't stand it. I couldn't think—I couldn't study."[506]

At the conclusion, dozens of people rushed forward to shake Jerry's hand, and to comfort Billik's small children, who could not escape the hugs and kisses of well-meaning spectators. "Do you really think they'll take my papa from me?" Edna asked one woman who picked her up to hold her in her arms. "My papa is a good man." The heartbroken woman could only offer a prayer that God would spare him.[507]

The meetings continued long into the evening. By the time the last one concluded on the city's western edge, in suburban River Forest,* it was approaching midnight. Father O'Callaghan was so hoarse he could hardly speak. "O God, what a lasting disgrace to the name of justice and to this community if this human being is sacrificed upon the gallows tomorrow," he said, tears streaming

---

* Held near the border of the adjacent suburbs of River Forest and Forest Park.

down his face. He concluded his final address by telling the large crowd, "There is little more that can be done for the unfortunate man but prepare him to meet his God."⁵⁰⁸

Billik spent his evening with his wife, reading from the Bible, and praying at the small altar that officials had constructed for him inside the "death chamber." A new glimmer of hope appeared when Jailer Will Davies publicly announced his belief in Billik's innocence. Unfortunately, the optimism was short lived, as Davies proclaimed that he would, nonetheless, "do his duty, and hang him anyhow."⁵⁰⁹

At about ten-thirty, Edna arrived at the jail. She rushed to her father and threw her arms around him, excited to bring him news of the amazing rallies taking place. The entire city was in an uproar, she told him, and Hinckley and a group of citizens were on their way down to Springfield. There was still hope.

After Edna and Mary left for the evening, Father MacCorry from St. Mary's stayed with Billik. The two talked and prayed for most of an hour. As they did, just outside of Billik's cell, Davies' men were securing a 205-pound sandbag to the end of the rope dangling from the crossbeam of the just-completed scaffold. When the knot was fastened, Davies gave a signal. Just before midnight, the platform was dropped and an immense *Thud!* echoed through the corridors of the jail. It was followed by the ominous and gentle creaking of wood, as the large bag swayed softly from the end of the noose. The gallows were ready.

It was about this time that Hinckley and his committee were arriving in downstate Springfield. They carried with them a large suitcase filled with petitions and letters to the governor asking that Billik's sentence be commuted. Governor Deneen had already been overwhelmed by thousands of letters and telegrams, which flooded his office on Billik's behalf. Almost 20,000 letters were delivered to the governor, with another 15,000 or so signatures gathered on petitions.[510] It was a completely unprecedented show of support for a condemned prisoner.

The delegation arrived at the governor's office around midnight. The governor and the members of the pardon board were all there. Hinckley told Deneen that the group had made the journey "on behalf of the thousand persons left in tears in the city of Chicago, and the 40,000 that have signed petitions asking for a commutation of sentence."[511] Several members of the volunteer committee made statements begging for clemency. Deneen said only that he would take the matter under advisement. As soon as the group left, Deneen placed a call to his friend Charles Vail, the Clerk of the Cook County Circuit Court. What was going on up in Chicago? Vail told him about the massive demonstrations, then phoned Father O'Callaghan.[512]

O'Callaghan went to see Billik not long after midnight, and told him about the dramatic close of the meetings, and the phone call from Vail. While the governor had promised nothing, O'Callaghan believed the public pressure might force him to act. At about one o'clock in the morning, O'Callaghan announced, rather optimistically, "Billik will not be hanged this morning. I have aroused the people of Chicago so that they will influence Gov. Deneen in his favor.[513] As it stood, however, the execution was still set for eleven o'clock, less than ten hours away.

34

Execution Day

On Friday, June 12th, Billik was up just after seven o'clock—on a morning which could be his last. This was his fourth date with the hangman, but it was the first time it had arrived without a reprieve already in hand. The tension was palpable, though Billik himself was fairly calm and collected, at least for a man who was just a few hours away from being executed. After talking to O'Callaghan the night before, and hearing about the wild demonstrations, he was optimistic that Governor Deneen might commute his sentence. He hoped a decision would come early. He paced back and forth for more than an hour, anxiously awaiting word from Springfield, but there was nothing. Finally, he was told that the pardon board had scheduled a meeting for nine o'clock. Maybe they would make an announcement then.

Outside, hundreds of people crowded around the entrance to the jail on Dearborn St., pushing and jostling for position. Some even tried to force their way inside when the door was opened for guards and officials reporting to work. Police used their clubs repeatedly to keep control, hoping to prevent anyone from being seriously injured in the scuffle. By nine o'clock, all traffic on Dearborn St., between Illinois and Hubbard St., had come to a halt as boisterous crowds overflowed into the streets.[514] There were always crowds on execution days, but this was far beyond the norm, and the mass kept growing as the hour of execution neared.

Down in Springfield, Deneen met with his Board of Pardons at nine o'clock sharp. Hinckley and the committee from Chicago waited outside his office, eagerly anticipating some sort of statement. As time dragged on, though, it became apparent that the governor was still undecided.

At about ten o'clock, Billik asked Will Davies if he had heard anything. "Nothing as yet," the big jailer told him. "There still is hope, however."

"You needn't say that," Billik replied. "In an hour I will be dead. I know there is no chance of a reprieve now."[515]

Over in federal court, Judge Landis called the room to order at ten o'clock. When he was once again assured that Billik would not be executed until he made his decision, he moved on to handle other matters. Attorney Stephen S. Gregory was not at all encouraged. He sat down and waited to present his argument, nervously eying the clock.

The scene outside of Cook County Jail was starting to get out of hand. Thousands packed the streets. By ten-thirty, Dearborn, Illinois, and Hubbard streets were filled from curb to curb with anxious onlookers.[516] It was the largest crowd ever congregated around the jail on the morning of an execution,[517] and its numbers continued to swell. Eventually, additional officers were dispatched from Chief Shippy's office to try to maintain some semblance of order. Ropes were secured around the perimeter of the building to contain the crowds, and to permit employees and officials to come and go from the jail.

Inside, Father O'Callaghan was with Billik in the "death chamber." Together, they prayed Billik's final prayer, and O'Callaghan administered the sacraments of the Last Rites to him. Billik solemnly removed his necktie and loosened his collar for the noose that would soon be fastened around his neck.

Down in Springfield, Governor Deneen and the Board of Pardons were still in conference. It wasn't clear exactly what was being discussed, but there may have been some differing advice being offered. Hinckley and the volunteer committee waited . . . and waited. As it approached eleven o'clock, there was still no word at all.

The final formality of the case was playing out back in Chicago, in Judge Landis' courtroom. When at last he finished with the routine cases before him, Landis turned his attention to Billik. He finally called the case at about ten minutes to eleven, and asked Gregory to step up to make his argument. Gregory quoted an opinion from the Supreme Court and an amendment passed by Congress to support his claim that Billik was entitled to appeal Landis' original decision. As Gregory spoke, all eyes were fixed on the large clock on the wall. When it reached eleven o'clock, a nervous hush fell over the courtroom. Everyone held their breath for a moment, then Gregory continued.

At the jail, Billik and jittery prison officials were preparing for the "death march," the procession of the prisoner to the scaffold. In the "death chamber," the guard who had spent most of the last three days with Billik was no longer able to console him. When eleven o'clock passed without word of a pardon, Billik sat back in a chair in the corner and covered his face with his hands.[518] It was all over. The jailer would be there at any moment to walk him to the gallows. Father O'Callaghan sat down at the small table beside him. He took out a pen and paper, and Billik began dictating his final statement.

In the jailer's office downstairs, Davies sat in front of the special phone that had been set up, waiting for word of a last minute reprieve. Everyone had expected a decision, one way or another, from both Governor Deneen and Judge Landis well before eleven o'clock. Officials were somewhat divided as to how to proceed. Earlier, Sheriff Strassheim had announced that he would hold off the execution until the last possible moment, but there was some disagreement as to what time that actually should be. They eventually decided they would move forward at eleven o'clock if they didn't hear anything by then.

When eleven o'clock arrived, everyone was so panic-stricken they could scarcely decide what to do. Will Davies, who would soon have to tie the noose around the neck of a man he believed to be innocent, was possibly the most anxious man in the building. He could no longer even think clearly. When no word from the governor came, at a few minutes after eleven Davies took the death warrant out of the safe in his office and assembled the deputies, physicians, and other officials for the procession to the gallows. At ten minutes after eleven, they began the grim parade to Billik's cell to read him the death warrant and march him to the scaffold.

At practically the same time, in U.S. District Court, Judge Landis was delivering his opinion. He spent little time making his decision, which seemed inevitable. But Landis would never be known for being predictable. "You would not contend that in a civil case this court could prevent having its own decision reviewed by a higher court . . ."[519] he began, apparently accepting Gregory's argument. The day before, he had practically discounted even the possibility of allowing an appeal. Now, he said that he may not have had the full picture when he made that hasty statement. "Yesterday I was informed by the state that the United States Supreme Court had passed upon this question, but I find upon investigation that it had not,"[520] he said, sounding as if he felt misled by the state's attorney's office. "I have no right to stand between this defendant and the United States Supreme Court,"[521] Landis announced to the startled courtroom. It was ten minutes past eleven when he concluded, "As long as there is a doubt of this man's guilt, under the Constitution of the United States, he has a right to fight for his life before the nation's highest tribunal and this court therefore allows this appeal, and hereby orders the state's attorneys and the Sheriff of Cook County not to carry out the execution of this person until the Supreme Court of the United States has passed on the case."[522]

Gregory could hardly believe it. Neither could the assistant state's attorney, who asked Landis if he would delay formal entry of the order for several hours so he could confer with State's Attorney Healy. It's not clear if he was intentionally trying to delay the order to ensure Billik's execution, but Landis shot down the request in an instant. "These orders will be entered by the clerk of court *at once*," the judge barked.[523] Gregory raced across the courtroom to the telephone. While official notice would be made in another minute or so, Gregory was the first to call Cook County Jail with the news. He only hoped that it wasn't too late.

35

Unnerved

JUNE 12, 1908

Davies' procession had taken the first few steps of their "death march" when, suddenly, a *RING!* of the telephone startled them all. Davies froze in disbelief. When it rang again, he realized he hadn't imagined it, and practically jumped for the receiver. In a few seconds, he shouted the news to the guards and officials lining the hallway that Landis had ordered a stay of execution. He practically threw the receiver at one deputy, and ran to give Billik the news.

A small handful of the crowd outside had been allowed to stand in the doorway of the prison entrance. When the phone inside rang, they listened carefully, and were among the first to hear the news from the jubilant Davies. One of them, a priest from suburban Wilmette, jumped back from the inner doorway to the steps outside, making himself visible to the thousands gathered on Dearborn Street.[524] "Billik lives!" he shouted. "Reprieved!" Then he took off his panama hat and waved it wildly over his head, jumping up and down.[525] The enormous throng roared its approval. They cheered madly, waving their own hats and handkerchiefs. They rushed past the ropes and police line, and approached the doors and the windows on the lower floor of the prison, as if hoping to congratulate Billik personally. Police had to use their clubs to keep people from actually going inside the jail.

Prisoners on the lower level heard the cheers through the windows and saw Davies scurry down the hall. As they realized what was happening, they gradually joined in the celebration. Their shouts soon became so fierce that those on the street took pause and, for a few moments, stood in silence, listening to the surge of "*Hurrahs!*" that thundered from within. The mighty holler was reportedly so loud it could be heard for blocks around.[526]

Inside, up in the "death chamber" of the prison library, Billik had just finished dictating the last sentence of his final statement to Father O'Callaghan when he heard the yells from the prisoners on the lower tier. It spread quickly, and soon the violent clamor enveloped the whole prison. "What is it?" asked a bewildered Billik. "My God! Can it be the death yell of the prisoners?" he wondered. "Do you suppose that it's the jailer with the death warrant?"[527]

"I'll see just as quickly as I can,"[528] said the guard, jumping up from his chair. Just then, Davies rushed in. Billik was seated at the table with O'Callaghan. He was pale and trembling. He assumed this was his summons to join the procession to the gallows. But instead of reading the death warrant to him, Davies extended his hand and smiled. "Reprieved!" he exclaimed.

"I don't understand," said Billik, so panicked he couldn't comprehend what he was being told.

"Judge Landis has granted your plea for an appeal to the Supreme Court," Davies told him. "You are saved."[529]

Billik stood up, and dropped his head so that his chin rested on his chest. "I thank God," he said.[530] He was so completely overcome that he nearly fell back into his chair as he sat back down and covered his face, tears running down his cheeks. The apprehension on Father O'Callaghan's face melted into a broad smile. Beaming with joy, he took hold of both of Billik's hands. "Herman," he said earnestly, "God is all merciful."[531] Billik was still dazed. He barely responded as the guards gathered around him offering their congratulations.

The noise inside the jail was almost deafening by this time. Out on the street, people were wildly out of control. Many narrowly escaped serious injury.[532] Assistant Chief Schuettler arrived with still

more officers right in the middle of the melee, and police were eventually able to push the mob back away from the building and across
Hubbard and Dearborn Streets. Still, the wild uproar continued.
People began calling for Billik to come to the window. "That's a
phase of human nature that cannot be accounted for," Schuettler
marveled. "They would stand here all day, miss their meals and
never feel the fatigue if they could get a glimpse of Billik."[533] After
about thirty minutes, things quieted as people became hoarse and
exhausted, and the crowd gradually dispersed.

When Billik regained his composure, a reporter from the *Chicago
Daily News* asked for his reaction. "I was all ready to die, and,
knowing I am innocent, my feelings were indescribable," he replied. "This sudden hope has unnerved me. I cannot express deep
enough thanks to Almighty God and to Judge Landis, whom
I regard as His instrument in saving my life."[534] He gratefully
acknowledged the efforts of Father O'Callaghan and Gregory,
who had raced to the jail from Landis' courtroom to join the
celebration. Billik clutched each by the hand and thanked them
profusely.

They still had a long way to go, however. "The work is not over
yet," O'Callaghan told Billik. "We are going to save you altogether.
This is but a respite, but we will not be satisfied with less than
justice."[535] He said they would need to raise more money to bring
the case before the U.S. Supreme Court, but he wouldn't give up. "I
will hold mass meetings every day for the next year if necessary to
complete this work which just has been begun."[536]

Absent from the festivities was Francis Hinckley. He and the
nine committee members waited all morning in Springfield for
Governor Deneen to decide on the clemency petition. A full hour
after Judge Landis granted Billik's appeal, Deneen finally issued a
statement: "It has been the uniform practice of the governor and
the board of pardons not to pass upon questions which are pending
in the courts. Accordingly, action was deferred until a decision has

been rendered in the federal court."[537] Landis had taken Deneen off the hook. Hinckley and the committee headed back to Chicago, relieved that Billik had been spared for now, but undoubtedly disappointed by the governor's inaction.

Billik looked around for his wife and children, but they were nowhere to be found. Mary Billik was far too upset to go to the jail that day, certain there was no longer any hope of a reprieve. Davies sent a guard to deliver her the news, and to bring her to the jail to see her husband. Billik's mother Barbara was notified by a reporter from the United Press association, who phoned her at her home in Cleveland.[538] "Oh my God," she cried. "God be praised, he saved my boy."[539] Already quite ill, she almost fainted at the news. Doctors watched her closely.

Mary Billik arrived at the jail at about twelve-fifteen. She was weak, her walk unsteady. When she saw her husband seated in the prison library, she became hysterical. "Oh, Herman. Is it true?" she screamed. "Can it be possible that you really are saved?"

"Yes, Mama; the highest court in the land is going to hear the case now. I will get justice," he assured her. Then he noticed that the children weren't with her. "But where are Edna and Emil?" he asked.*

"I wasn't sure the good news was really true. I couldn't believe it until I saw you," she explained. "I didn't want them to have to bear another disappointment."[540] An hour later, Edna and Emil charged into the room. "Papaaaa . . . !" they shrieked. They ran and jumped onto their father's lap, clutching him tightly, and kissing him again and again. It was the happiest reunion one could imagine. After a long visit, Billik, having spent the last three sleepless nights pacing the "death chamber," was happy to return to his old cell.

---

* The older boys, Frank and Herman Jr., were not around, likely in Cleveland at the time.

Part V

Benefits
and Battles

36

Another Body

The following week, Chicago's attention again turned to politics. On June 16th, the Republican National Convention assembled in the city's largest arena, the Coliseum. It was on Wabash Ave, spanning from about 14th St. to 16th St., just two blocks north of the Levee district and a few blocks south of St. Mary's Church on 9th St. The Coliseum held 15,000 people, and hosted all of the city's biggest events, such as the annual horse show, which gradually gave way to the annual auto show.*

The Republican National Convention of 1908 was Chicago's seventh.† The city's central location and ample amenities made it a natural choice. There was quite a bit of apprehension in the months leading up to the event, with strikes threatened by a multitude of the city's labor unions including truck and wagon drivers,

---

* The Coliseum was also the venue for the infamous First Ward Ball, held every December. That event attracted not only the saloon keepers, gambling chiefs, madams, and "ladies" of the Levee, but also politicians, judges, and police officers. It amounted to a large-scale drunken orgy, which grew further out of hand each year, with all of the proceeds benefiting the First Ward Democratic Organization and its' bosses, who ruled the Levee.

† The 1860 Convention in Chicago saw the nomination of Illinois' favorite son Abraham Lincoln. The Coliseum would be host to every Republican National Convention from 1904 to 1920.

commercial telegraphers, elevator engineers, and street car workers. The convention itself, however, lacked any real drama. Secretary of War William Howard Taft, the hand-picked successor of popular President Theodore Roosevelt, was nominated on the first ballot. He would go on to become the next President of the United States.

The Supreme Court wouldn't consider Billik's case until October, so he was safe for the time being. Ultimately, though, the appeal had very little chance. His only real hope was still for the Governor to commute his sentence. They would have to keep the pressure on Deneen. "It is because of the efforts of the public that Billik has been saved from this gross injustice," O'Callaghan said, "and I do not believe the public will desert him now."[541] He planned a series of benefits to raise money for Billik's defense, hoping to keep the case in the spotlight long enough to force Deneen to do something. Former Mayor Dunne was made chairman of the planning committee.

July 1-2, 1908

Four benefit performances were held, on the 1st and 2nd of July. Dozens of performers, representing virtually every theatrical company appearing in Chicago,[542] donated their efforts. The acts included popular performers such as singer Joe Howard and his wife, stage actress Mable Barrison, and ranged from the classic opera of the Baroness de Merkle of the Royal Weimar Opera, to the comedic antics of "the Juggling Parrotts" (who were not, as their name might suggest, a poor-spelling animal act, but a couple named William and Lillian Parrott). At the start of each performance, Edna took the stage and thanked the audience for helping her father. Then everyone was treated to a spectacular, full-blown vaudeville show. There were sketches and songs, dancing, acrobats, and beautiful girls. The show opened with a musical sketch of Bohemia that included twenty chorus girls.

Father O'Callaghan followed the entertainment. He took note of the flimsy costumes and slightly wild music (at least by his standards), and joked, "That doesn't sound much like church music."[543] But the light nature of the gathering didn't last. O'Callaghan had promised a dramatic presentation, and he did not disappoint. "The details of a political conspiracy have not half been told," he announced cryptically. Then, in apparent reference to the upcoming election, he said, "When the proper time arrives—and it is not far distant—we will make those who are occupying the chair of justice suffer for their political future as well as their eternal happiness."[544]

Billik, he said, simply wanted a trial free of perjured testimony. Unfortunately, there were those who feared the political consequences. "The opposition arrayed against us is based upon the desire to protect those who caused Jerry Vrzal to commit the perjury which he admits now."[545] O'Callaghan chastised police and prosecutors. He claimed that he had more information than anyone about the case, and was never more certain of Billik's innocence. He hinted that there might be some startling revelations yet to come and promised that as soon as he had a little more information, he would have a lot more to say. "I will tell a tale that will ring from the housetops of this city, that will make the blood boil in the veins of certain politicians,"[546] he said.

At the last performance, Jerry Vrzal took the stage, telling his story of police intimidation and perjured testimony, and voicing his confidence in Billik's innocence. The benefits were a great success, with large enthusiastic crowds. Most importantly, $1,200 was raised for the next stage of Billik's crusade.[547]

July 24-31, 1908

By the end of July, it became apparent how some of that money was spent. For several weeks, a private investigator hired by Father

O'Callaghan had been in the western suburbs of DuPage County looking into persistent rumors regarding the family of Emma's deceased husband, William Niemann. The fruits of those labors were soon realized. In the late night hours of July 24th, 1908, officials secretly removed the body of William Niemann's father, Henry, from his grave at Trinity Lutheran Cemetery in Lombard. The internal organs were sent to chemists at Northwestern University for analysis.

They were looking for evidence that the 77-year-old, who had died three years earlier, was poisoned by arsenic. Chicago officials quickly dismissed it as a wild goose chase, but this mystery was not in Cook County. It was in DuPage, and the DuPage County Coroner, Newton E. Matter, felt there was plenty of reason to be suspicious. "[The burial] had taken place under strange circumstances," said Matter, "it being reported that alcoholism had been the cause of death."[548] He ordered the exhumation after learning that no death certificate had been issued and no autopsy, nor coroner's inquest, was conducted. Other circumstances raised questions. "After the death, property interests became involved," said Matter. "There was some trouble over the disposition of the property, which amounted to about $15,000. William Niemann, the son who married Emma Vrzal, is dead, but there is another brother, Fred Niemann, who lives at Joliet."[549]

Fred Niemann, William's younger brother, was in the Illinois State Penitentiary in Joliet for defrauding several undertakers. His unusual scheme involved pretending that his father had just died, and that he wanted to hire them to handle the burial. He then borrowed money from the sympathetic funeral directors, claiming he was awaiting an insurance settlement. There was, of course, no settlement, and Fred disappeared with their money. It wasn't his first brush with the law. Around the time that their father died, his brother William had accused him of stealing his horse. Fred was convicted and served eleven months at Joliet. Some alleged that his prosecution had been a "railroading"[550] to cut him off from a share of the estate.

Coroner Matter declined to say if it was Fred Niemann who provided the information that sparked the inquiry into Henry

Niemann's death, but he said an inquest would be held once the test results were announced. "I have not received any report as yet from the Chicago doctor who is examining the stomach," said the coroner. "Until I have there will be no arrests or no one placed under surveillance."[551]

Father O'Callaghan put up his last cent to pay for the inquiry and he left no doubt who the main suspect was. "Who poisoned him?" he asked. "Not Herman Billik, but the same person who poisoned the Vrzal children, the father, and the mother. The father died in March 1905, Mary died in July, and it was just at that time that Emma Vrzal went to visit the Niemann farm."[552] On August 21st, 1905, just a little more than a week after Emma's arrival on the farm near Downer's Grove, Henry Niemann was dead. Emma's "visit" soon became permanent. She lived there with William for more than a year, until he purchased the Vrzal home on 19th St.

O'Callaghan hinted that Emma may also have had a hand in the death of her mother, which the police still considered a suicide. "How can anyone figure that Mrs. Vrzal, the mother, was the co-conspirator with Billik?" he asked. "Any poison taken on [the day she died] would have been found only in her stomach," he said, "but there was poison in her liver. It had been in her system for days, for months perhaps."[553]

"There was suspicion of the real poisoner at the time," O'Callaghan continued. "William Niemann, who after living with Emma Vrzal for two years, married her in February 1907, died the following November. Five months before his death he canceled an insurance policy upon his life, believing that would save him from the danger hanging over him."[554] What motive could Emma possibly have had for killing them all? O'Callaghan didn't hesitate. "She did it for the property," he said. "She got possession of the Niemann farm, and then she wanted the Vrzal home and the milk business. She got it when all the other members of the family died."[555]

Cook County Coroner Hoffman claimed that his office had already investigated Henry Niemann's death. "I feel confident there is but the slightest foundation for Father O'Callaghan's claims, and that no benefit will result from the spectacular step he has taken," said Hoffman. "I have every reason to believe that all of the deaths in the Niemann family were from natural causes."[556] He maintained that he had followed every lead, and found no evidence of any wrong-doing. "The investigation is bound to fall flat,"[557] he declared. Predictably, Chief Shippy and State's Attorney Healy made similar statements. Henry Niemann's physician, Dr. William Tope, had told them that the old farmer died of natural causes, and that was good enough for them. Not everyone agreed, however. "I have known for some time what formed the basis for my investigation," said Father O'Callaghan. "I presented it to the state's attorney. He wrote to the physician who attended Niemann, that man Tope, and when he received as reply that the old man died of alcoholism he went no further. He did not investigate as I have done."[558]

Unable to get any action from Healy's office or Chicago police, O'Callaghan said he was forced to hire a private detective to look into it. Posing as an insurance agent, the investigator spoke to dozens of Henry Niemann's relatives and neighbors in DuPage County. While Dr. Tope may not have had any suspicion about Henry Niemann's death, there were people who did. Dr. George M. Fox, who had also treated the old man, said Henry complained of a particular weakness in his legs that was similar to that which he once found in a man who had swallowed roach poison containing arsenic.[559] Fox had also treated Louise Niemann, William's first wife. She died in August of 1903, at the age of thirty-one. Fox said she suffered from some affliction of the throat. At the time he attributed both deaths to natural causes, but said he now was inclined to believe that arsenic poisoning may have caused either death.[560] If it were shown that Henry Niemann had been poisoned, Louise Niemann's body would be exhumed next.

Some in the Niemann family weren't exactly thrilled about the inquiry. "The death of my wife's father is ended so far as we are concerned," said Charles Mech, who was married to William Niemann's sister (also named "Louise"). "We were solid against reopening the case. The old man was sick long before Emma ever visited the house." Mech went so far as to hire an attorney and threatened to take action if it was determined that the exhumation was illegal.[561] Oddly though, Mech seemed to acknowledge that his father-in-law might well have been poisoned. "Even if they do discover traces of poison in the old man's stomach, which is probable, how can they prove that Emma poisoned him?" he asked. "There were others present in the house," he said, "and why they should single out Emma is more than I can tell."[562]

Newsmen tried to get a comment from Emma, but she wasn't talking. "I don't care what they do," she yelled at one reporter, slamming the door in his face.[563] Another showed up at the milk depot on 19th St. pretending to be a customer. When Emma discovered who he was, her eyes flashed with anger. "I will say nothing at all to anyone," she told him, her voice quivering. "I have nothing to say."[564]

37

Politics

Billik was excited about Henry Niemann's exhumation, but feared someone might try to tamper with the test results, maybe even steal or replace the organs that were sent to the lab. He sent a note to Father O'Callaghan begging him to make sure they were guarded closely.[565] Billik and his friends didn't exactly trust officials from Cook County. On Friday, July 31st, Father O'Callaghan had his harshest words yet for the Cook County State's Attorney. "Healy would have hanged Billik for nothing but political reasons," said O'Callaghan. "If anyone ought to be hanged, he is the man. He would have been guilty of taking a human life to gain his own ends. I know that if he could he would put me under the ground tonight."[566]

O'Callaghan said he was made aware of a phone conversation between Healy and Governor Deneen in which Healy urged the governor to deny Billik's request for a pardon. "I was in Billik's cell at the time Mr. Healy talked with Gov. Deneen over the long-distance phone," recounted O'Callaghan, "and their conversation was overheard by some overzealous person who had tapped the wire. Gov. Deneen was pleading with Healy to allow him to pardon Billik. Healy said: 'No; to do that would be fatal.'

'I think you are making a mistake,' interposed the governor, and Healy replied: 'No; on the contrary, the political situation demands it.'"⁵⁶⁷ O'Callaghan said it was morally reprehensible for politics to even be discussed when a man's life was hanging in the balance.

Healy vehemently denied the accusation, all but calling the priest a liar. "I never had any such conversation with the governor, and Father O'Callaghan's informant is mythical," he protested. "There is no politics in the Billik case. It is simply a question of guilt."⁵⁶⁸ He then tried to take himself out of the controversy altogether. "I had little to do with Billik's case," the county's chief prosecutor said. "He was tried in court, found guilty by a jury, the case went to the Supreme Court which, after reading the record, said Billik was guilty. Then the pardon board heard all of the case and refused to act and since then Father O'Callaghan has not furnished us with a particle of tangible proof showing Billik's innocence."⁵⁶⁹

In reality, Healy's adamant stand that Billik should be executed greatly influenced the governor and board of pardons, and the trial jury based their decision on perjured testimony, as did the Illinois Supreme Court, who denied Billik's appeal, but (contrary to Healy's claim) never made any decision regarding his guilt or innocence.⁵⁷⁰ The state's own argument to the court was filled with references to testimony that was later admitted to be false. Healy's use of the term "Supreme Court" was itself deceptive, as it implied that the case had been heard by the *United States* Supreme Court, and not simply the Illinois Supreme Court. This same misrepresentation almost cost Billik his life when Healy's assistant told Judge Landis that the case had already been before "the Supreme Court." Landis assumed he meant the *U.S.* Supreme Court (particularly since they were standing in U.S. Federal Court) and quickly rejected Gregory's request for an appeal. When Gregory clarified the issue, the judge realized he had been misled and ordered the stay of execution.

None of this was lost on Father O'Callaghan, who now considered Healy the main, perhaps only, obstacle in the road to justice for Herman Billik. Maybe a new state's attorney would be slightly less zealous about seeing Billik hanged. With the primary election just a week away, O'Callaghan decided that if Healy would allow politics to enter into the Billik case, then perhaps the Billik case should enter into politics.

August 1-2, 1908

O'Callaghan organized a series of public meetings to discuss the case and Healy's handling of it. "The first meeting will be held at Forest Park next Thursday," he announced. "It will be in the nature of a benefit for Billik . . . I shall not take the stump against Mr. Healy, although my meetings, being public, may have a political effect."[571] It was no coincidence that it was to be held just two days before the primary election of August 8th. Since the governor had ultimate authority over Billik's fate, one might have expected him to be a target, but he wasn't. "Governor Deneen is in no way involved in the agitation at this time," said O'Callaghan. "I do not expect Gov. Deneen will in any way be attacked."[572] O'Callaghan never said a harsh word about Deneen, or challenged his integrity or competence in any way. Those things he saved for the state's attorney.

John J. Healy had two opponents in the Republican primary for the position of Cook County State's Attorney. Neither had a strong political organization behind them, and they weren't expected to give the incumbent much trouble. The issue in the race for state's attorney, for both Republicans and Democrats, was very clear: enforcement of the city's liquor regulations, particularly the closing of saloons on Sunday. Healy had upset many by ordering strict enforcement of the Sunday closing laws, which until then had been largely ignored in many neighborhoods. The issue brought out passionate opinions on both sides. There were liquor opponents and also "pro-saloon" people in both of the major political parties. Healy strongly favored the Sunday closings. His main opponent in the primary, a young attorney named John Wayman, announced himself a "personal liberties" candidate, believing, basically, in a man's "right" to drink.

The liquor interests in the city were well organized. They had decided that their best strategy would be to have their supporters vote in the Democratic primary to ensure that there was a strong pro-saloon candidate to defeat Healy in the general election.[573] If they tried to take him on in the primary they might well lose, and risk having another anti-liquor candidate nominated by the Democrats (who had eight men running for the office). It seemed like smart politics, and it left Healy without much opposition until the general election. On Sunday, August 2nd, less than a week before the primary, the *Chicago Daily Tribune* said of Healy, "Among the politicians, his nomination is regarded as a foregone conclusion."[574]

DuPage Investigation

On Monday, August 3rd, DuPage County Coroner Matter was notified that arsenic was discovered during the analysis of Henry Niemann's organs. Matter ordered an inquest to begin at the courthouse in Wheaton the following day. "[W]e feel certain that we will be able to fix the responsibility on the guilty person," said Matter.[575] Billik's case was now getting massive publicity. Tickets for the benefit at Forest Park sold so quickly that O'Callaghan had to schedule several more events to accommodate the demand. He promised to talk about the DuPage investigation at a benefit scheduled for the following evening.

DuPage residents were besieged by reporters and investigators. Not only were local officials interviewing the friends, family, and former associates of Henry Niemann, but detectives hired by Billik's supporters, and Healy's office were doing the same. August Tielk, who owned an adjacent farm, said he stopped visiting the Niemann house after becoming ill from a meal he ate there.[576] However, another neighbor, Richard Ulhorn, said that locals were divided as to whether or not they believed Niemann had been murdered. Ulhorn thought the elder Niemann had used patent medicines, some of which probably contained arsenic, and was ill for years before he died.[577]

A reporter from the *Chicago Daily News* caught up with Emma at her home. She was calm at first, but when asked about arsenic being found in Henry Niemann's body, the reporter said, "She burst out excitedly in protestation that she would not talk."[578]

"I don't care what others think," Emma said, "I wish they would let me alone." She claimed to be sick, and the reporter said she looked to be on the verge of a nervous breakdown. "I am being persecuted," she complained, "but I will fight to the end. I am not alone in my struggle. My sister, who usually is with me, has joined hands in this fight. She is not here today and her presence will be known to no one but myself and the State's Attorney of Cook County."[579]

She was referring to her little sister Bertha. Billik's supporters had been trying for weeks to interview the girl, believing she could help their case, but Emma wouldn't allow it. It wasn't clear where Bertha had gone, but apparently Emma wasn't going to let her speak to anyone but State's Attorney Healy. A spokesman for Healy's office said they didn't know anything about Emma's peculiar statement, or Bertha's whereabouts, but offered, "I know that the defense has visited Mrs. Niemann often since this case began and as I recall it somebody tried to kidnap her sister from her home while Mrs. Niemann was at the Criminal Court Building."[580] Whether it was an actual kidnapping attempt or, more likely, someone trying to interview the child, is not clear.

Healy himself didn't seem surprised that arsenic was found in Henry Niemann's body. He said it was too early to make any judgment, as it would take a month to determine exactly how much of the poison was present. "If a mistake has been made we want to know it and no one ought to take any decided position on the matter now, until we find out what the facts are," said Healy, sounding open-minded. "I didn't prosecute Billik. I shall be as glad as anyone if it is proved that [he] is innocent, for I personally am opposed to hanging."[581] Healy defended his limited investigation into Henry Niemann's death, oddly, by implying that it was Father O'Callaghan's responsibility rather than his own. "Father

O'Callaghan came to me in February or March of this year and told me he suspected that Henry Niemann and his wife had come to an untimely end," he said. "It is strange he should have waited so long before he took action."[582]

Healy claimed he saw nothing peculiar about the deaths. "At that time, I investigated and found that Mrs. Niemann died eighteen years ago and that the doctors had no suspicion of arsenical poison as to Niemann's death. Finding that at least half of Father O'Callaghan's suspicions were baseless, I dropped further investigation of the case."[583] Healy was either intentionally distorting the facts, or demonstrating a lack of familiarity with the case. In fact, there was no controversy about the death of Henry Niemann's wife, who died back in 1890. The suspicions that *were* brought to Healy (along with those concerning the deaths of William and Henry Niemann) centered on *William's* first wife, Louise, who died in 1903. Though she was only thirty-one at the time of her death, no death certificate was issued* and no autopsy or inquest was conducted. Healy either made such a cursory review of the case that he looked into the wrong death, or he was trying to mislead the public to justify his lack of inquiry.

Father O'Callaghan was livid. "I wish to emphasize the one fact that stands out clear in this case at this time," he declared. "If Henry Niemann had died and been buried in Cook County, the machine of the Cook County officials who have been seeking to justify the conviction of Herman Billik would never have permitted the facts to get into the sunlight of truth. I thank God that DuPage County is not under the lash of the clique which governs here. That does not include all Cook County officials," he said, trying to temper his remarks, "but the group which commit judicial murder if need be to protect its own work of causing Jerry Vrzal to commit perjury and to carry out political ends. The public conscience is being aroused and I am glad of it."[584]

---

* Neither the DuPage County Clerk, nor the Illinois Secretary of State has any record on file. Her tombstone indicates that she died August 29, 1903.

The inquest in Wheaton Tuesday night drew a lot of attention. Coroner Matter presided, with DuPage County State's Attorney Charles W. Hadley interviewing witnesses. Several officials from Cook County attended, including Dr. Harold Moyer and Assistant State's Attorney James Barbour, who had conducted the questionable prosecution of Knute Knudson so vigorously. Coroner Matter allowed Barbour to cross-examine witnesses, almost as if it were a criminal trial. It's safe to say that Cook County Coroner Hoffman would have never granted anyone such leeway. For his part, State's Attorney Hadley, who was a Republican himself, wanted to remain as neutral as possible in the underlying battle between Healy and Father O'Callaghan. "I have no axes to grind and would do nothing to antagonize the state's attorney from Cook County, who is a personal friend of mine,"[585] said Hadley. He began by interviewing the undertaker who prepared Henry Niemann's body for burial. He stated unequivocally that there was no arsenic used in the embalming process. Any arsenic discovered must have been ingested by Niemann when he was still alive.

Then Professor Harry M. Gordin, a chemist from Northwestern University, described how he conducted the analysis of Niemann's internal organs and found arsenic. Gordin said he felt pressed for time, believing that Billik could be executed any day. Unfortunately, in his haste, he took a shortcut that now made it impossible to know which organs contained arsenic, and exactly how much was contained in each. Rather than testing the organs separately, he combined them, tested a sample, and then estimated the total amount of arsenic. After analyzing one-third of the organs, and finding 1/15th of a grain of arsenic, Gordin projected a total of about one-fifth of a grain of arsenic present in the body, considerably less than that found in the Vrzals. Gordin said he spent only about fifteen minutes looking at the tissues under a magnifying glass.[586] Dr. Haines, of course, had spent several weeks examining tissues in the Vrzal case to find the amount of arsenic that he did.

Likely, Gordin found only a portion of the arsenic that was actually present in the sample. Unfortunately, that made it much harder to prove whether or not Henry Niemann was murdered.

Hadley had planned to call Dr. Tope to the stand. He was the last physician to treat Niemann, and was the one who decided that no autopsy or inquest was necessary. Tope was summoned, but said he was ill and didn't appear. However, Niemann's other physician did testify. "It was a rather peculiar case," Dr. Fox recalled. He said he observed signs of heart disease, but also stomach trouble, and a complaint of weakness in the old man's legs. "I didn't feel altogether satisfied about the case,"[587] he said. Fox also pointed out that the organs retain only a moderate portion of the total amount of arsenic ingested. Niemann, therefore, probably consumed far more than the 1/5 grain estimated to be in his system at the time of his death.

Dr. Moyer said that that amount would not normally kill someone directly, though it could in the case of an elderly man like Henry Niemann, and that it was consistent with poisoning by small and repeated doses.[588] He said it would cause irritation of the stomach and nerves, pains in the arms and legs, a partial paralysis he termed "drop foot" and "drop hand," and, eventually, death.[589] Coroner Matter continued the inquest for the following week to bring in more witnesses.

39

Get Busy For Wayman

AUGUST 4, 1908

While the inquest was going on in Wheaton, thousands braved a stifling (and deadly) heat wave to attend the latest benefit for Billik at one of Chicago's finest venues. The massive Auditorium had been commissioned in 1886 in the wake of the unrest following the Haymarket Affair. Wealthy business leaders hoped to bring culture to the city's working class (and thus calm them) by building the world's grandest theater. It was designed by famed architects Dankmar Adler and Louis Sullivan (considered the father of the modern skyscraper).* Luckily, it happened to be the first building anywhere to have central air-conditioning,[590] consisting of a series of vents that moved air cooled by huge blocks of ice.

Temperatures were still in the 90s as night fell. Out in front, on Congress and Michigan Avenues, volunteers for candidates for Cook County State's Attorney handed out "palm cards" advertising their favored candidates, along with free tickets to the upcoming benefit in Forest Park. Father O'Callaghan had planned to provide

---

* The Auditorium was ten stories tall, with a seventeen-story tower. Its centerpiece was the spectacular gold and ivory theater, which boasted more than 4,200 seats, three balconies, and near-perfect acoustics. The building also housed a 400-room hotel, restaurants, banquet halls, and more than 130 offices, all of which generated revenue to keep ticket prices for the theater low enough that it could be enjoyed by everyone.

live updates from the inquest in Wheaton via a telephone hook-up, but was disappointed when those proceedings ended early. He still had a full program planned, however. He was joined on stage by former Mayor Dunne, Stephen Gregory, Francis Hinckley, Jerry Vrzal, and a half dozen clergymen. Mary Billik, Herman Jr., and, of course, Edna also made appearances. William Henry Rose, a popular singer, warmed up the crowd, but the real entertainment of the evening was O'Callaghan's scathing oratory.

Dunne offered his own criticism of both the governor and the state's attorney for failing to vacate Billik's conviction as soon as Jerry recanted his testimony.[591] He also defended O'Callaghan. "The story that Father O'Callaghan was told by an attaché of the Criminal Court building that Governor Deneen and Mr. Healy conferred about the advisability, politically speaking, of commuting the sentence of Billik, while the fortune teller was waiting to be led to the gallows was not a myth,"[592] Dunne told the audience. He said he knew it was true because he was there, and heard the employee tell O'Callaghan about the conversation.

Father O'Callaghan picked up right where Dunne left off. "That informant is a reality," reiterated the priest. "I learn[ed] from more than one source that upon that fateful morning when I sat beside Herman Billik fearing the next moment he might have to ascend the gallows, there were hearts burning to tell me that the Governor of Illinois was begging the State's Attorney of Cook County to permit him to commute the sentence."[593] Apparently, Healy didn't budge. "When I attach blame or most of the blame to the State's Attorney of Cook County, I place it where it belongs," O'Callaghan declared. His efforts to talk with Healy about the case got him nowhere. "I went to Mr. Healy, and laid before him my reasons for believing that a great mistake had been committed. Mr. Healy said it was impossible that one of his assistants had tampered with a witness. He said that had Jerry Vrzal come without trying to reflect upon one of his assistants, he would have been more ready to believe him. I came away convinced that I would obtain no justice from Mr. Healy and absolutely distrustful of his protestations.

What I gained was a belittling of the withdrawal of Jerry Vrzal's testimony and an insinuation that I had offered the boy money."[594]

"Shame! Shame!"[595] came the shouts. The audience was enthusiastically behind O'Callaghan, the only possible exceptions being the two plainclothes detectives Healy sent to sit in the audience and observe things for him. "The state's attorney spoke to me insultingly before the pardon board," O'Callaghan continued. "He was as devoid of justice as any man I have ever met in my long and eventful life. He said 'You do not need to go beyond me.'"[596]

"I looked into his eyes as far as I could, for he cast them down often, he looking at me much as such a man can look an honest man in the face. I read his soul. I stated to a friend what his judgment would be, and I was correct. I know that the pardon board kept its ear to the ground and listened principally for John Healy. Their finding emphasized the opinion of the state's attorney."[597] O'Callaghan compared Healy to Pontius Pilate,[598] and to the pious priest in the story of "the Good Samaritan," who chose to pass by the wounded traveler, leaving him to die. He said Healy was "capable of taking the blood of an innocent man," and he warned the audience against sharing guilt by "perpetuating" a public servant who was willing to do so.[599]

August 5, 1908

It's not clear how much money was raised by the event, but it certainly raised plenty of attention. A spokesman for Chicago's Archbishop released a statement indicating that Father O'Callaghan and other priests taking part in the crusade for Billik were acting on their own, and that the Catholic Church had taken no official position on the matter. Catholics generally opposed the death penalty and, for that reason, most wished to see Billik's sentence commuted, but the Church wanted no part in the controversy with State's Attorney Healy.[600]

Healy made no comment on O'Callaghan's vitriol. His staff, however, had plenty to say about the Niemann inquest. Assistant State's Attorney Barbour ridiculed DuPage authorities, calling the proceedings at Wheaton "farcical."[601] Assistant State's Attorney Popham made a more peculiar statement, announcing, "We can prove that if [Henry] Niemann was poisoned, Billik did it."[602] It seemed more than a small contradiction for the prosecutor to say he had the evidence to "prove" Billik guilty of a crime that his own office was arguing never occurred.

Meanwhile, the city's organized liquor interests suddenly announced that they were shifting their efforts from the Democratic primary to the Republican contest, and were throwing their full support behind Healy's opponent, John Wayman, for Cook County State's Attorney.[603] It was a bit of a gamble on their part, not only switching candidates, but jumping to a different party's primary altogether, just three days before the election. There's no way to know just how much influence O'Callaghan's campaign against Healy had on their decision, but they obviously sensed a vulnerability in Healy's candidacy in the closing days of the campaign, only a few days after his victory had been considered a near certainty.

Ironically, it was a Bohemian immigrant from the Pilsen neighborhood now organizing Healy's opposition. Anton "Tony" Cermak* was the head of the most powerful pro-liquor organization, the United Societies For Local Self Government (or "United Societies"). They, along with the Liquor Dealers Protective Association, prepared 150,000 sample ballots with Wayman's name marked on them to distribute to voters. Posters and placards were sent out to beer wagon drivers bearing the words "Vote For Wayman against Healy for State's Attorney," and saloon keepers were ordered to "get busy for Wayman at once."[604]

---

* Cermak would eventually help establish the Democratic "machine" that ruled Chicago for more than 50 years, beginning with his own election as Mayor in 1931.

In the basement of the old Vrzal family home on 19th St., Emma Niemann sat with a reporter from the *Chicago Daily Tribune* and gave her first real interview since her family had been murdered. "If I were as I am painted by Father O'Callaghan and others, do you think I could still continue to live in this house where the murders occurred?" she asked. "Why, if I had got all the money from the insurance policies on the lives of the members of my family, you don't think I would be slaving myself sick here in this little milk depot, making just enough to live on. I would buy an auto and a city mansion."[605] Of course Billik's supporters had been saying all along that there wasn't enough insurance money to have been the motive for anyone to commit the murders. Had Billik collected a fortune, he could have afforded an experienced attorney and been able to pay for an appeal without relying on Father O'Callaghan to beg for the money to keep him from the gallows.

"I saved the life of my brother Jerry at the hands of Herman Billik and see how he turned on me?" Emma said, adding a new twist to her story. "Why, he even came to my house and wanted me to sign an affidavit that I had sworn falsely against Billik."[606] Emma couldn't explain why Jerry would now want to blame her and seek to free the man who supposedly tried to kill him and their whole family. "Maybe he and others know. I will wait my time,"[607] she said.

O'Callaghan said it was Billik who narrowly saved Jerry from being murdered. "Jerry was sick and it was Billik who said he should be sent away," O'Callaghan countered, "and it was Billik who took him away until he recovered."[608]

As for the death of her father-in-law, Emma admitted to visiting the Niemann farm while Henry Niemann was still alive, but denied ever feeding him or caring for him. "The old man was sick for a long time before I ever went to the farm," she said, adding, "Herman Billik was on the farm a long time before I went there, too."[609] She said she was completely innocent. "My time will come and I will make these people who are slandering me now jump hurdles. I don't intend to do anything, however, until Billik is hanged."[610]

Emma Vrzal Niemann. *Photo courtesy of the Chicago History Museum, DN-0004386.*

40

The Election

AUGUST 5-6, 1908

Late Wednesday, State's Attorney Healy released an affidavit from Dr. Tope. The doctor said he treated Henry Niemann for twelve years, and was familiar with the symptoms of arsenic poisoning. The only one his patient ever displayed was a palsy, or partial paralysis, which Tope attributed to an electric shock Niemann had received in an accident several years before his death. He said the presence of arsenic could be explained by Niemann's use of patent medicines that may have contained the compound. He concluded: "In my judgment, Henry Niemann died of natural causes as the result of mitral disease of the heart and old age and not by any chronic or recent arsenic poisoning."[611]

Tope's affidavit was assumed by many to be the final word on the death of Henry Niemann. But there was reason to be skeptical. Since Tope had failed to issue a death certificate, let alone call for an autopsy or inquest when Niemann died, he had little choice but to say that he saw no hint that Niemann had been poisoned. Otherwise, he would be in trouble himself. And there's no doubt that the detectives dispatched by Healy and Chief Shippy pointed that out to him. Tope claimed to observe no stomach problems, which Dr. Fox very specifically noted. Moreover, the paralysis Tope observed in Niemann was consistent with the weakness in his legs that Dr. Fox considered suspicious; and matched what Healy's own expert, Dr. Moyer, described as "drop-foot," something he said he would expect to see in a person suffering from chronic arsenic poisoning.[612]

Nevertheless, the next morning Cook County officials publicly declared that Henry Niemann had not been murdered. Chief Shippy, who was mostly away from work in the months following the Lazarus Averbuch incident, stepped up to join the attack on the DuPage investigation. Shippy claimed that his officers had thoroughly investigated Henry Niemann's death, and that Emma couldn't have been involved because she didn't arrive at the Niemann farm until shortly before he died. Healy claimed to be getting correspondence from experts all over the country telling him that the small amount of arsenic found in Niemann's body could not possibly have been the result of poisoning. He made much of the fact that so little arsenic had been found, though he knew the results were only preliminary estimates, and had said himself that he expected it to take weeks to get a complete and accurate total.

When told of Dr. Tope's statement, Father O'Callaghan was more riled than ever. Luckily, he had ample opportunity to air his frustration. That night, the biggest benefit events for Billik yet were held, with a series of three addresses at vaudeville theaters in west suburban Forest Park. Each performance began with Edna Billik singing a song for the charmed audience, and culminated in a blistering attack on Healy by Father O'Callaghan. Some thought the priest had been too harsh in his last address at the Auditorium. To those, O'Callaghan said, he was sorry. "I wish to offer an apology," he said, "to Pontius Pilate, for comparing him to Healy. That sturdy Roman was a gentleman if he was a scoundrel . . ."[613] The line undoubtedly drew a laugh, but O'Callaghan's clever wit couldn't conceal the fact that he meant every word of it.

"All the waters of heaven will not wash clean John Healy's scarlet soul," he proclaimed. "I am confident that if he is not condemned by this people God's curse will still rest upon him and upon his children."[614] It was harsh, but O'Callaghan felt it was justified. "John Healy's conscience . . . ought to be good—it has never been used," he told one audience, paraphrasing an old joke. "The man is unfit to be trusted with the lives of the meanest citizens, and you are responsible so long as you keep him in office."[615]

He also told what he thought of Healy's efforts in the current investigation. "Mr. Healy . . . judicial and just as he pretends to be, before the inquest on the body of Henry Niemann is fairly started, publishes an affidavit of a poor old country doctor, and because the doctor thinks Niemann might have taken medicine with arsenic in it he sets aside the other evidence in the case."[616] O'Callaghan was particularly incensed by Healy and Barbour's interference. "He reveals what a hypocrite he is when he sends his assistant to DuPage County, saying that he wished to assist in the inquest, when the proceedings revealed the fact that his purpose was to belittle the facts and make farcical the most solemn and tragical of all events."[617]

He said people were being naïve if they thought Healy honestly investigated the matter. "Even wise doctors have been fooled in this Billik case, and yet Mr. Healy takes the word of an old country doctor, who did not even sign a death certificate, and stops there with his investigation."[618] O'Callaghan recounted how he was forced to take up the case himself, hiring a detective, and convincing officials to exhume Niemann's body. "I have had the feeling of a gambler who wagers his last dollar," he told the crowd, "but every suspicion I had has been corroborated. There was arsenic in Henry Niemann's body . . . John Healy is a hypocrite—he has been given ample proof of murder and has done nothing of consequence with it."[619] He concluded, "There is no way to secure a fair hearing for Billik except by removing from office this man, absolutely lacking in a sense of official responsibility. John Healy gave Billik a bad name to hide his cowardly self and justify his own miserable office. No doubt he would sacrifice his own mother, as he has sacrificed things as sacred before this to further his own prospects. Get him out, and jump on him."[620]

AUGUST 8, 1908: ELECTION DAY

Just two days later was Election Day. While voters may not have jumped on him, when the ballots were finally counted, John Healy was out. John Wayman was the winner of the Republican primary for State's Attorney. Healy failed to ride the coattails of his friend Governor Deneen, who won his contest fairly handily. A dejected Healy refused to even comment on the results. "What's the use? Let the other fellow do the talking,"[621] he told a reporter as he left his campaign headquarters for home. Soon after, Healy left town altogether, and headed for his vacation home in Massachusetts. Assistant State's Attorney Barbour took charge of the office temporarily, with instructions to fight the election results if there was any hint of impropriety. When it became apparent that some Democrats voted in the Republican Primary, though it was technically not allowed, Healy supporters complained loudly, particularly since virtually every Democrat to vote in the Republican primary was assumed to be a vote for Wayman.

As state's attorney, Healy was in a unique position to investigate and prosecute vote fraud, which he could then use as evidence to overturn the results of the election. He had Barbour look into more than a hundred complaints, including the cross-over voters and the usual assortment of unqualified and "repeat" voters, who were often paid by ward bosses to vote at multiple polling places under assumed identities. Particular attention was paid to certain Jewish precincts, where many people did not vote for religious reasons, as the election was held on a Saturday. Unscrupulous precinct workers had supporters pretend to be voters that they knew were staying home, and cast ballots in their names. One voter, described as a "drunken hobo," reportedly showed up at a polling place claiming to be a well-known rabbi.[622]

When the final canvass was completed however, Wayman was declared the official winner. Healy challenged the result, but Wayman argued his own case, and his victory was ultimately upheld. The saloon interests provided the deciding vote for Wayman, but it's fair to say that Father O'Callaghan's involvement was a key ingredient in the victory. Without his public pressure on Healy in the closing week of the campaign, the saloon men might well have concentrated their efforts on the Democratic primary. It is ironic that O'Callaghan, an outspoken and prominent foe of alcohol consumption, helped deliver victory for the saloon keepers' candidate, but he obviously thought it was more important to be anti-Healy than anti-saloon, and convinced many of his supporters to think the same way.

With Healy out of the way, Billik would at least have a chance at a pardon from Gov. Deneen, who had been boxed in by his colleague's unflinching demand that Billik be executed. John Wayman was truly an independent man, not beholden to any faction or political power brokers. He had made his name as a criminal defense lawyer, and Billik hoped that would make him more sympathetic to his situation.

August 9, 1908

From the pulpit of St. Mary's that Sunday, Father O'Callaghan vividly described an odd encounter that summed up his view of John Healy. A few days before his execution date, Billik looked out of a window at the jail and saw staring at him from the building across the courtyard, State's Attorney Healy and his assistant, Popham. "As soon as he looked towards them," said O'Callaghan, "they fell down below the windowsill and peeped over it, with just their eyes above the sill, glaring at their victim. I would that I might have the power of eloquence to paint that picture, that I might show you those two vultures in human form feasting their eyes upon their victim—or two rats, as it were, watching the mouse in his trap. Though the mouse is still in his cage he has been able to smite those that watched him from across the courtyard that morning, and I feel that it has been the judgment of high heaven that this wretched hypocrite has been brought at this moment into disgrace, and I do hope that his name will be held in the infamy which it deserves."[623]

41

A Raucous Hearing

The Henry Niemann inquest resumed in Wheaton on Monday. Emma was there with Benson Landon, a prominent attorney she had hired to represent her. She glared at her brother Jerry as she took the stand. She said she first met Henry Niemann about twelve years earlier. The Vrzals purchased their milk from the Niemanns, and the families became friendly. Emma went to the Niemann farm in Downer's Grove numerous times over the years, sometimes staying as long as a week. She was there for a visit in May 1905, then moved there permanently a few months later, on August 13th, two weeks after her sister Mary died. She said she initially planned on staying only for a short vacation, at the recommendation of her doctor. A little more than a week after Emma's arrival, the elder Niemann was dead. She said the old man was already sick by the time she got there, and that she had little interaction with him, as he spoke only German. There was a housekeeper, named Anna, but she left the house the day after Emma arrived. Emma then assumed the duties of William's housekeeper and eventually married him (though not until a year and a half later, in the closing days of the inquest into the Vrzal deaths).

Charles Mech, William Niemann's brother-in-law, testified that he wasn't even aware that Emma and William were married until reading it in the newspaper following William's death. And even though Emma had claimed at Billik's trial that she and William "were married in the old Bohemian fashion and promised to live as husband and wife"[624] almost a year preceding their actual marriage, Mech never saw her as anything more than William's housekeeper. "He never told me he was married to Emma," Mech said. "I don't know that Will and Emma were living together at the farm . . . she was doing housework for him."[625]

Emma claimed to know nothing about Henry's illness, and once again pointed to Billik. She said he was at the Niemann farm on at least two occasions, and once brought food for the family. The most interesting parts of Emma's testimony, though, had nothing to do with Henry Niemann. She dramatically retold the story of her parents and sisters' deaths. She broke down repeatedly, and her voice eventually became hoarse. She said that her mother collected insurance money from all the deaths[626] (which was not actually true[627]), and subsequently loaned money to Billik. She admitted that she visited her family regularly while she was living at Downer's Grove, and often brought them canned goods and preserves. William also came at least once a month to collect payment from the Vrzals for milk deliveries.

Emma said Jerry came to her shortly after Father O'Callaghan met with him in Valparaiso, and told her the priest had accused both her and William of murdering the family. Just a few days after that meeting, William died. Emma became flustered when questioned about her husband's death, and her description of his final day raised some serious questions. Piecing together her uncharacteristically disjointed and conflicting testimony, things happened something like this: The night before William died, he sat in his recliner smoking. At about one a.m. Emma saw he was "very bad," and sent Fred for a doctor. For some unknown reason, Fred returned without a doctor. She said William sat in the chair until two a.m., but later said she put him to bed at four a.m., and that he was at that time "feeling better." She said he slept until nine a.m., though for some reason she sent a neighbor for a doctor at seven a.m. The neighbor returned, saying the doctor wasn't in.[628] At nine a.m. William got up and asked for his pipe. He smoked a bit, then went back to sleep. Sometime between nine and ten o'clock, Emma decided he was "in pretty bad shape," and went to the drugstore to use the telephone, but instead of calling a doctor, she called William's brother-in-law Charles Mech to tell him she "didn't think William would live very long."[629] William awoke again around noon. At about one-thirty Emma gave him his pipe again, but still never went for a doctor. She waited on several customers in the milk depot, checked on him at about one-fifty—he was still alive— then returned at two o'clock and found him dead. She finally went for the doctor after William was already dead.

Living just a block from Pilsen's main thoroughfare, 18th St., there were literally scores of doctors within a short walk of the home, yet more than thirteen hours elapsed from the time Emma supposedly first tried to get a physician and when she finally contacted one. And that was some four or five hours after she called Mr. Mech to tell him William would likely die soon. Under questioning, Emma admitted that the first thing she said to the doctor when he arrived was, "Does he look as if he were poisoned?" When asked why she would ask such a question, she simply said, "I don't know how I came to say that."[630]

When it was Jerry's turn, Cook County Assistant State's Attorney Barbour, who had no official role in the DuPage proceeding, demanded to question him. Coroner Matter eventually relented, and Jerry was subjected to a brutal cross-examination by Barbour, who made no pretense of impartiality. The two engaged in several heated exchanges. At one point Barbour asked Jerry if he ever lied. "Only when the state's attorney instructs me to change my testimony,"[631] the boy shot back sharply.

Jerry refuted his sister's claim that she had been sick to her stomach like the other Vrzal girls, saying that she wasn't physically sick, but was on the verge of a nervous breakdown following Mary's death, and that the doctor advised her to go out to the country for a few weeks to rest. He said that William Niemann visited his family regularly, coming every month to collect payment for milk. He also confirmed that Billik had visited the Niemann farm once with his children, and again when Mrs. Vrzal paid him to work his magic to make William marry Emma (although that time he performed a spell down the road and never actually went to the house).

Magdalena Runge, the mother of William Niemann's first wife, Louise, told the jury that her daughter was diagnosed with tuberculosis when she died. Her power of speech was impaired and she constantly complained of a burning in her throat. Mrs. Runge contradicted Dr. Tope, saying repeatedly that Henry Niemann complained of stomach pain before he died. She also said he was unable to talk or walk as he neared death.

After William Niemann died, Mrs. Runge was appointed guardian of his sons Henry and Willie (who were her grandchildren). She described how she and her husband went to get the boys from Emma, accompanied by a police officer. She said that when they arrived, Emma told her she didn't want to give up the children and grew angry. "And then she got crazy," said Mrs. Runge, "and she scared me and she said, 'You only come to get the children on account of the money.'"[632] But it sounded like Emma was the one thinking about money. Mrs. Runge said Emma only wanted to keep the children temporarily, just long enough to settle their inheritance, which included the old Vrzal home and milk business. "I don't know that she said anything about retaining them or wanting to keep them except for about a year," Mrs. Runge said of Emma. "She said, 'You could have the children not before a year is around.' So I says, 'I have a right to the children and I am going to take them.'"[633]

Interestingly, in a 2004 interview, William Niemann's granddaughter Doris said the family suspected Emma was responsible for William's death, but she didn't know anything at all about the mystery surrounding the elder Niemann's (Henry's) demise.[634] She said her father never discussed it, even though records indicate that both he and his younger brother testified at the DuPage inquest.[635]

Rumors swirled around the Henry Niemann case just as they had the Vrzal murders. The investigator Father O'Callaghan hired was told that the Niemann's housekeeper, Anna Stoeck, disappeared the day after Emma's arrival, following a violent argument. She was rumored to have been murdered and dumped into the old well at the Niemann farm. The well was filled with debris, presumably in an effort to conceal the girl's body. DuPage authorities prepared to dig up the well to search for her. Friends and neighbors of the Niemanns weren't so sure, however. They said that the girl left for Chicago, and at least one saw William driving her to the train station in his milk wagon.

August 21, 1908

When Coroner Matter reconvened the inquest a few weeks later, Cook County Assistant State's Attorney Barbour surprised everyone by announcing that Chicago detectives had located a witness who, if called to testify, could clear up at least part of the mystery: Mrs. August Zaczeck of Chicago. *She* was Anna Stoeck, now married and living in the city on Belmont Ave. Newspapers had a great time with a variety of puns about the girl, whose name was pronounced "stuck," and was now known to be alive and well, and not "stuck in a well."

The coroner questioned the Niemanns' next door neighbor, Henry Roeder. He testified that Henry Niemann's limbs pained him (a classic symptom of chronic arsenic poisoning), but said he doubted that Emma was involved in his death, since Niemann was sick for weeks.[636] "They expected him to die the week before her arrival on the farm,"[637] Roeder said. Another neighbor, Peter Felde, had helped care for Henry Niemann during his final illness. He said Henry was sick for several months before he died, and that William Niemann, Fred Niemann, and their sister Louise Mech all took turns caring for their father. Oddly, Felde became sick himself and left the farm before Emma arrived.

Several other neighbors and relatives testified. None were aware of Henry Niemann using any patent medicines, and they said he rarely drank alcohol. It cast doubt on Healy's assertion that he died of alcoholism, and Dr. Tope's claim that he might have ingested arsenic from patent medicines. All of the witnesses agreed that Henry became sick around the middle of June 1905, about nine weeks before he died. They also remembered Emma, as well as Billik and his wife and children, visiting the farm over the Decoration Day (now Memorial Day) weekend (May 28th-30th) of that year.

When they were done, the coroner's jury couldn't reach any conclusion and was adjourned. Coroner Matter said they would be called back when any new evidence was brought forward. Both Emma's attorney and Barbour were livid. They wanted Emma to immediately be cleared of any wrongdoing. Barbour called DuPage officials "cowardly," and berated them. He and DuPage County State's Attorney Hadley became so excited trading insults and invectives they practically had to be separated by Coroner Matter.[638] Another confrontation turned ugly when Emma denounced her brother Jerry as she left the courtroom. "You are an unnatural brother, and are the cause of all of my troubles!" she shouted. "From now on I disown you and forbid you coming to my house!"[639]

42

Decisions

By the time Coroner Matter reconvened the jury a month later, doctors had determined that Henry Niemann's organs contained approximately .58 grains of arsenic,* almost three times the estimate made at the start of the inquest. Dr. Ernest C. Riebel said that his postmortem exam indicated Niemann died of chronic arsenic poisoning, and that he observed no signs of heart disease. He was certain that the arsenic had not been absorbed from the ground after burial, and said he strongly suspected intentional poisoning.[640]

Mrs. Anna Stoeck-Zaczeck, the mysterious domestic once thought to have been murdered, also testified. She said that when she worked on the Niemann farm, William proposed marriage, but she didn't accept his offer. She became ill, and left the morning after Emma's arrival. "I didn't feel good and then came this girl and I didn't feel like waiting on her too," she told the coroner.[641] She said Henry had pains in his stomach, head, and chest, and was incoherent at times; his stomach was swollen, as were his limbs, and his feet were so sore he could barely walk for the last few weeks she was there. He also trembled so much near the end that he couldn't feed himself. Anna never saw any patent medicines in

---

* .0667 (1/15th) gr. found initially, plus .5108 gr. discovered in the remaining sample = .5775 gr. total.

the house. "The old man never took any medicine but what the doctor gave him,"[642] she said.

Anna said that William and Fred occasionally argued with their father and that their relationship was "not very pleasant all the time."[643] She remembered both Emma and Billik visiting on a few occasions. William told her that Billik was trying to convince him to marry Emma, but that he wasn't interested. Over the Decoration Day weekend, Billik brought coffee and beef, and Emma had fruit for the children and a gift of tobacco for Henry. Anna said that everyone, including herself, ate Billik's food with no ill effects. A few weeks later, though, she, Henry, and his caretaker Felde all began feeling queasy and run-down. Anna said that they did drink the coffee Billik gave them over the course of several weeks, but she remembered Billik, his wife, and even little Edna drinking it, as did many others who never felt sick, so that wasn't likely to have been the source of their illness, either.

Was the tobacco Emma gave Henry poisoned? Anna and Felde spent the most time around him, and would have had the most exposure to Henry's smoking; however, William, Fred, and their sister Louise also spent time with their father, and none of them became ill. Felde eventually left the farm, and was followed a short time later by Anna. Their symptoms, particularly Anna's, were very consistent with arsenic poisoning. "My stomach troubled me. I had pains in the stomach and no appetite," Anna recalled. "After I left the Niemann household it took several months before I was right again," she said. "The weakness and pains in my limbs prevailed a long time."[644]

After hearing the testimony and reading the lab reports, the jury reached a verdict: "Henry Niemann . . . came to his death . . . from arsenical poisoning administered by a person or persons unknown." They added, "We recommend that the State's Attorney conduct a thorough investigation and bring the guilty parties to justice."[645] Emma's face flushed as the verdict was read. Her hands gripped tightly together. She whispered in the ear of her attorney, then left the courtroom without saying a word.[646] The verdict certainly helped Billik's cause, but disappointed many who had hoped that Emma would be charged with the murder. There was never enough evidence to charge anyone with Henry Niemann's murder, and the body of Louise Runge-Niemann, William Niemann's first wife who died so young, was never exhumed.

OCTOBER 12-20, 1908

In October of 1908 Chicago was basking in the glow of its third straight World Series victory. It was the second in a row for the Cubs, following their bitter loss to the cross-town White Sox in 1906.* The Cubs' home field, West Side Grounds, was at Polk and Wood Streets, just eight blocks directly north of the Vrzal home. While most of Chicago celebrated its baseball supremacy, Herman Billik was hoping that he would soon have his own reason to celebrate as the U.S. Supreme Court began hearing his appeal.

Hinckley and Gregory maintained that Billik was denied his constitutional rights by not being allowed to make a statement before being sentenced to death. Opposing them was State's Attorney Healy, who was still in office for a few more months, and still determined to see Billik hang. He referenced a recent Act of Congress which required federal judges to certify that there was probable cause for an appeal before granting it. Judge Landis issued no such certification, and had even said publicly that he thought Billik had no case. Healy argued that the appeal was therefore invalid, and the case should be sent back to the Circuit Court for Billik to be sentenced again. It was the first time the new federal statute was ever invoked.[647] Had the assistant state's attorney pointed out the requirement at the time Billik was preparing to march to the gallows, Landis would almost certainly

---

* Far from the "lovable losers" who have disappointed fans at north side Wrigley Field for most of the last hundred years, the Cubs of the early 1900's were the most successful team in baseball, and were actually the city's "West Side team."

have denied the appeal, and Billik would have been hanged. A lucky break saved his neck the last time. But Billik's luck would soon run out.

The U.S. Supreme Court considered arguments for several days. They eventually agreed with Healy and dismissed Billik's appeal. The *Washington Post* reported, "[The ruling] brings to an end one of the most notable struggles ever made in the history of American jurisprudence to save the life of a condemned man."[648] Billik's legal avenues appeared to be exhausted. He tried to stay upbeat, but he was also realistic. "I do not altogether give up hope, but it appears they are determined to hang me," he told a reporter. "My only hope it would seem is with the governor."[649] Unfortunately, Governor Deneen was already hinting that he didn't plan on intervening.[650] Father O'Callaghan was undeterred. He said that if necessary, he would appeal directly to President Theodore Roosevelt.[651]

OCTOBER 29-NOVEMBER 17, 1908

Over the course of several brief court appearances in the following weeks, it became apparent that Billik's lawyers had yet another plan to free him. Hinckley argued that the Criminal Court had lost jurisdiction. He refused to make any motions, or even agree to a continuance, as it might infer that he was acknowledging the court's authority. When it came time for Judge Barnes to re-sentence Billik, the courtroom was nearly empty. The only spectators were Mary, Edna, and Emil Billik, and a few reporters. Hinckley and Gregory then raised a most unusual argument. They claimed Billik was already "dead"—at least as far as the court was concerned. He had escaped his previous execution date because Judge Landis granted an appeal in Federal Court, but the State Court never issued a stay of execution, as was required. Since the execution date passed without the court taking any action, they reasoned, the state no longer had any jurisdiction, and could not even pass sentence on him.

Judge Barnes wouldn't accept the notion that Billik was "dead," and declared that the court did indeed have jurisdiction. Hinckley and Gregory immediately made a motion for a new trial. If the court had jurisdiction to sentence Billik, they contended, then it should also have jurisdiction to order a new trial. They submitted Jerry Vrzal's affidavit recanting his original testimony and a certificate from the coroner's jury in Wheaton indicating that Henry Niemann was murdered by arsenic poisoning. But the points barely registered with the judge. Barnes brusquely denied their motion, and called the defendant forward. "Have you anything to say, Herman Billik, why sentence of death should not be pronounced on you?"[652]

"I swear before God I am an innocent man," he told the judge. "I never even thought of poisoning anybody in all my life. It was never in my mind. Perjury has been committed against me . . . Jerry Vrzal lied, and so did others at the trial. In view of these facts I expected your honor would give me a new trial, and I am disappointed. I am innocent, but not afraid to die. May the Lord have mercy on the souls of those who are responsible for my conviction."[653]

Barnes formally sentenced him to death by hanging, again, and Billik was returned to his cell. This, his fifth execution date, was set for Friday, December 11th. The *Washington Post* jested, "Sentencing Billik to death is becoming a confirmed habit of the Chicago courts."[654]

In the evening, Father O'Callaghan issued a statement: "Herman Billik never murdered anyone. He must not and he will not hang . . . We have been hampered at every step by the smallness of our means and I have not a dollar left. I therefore beg all lovers of justice to hold up my hands a little longer. Send me what you can. Justice must and will prevail for the honor of our civilization."[655]

43

Mourning and Merrymaking

Soon after O'Callaghan's plea, Billik received a contribution from his staunchest supporter: his mother in Cleveland. She was ill, and too frail to come to Chicago to be with him. She said she never doubted his innocence, and wanted to do what little she could to help. "I am praying night and day that I may live to see the [resolution] of all my child's troubles," she wrote. "I am sending you $2, all I can spare." The letter was signed, "With a dozen kisses, your heartbroken mother."[656] Heartbroken himself, Billik prepared a letter to tell her of his latest setback in court. He realized that, with his execution looming, he would probably never see his mother again. Tearfully, he penned a final "goodbye."

Hinckley was working to once again bring the case before the Supreme Court, and O'Callaghan continued his campaign. But Billik's greatest weapon at this point was in the guise of his sweet little daughter Edna. Throughout the entire ordeal, she accompanied her mother to every single court appearance, even the most trivial of legal motions. By now, she had become the sorrowful face of Herman Billik's story. She could appeal to the hearts of the public, and keep the pressure on Governor Deneen.

The press played it up. Heartrending stories of Edna abounded, often with photos of her staring dejectedly into the camera, with captions such as, "Little Edna Billik Sadly Counting the Days That

Her Father Has to Live."[657] One story had a photo of Edna with her hands on her father's cheeks, as the two looked tenderly into each others eyes. It was captioned, "Little Edna Billik Bidding Her Father, Who Is to Be Hanged Dec. 11, A Fond Farewell." The accompanying text declared, "Unless he can secure the help of Governor Deneen and . . . have the sentence commuted, Herman Billik will hang Dec. 11, and little Edna Billik, the pathetic, silent sufferer in the case will be fatherless."[658]

In his memoirs, former Mayor Dunne described Deneen as "unemotional,"[659] but it's hard to imagine that such stories didn't affect him. Little Edna prepared to make a trip down to Springfield. Newspapers were notified that she would be making a personal appeal to Deneen.[660] As Billik's execution drew near, all the pressure was on the governor.

November 28-December 4, 1908

On November 28th, Billik received an urgent telegram from Cleveland. Upon reading his emotional farewell letter, his mother had collapsed. She never fully recovered, and died at her home. Her health had been failing gradually, largely from the stress of watching her only son near execution. When she learned that the last efforts to save him had failed, it was simply too much for her to bear. Newspapers reported that she died of "a broken heart."[661] Billik was overcome with grief. He broke down, and collapsed in his cell.

Mary and the children went to Cleveland for the funeral. When they returned a week later, they visited Herman at the jail. They talked about the service and their trip for a bit, then their thoughts turned to his impending execution. "Just one more week,"[662] he reminded them glumly. Mary began crying, but then Edna jumped in. "They ain't going to kill you, Papa," she reassured him. "The governor is going to save you. Father O'Callaghan told me this morning that you weren't going to be hanged."[663] Was it a child's innocent optimism, or maybe just positive thinking on O'Callaghan's part? What the Billiks didn't know was that, behind the scenes, Governor Deneen was tiring of the controversy.

O'Callaghan and Gregory had quietly met with Judge Barnes during the week. The judge told them that he planned to meet with the Deneen, and promised that they would both, in his words, "give the matter the fullest and fairest consideration."[664] That was about as close as Barnes could come to saying that he was going to recommend that the governor commute Billik's sentence. The law required that both the trial judge and state's attorney submit recommendations to the governor whenever a petition for clemency was considered. Healy still refused to budge on the issue of Billik's execution, but he was in the closing days of his term as state's attorney. He would be gone soon, and State's Attorney-elect Wayman was said to be favorable to commuting Billik's sentence.[665]

Somewhat conveniently, Governor Deneen was headed to Washington for a meeting. That meant that Acting-Governor Lawrence Sherman could grant a stay of execution for a few weeks, until Deneen returned to Springfield and Healy was out of office. Someone, perhaps even Deneen himself, must have assured Billik's supporters that Sherman would order the stay, because they suddenly seemed confident that Billik would not be executed on December 11th. Hinckley even canceled the trip he had planned to file a new motion with the Supreme Court. During the week, there were no mass meetings or dramatic protests in the streets of Chicago. Father O'Callaghan was practically silent. And the sad stories of "soon-to-be-fatherless" Edna Billik disappeared from the news.

DECEMBER 7, 1908

On Monday, December 7th, the new State's Attorney of Cook County, John E. Wayman, was sworn in to office.[666] That same day, Francis Hinckley presented Acting-Governor Sherman with a petition asking simply that Billik be granted a temporary reprieve until

Governor Deneen returned to the state and heard his appeal for clemency. Sherman promptly granted the request and set January 29th, 1909 as the (now sixth) date for Herman Billik's execution.

Jailer Will Davies brought Billik news of his fifth reprieve, this just four days before his execution. Billik knelt down and kissed Davies hand. "I will never hang," he cried. "Governor Deneen, when he returns to Springfield, will grant me full reprieve."[667]

The Pardon Board accepted a new petition from Hinckley. The only new evidence was a letter from Judge Barnes to Gov. Deneen. It reflected a new tone from one of Billik's harshest opponents. Barnes wrote:

> *The more I reflect upon the matter the more convinced I am that the sentence of Billik should be commuted to life imprisonment ... there are features of the case that will always provoke discussion and dissent with respect to the propriety, if not the justice of imposing [the death] penalty in this case ... First ... the character, antecedents, and environments of many witnesses were such that ... their testimony . . . was not all as satisfactory as if it had come from other sources ... I felt we hadn't gotten the whole story ... Second: Had Jerry Vrzal furnished the same affidavits as to his perjury while the trial court had jurisdiction, it probably would have been error not to have granted a new trial. No tribunal can now give a new trial, and inquiry into the truth and effect of such affidavits is left entirely to you and the Pardon Board to determine. Third: . . . The jury . . . is presumed to have considered testimony now claimed to have been perjured . . . It has the effect of casting suspicion upon the testimony of others, and of creating doubt as to some matters considered by the jury, and, with some people, as to Billik's guilt. To enforce the penalty of death under such circumstances will not in my judgment meet with general approbation . . . and an opportunity should be left to rectify any possible wrong . . . We therefore feel that under*

the circumstances the death penalty should not be inflicted, and
that the sentence should be commuted to life imprisonment . . .
While I deprecate a precedent . . . this case is so unusual I feel
warranted and compelled to make such recommendation . . .
                          Very Sincerely Yours, Albert C. Barnes[668]

JANUARY 22-23, 1909

When the Pardon Board made their formal recommendation a
month later, Judge Barnes' letter to the governor was quoted practically in its entirety. They acknowledged that there was a widespread
belief that Billik was convicted unjustly, and concluded that, since
the jury was influenced to inflict the death penalty by testimony
from Jerry that was not testified to by any other witnesses, the
sentence should be commuted. On January 22nd, 1909 Governor
Deneen commuted Herman Billik's sentence to life imprisonment
at Joliet State Penitentiary. Six times he stood in the shadow of the
gallows, and six times he was reprieved. The announcement was
made late in the evening. Billik was awoken in his cell by the guard
on duty, and given the news. He looked dazed at first, then finally
dropped to his knees and wept, uttering a few incoherent words of
thanks as he finally realized that he wasn't dreaming.

The next day, Mary and the children came to the jail and the
family celebrated like never before. They felt it was now just a
matter of time before Herman would be freed altogether. "Life imprisonment means liberty," Billik declared. "I shall now have the
chance I have been fighting for to prove my innocence."[669] Hinckley
planned another appeal to the Supreme Court, and promised to
continue until Billik was freed.[670]

Part VI

The
Final Act

44

On to Joliet

News of the commutation was reported and debated across the country. Apparently the only one who didn't hear about it was Cook County Sheriff Strassheim, who forged ahead with plans for the execution. "If the governor has commuted the sentence it will be unlucky for Billik unless I am officially notified,"[671] said the Sheriff, as he sent out invitations to the hanging to various officials. Strassheim was finally notified, and called off the execution two days before it was scheduled. On February 1st, 1909, Billik was taken from Cook County Jail forty-five miles south to Joliet. It was the first time in two years that he was outside the prison walls. As he left, he expressed confidence that he would soon receive complete freedom.

His new home was the Joliet Prison, a massive limestone complex built in 1858, which at one time housed Civil War prisoners. When Billik arrived, it was already old and outdated. It had no running water or toilets in the cells. Modern audiences would recognize it from the opening scene of *The Blues Brothers*, or from the television series *Prison Break*. Billik undoubtedly figured it would be just a brief stop on his way to freedom. But Hinckley's legal maneuvers hit a dead end. The Supreme Court would not hear his case. And he would not be granted a new trial. As weeks turned into months, it became clear that, barring some amazing new evidence, his only hope for freedom would again lie with the governor.

Governor Deneen, however, was in no position to risk any political damage by freeing Billik. He was in the middle of a civil war within the Republican party, struggling to maintain his own political future. Shady West Side Republican boss, William "Bill" Lorimer, was trying to settle a score with fellow Republican Albert Hopkins by denying him the U.S. Senate seat for which he had recently run for re-election. Hopkins received the most votes, but at that time the state legislature actually elected senators. The votes of the people were merely "advisory." Legislators normally went along with the choice of the people for political reasons, but they could in fact choose *anyone*. That included Lorimer, though he wasn't even a candidate in the election. Deneen feared his own ouster from the governor's chair, and struck a deal with the morally-impaired Lorimer, who was made U.S. Senator from Illinois. Hopkins, the man chosen by the people, was deposed. Some questioned how Lorimer managed to secure the votes to take the seat, and a full-scale investigation was launched. That was just one of many scandals Illinois Republicans faced.

In Cook County, the charges of Sheriff Strassheim underfeeding prisoners to line his own pockets were coming to light, and the new state's attorney, John Wayman, was proving his independence by looking into allegations of jury-fixing in the courts, and bribery and corruption within Chief Shippy's police force. Since the Levee district ran gambling and prostitution operations so openly and with such little fear of intervention, most people just assumed police were being paid to look the other way. Shippy agreed that there might be isolated instances, but insisted there was no organized system of graft, as was charged. Shippy was personally implicated in the scandal, however, when one of his inspectors testified that the chief was aware of bribes to officers in the Levee, and that he even ordered inspectors to leave alone one particular gambling boss named "Monkey Face Charley" Genker.[672] Shippy, of course, denied any knowledge of it.

Shippy was rarely on the job in the year or so that had passed since the Lazarus Averbuch killing. He cited various mysterious health problems, and traveled to doctors and spas across the country and Europe seeking treatment. Some thought he had a nervous breakdown, while doctors cited such things as gallstones, liver disease, overwork, and even food poisoning as the source of his ever-declining health. In mid-1909, doctors finally determined he was unable to return to work, and Shippy retired from the police force.

Around that same time, the Illinois Legislature considered a measure to ban the death penalty. The *New York Times* reported:

> *Capital punishment will become a thing of the past in Illinois if a bill to abolish it, which passed the House today succeeds in getting through the Senate . . . In urging the passage of the measure, Rep. Chiperfield referred to the memorable Billik case in Chicago, and the boy who almost at the last minute admitted that he had perjured himself in giving the testimony which caused the death penalty to be imposed.*[673]

The House approved the measure handily, but the bill was never passed into law. Illinois kept its death penalty. Ironically, a hundred years later, Illinois was still grappling with the problem. In 2003, the *Chicago Tribune* reported: "Declaring the state's capital punishment system 'haunted by the demon of error' and citing the state legislature's failure to reform it, Gov. George Ryan on Saturday commuted the sentences of every inmate on Illinois' Death Row."[674] On March 9th, 2011, Illinois' next Governor, Pat Quinn, finally signed into law a bill banning the death penalty in Illinois, saying it was impossible to fix a system that had condemned at least twenty innocent men.

Billik eventually settled in to life at Joliet, which was harsh. The jail itself had actually been built by convict labor, a testament to the rigors endured by prisoners of the day. Inmates observed a "rule of silence," only allowed to speak to one another at designated times.

Other than work, they enjoyed virtually no activity. Billik was lucky enough to get a job as a baker and chef in the prison kitchen. It seemed a questionable vocation for a convicted poisoner, but it was a clear sign of just how much he was trusted. He worked long hours, which helped keep his mind off of his predicament. Billik was a model prisoner, well-liked by other inmates and prison officials, but he was undoubtedly quite lonely away from his family. Mary and the children lived at a rooming house near St. Mary's Church, and hadn't the time nor money to visit him very often.[675]

June 1910–December 1911

In June of 1910, the battle over the estate of William Niemann was finally settled. His sons' guardian and grandmother, Magdalena Runge, sold the house on 19th St. and the boys kept the proceeds. The house was sold at auction to the highest bidder, who also happened to be the occupant: Emma Niemann. She still operated the milk business and lived there with her sister Bertha. In 1911, Emma married again. She and her husband sold the house and moved a few miles west, taking little Bertha with them.

Father O'Callaghan remained active in the temperance cause and became the national President of the Catholic Total Abstinence Union. He wrote to Billik regularly, telling him to keep his faith strong, and promised he wouldn't forget him. But with Billik no longer on death row, there was no sense of urgency among the public to do anything about his case. All O'Callaghan could do was assure his friend that the Lord would see to it that one day he would be free.

Francis Hinckley, somewhat ironically, became an Assistant Cook County State's Attorney. He too kept in touch with Billik, but had run out of legal maneuvers to help his friend. Billik's name had disappeared from the news and he was largely forgotten. It looked like he might well live the rest of his life in Joliet Prison.

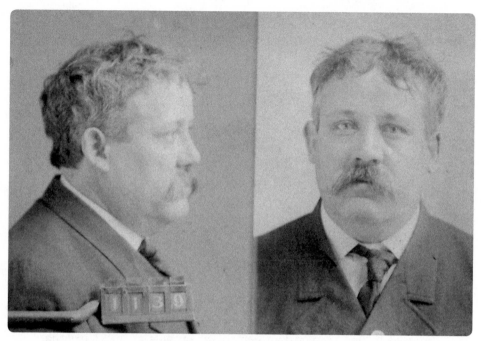

Herman Billik, mugshot Joliet Prison; Illinois State Archives, *Executive Clemency Files 1835-197, RS103.096.*

45

The Governor

1912

In early 1912, after more than five years of imprisonment, Billik suddenly saw a light at the end of that long tunnel. Democrat Edward F. Dunne, who had helped stir crowds at the rallies that quite literally saved Billik's neck, declared his candidacy for Governor of Illinois. Illinois' Republican Party was in a bit of a shambles. The investigation into Senator Lorimer's election had concluded that he bribed legislators to gain the seat, and he was thrown out of office. Governor Deneen's brief alliance with him was now a major liability. The Lorimer investigation also revealed what legislators themselves termed "jack pots," secret funds used for bribery to get themselves elected and maintain power.[676] Since the Illinois Legislature was overwhelmingly Republican, the party itself was branded as corrupt.

The Progressive wing of the party split from regular Republicans and fielded their own candidates. For governor, they selected State Sen. Frank H. Funk, while regular Republicans backed the incumbent, Deneen. The divide provided a rare opportunity for Democrats in a state that was still largely Republican. Democrats nominated Dunne, the honest and affable face of reform in Illinois. Dunne's reputation was impeccable. University of Illinois-Chicago political science professor Dick Simpson called Dunne "the most serious challenge to the existing order in Chicago politics until the election of Harold Washington in 1983."[677]

While Dunne and Deneen always shared a mutual respect, Dunne used the Republican party's tarnished image to his great advantage. "The state has been disgraced and its citizens humiliated by an unparalleled saturnalia of debauchery and corruption,"[678] he declared. Dunne accused Deneen of double-crossing voters by conspiring with Lorimer over the Senate seat, and he referred to the "Jack Pot Legislature" in virtually every speech he made.[679] He said Deneen was well aware of the corruption, but did nothing about it. "If he is so inefficient, so unintelligent, or so lacking in capacity to put a stop to it during the last eight years, what hope can be entertained that he will present any greater efficiency or earnestness during the four years to come?"[680] Dunne asked rhetorically.

In November of 1912, Edward F. Dunne, the man who had so eloquently argued Billik's case before the Pardon Board of Governor Deneen, was elected Governor of Illinois, and now held the power to free Billik himself.

1913

Dunne took office in February of 1913, and made reforming the prison system one of his first priorities. He believed prisoners should be treated humanely, to build their self-respect rather than degrade them. Under his leadership, conditions improved greatly. The "rule of silence" was ended, rules regarding writing letters and receiving visitors were liberalized, a system of privileges to reward good behavior was initiated, and prisoners were provided a one-hour recreation period each day.[681]

Morale, health, and discipline among inmates improved dramatically.[682] Dunne studied other state's prison systems for ideas, and visited Joliet himself. Letters from Billik to Governor Dunne held at the state library indicate that Dunne visited with Billik on at least one of those occasions, and promised to "grant him some consideration."[683] But that didn't mean an immediate pardon. Billik continued working, and praying, and waiting for Dunne to make good on his promise.

1914

Billik's health deteriorated and he was in and out of the prison hospital. By mid-1914, the doctor suggested that he write to the governor. "I sincerely hope that you have not forgotten your promise to me,"[684] he reminded Dunne. He then laid out his current situation:

> *I have many diseases which the doctor says he is unable to relieve me of because of my present environment . . . The good Father O'Callaghan writes me quite often and cheers me up and always says everything will be all right in time. May the good Lord bless him forever . . . I am praying constantly to the good God Almighty that he will give you strength and power to allow me to be at my famil[y']s side for the short time that is allotted me on this earth. I have in memory your great kindness of the past . . . you must know that the greatest joy of one in this life is to be with one's family before leaving this earth. Once again, thanking you for your kindness of the past and thanking you now for your great consideration . . .*
>
> *Herman Billik #1139*[685]

The Board of Pardons asked the prison physician for a report on Billik's health. The doctor said that he suffered from diabetes complicated by cardiac asthma. He confirmed that it was incurable, but concluded that Billik was in "no immediate danger."[686] That was apparently enough for the board to put aside his request for a pardon, and no action was taken.

In December, Billik wrote to the governor again, this time with a sense of urgency:

Once again I appeal to you to do something for me as my health is failing very rapidly. I have been confined in the Hospital for some time. I have been here close [to] seven years and not only have I suffered but my dear wife and children have suffered also. Rev. Father O'Callaghan has tried to help me and my family for he knows as the whole world will know some day I am here for some thing I did not do. You dear Sir know my case, as you saved my life . . . If you can see your way clear after going over my case again you will be doing a great kindness. For I would like to live to go out of here and be a help to my dear wife and children before I die. Hoping to hear from you soon.[687]

The response to Billik's plea was a somewhat terse letter from the Board of Pardons saying he had to file a formal petition for a pardon in accord with the rules, and duly laid out the legal requirements.[688] It was quite discouraging.

1915

Several months later, in April 1915, the Pardon Board again inquired into Billik's health. "I have made an examination of this man," wrote the prison physician, "and find that he has Chronic Heart and Bright's Disease which is accompanied by a great deal of shortness of breath. This man says he has a wife and family that would care for him."[689] Apparently, it was still not enough for the governor or the Pardon Board to take any immediate action.

Back in Chicago, Father O'Callaghan was informed that he would be leaving St. Mary's. He was being named Pastor of the Apostolic Mission House in Washington, D.C. It was part of Catholic University, set up by the Paulists to train diocesan priests in the art of preaching. He was perfect for the job. Billik congratulated his friend, but worried that he would never be free without the priest's continuing help. O'Callaghan promised Billik he wouldn't forget about him.

Eager to escape the notoriety that still hounded him, Jerry Vrzal tried to enlist in the Army, but was rejected due to a medical condition he described as "a permanent heart lesion"[690] (perhaps from arsenic poisoning years earlier). He eventually accepted a position from Father O'Callaghan as the advertising manager for the Catholic Missionary Union at the Mission House, and joined him in Washington.

January-April 1916

In February of 1916, Billik once again wrote to the governor:

> *Your Excellency,*
>
> *Please pardon my temerity in writing you, for I know you are very busy. May I hope that you will consider the fact that as time goes on I am growing noticeably older and am worrying quite a [bit]. However, I am enjoying good health at present and sincerely hope that you are likewise. My dear friend—yes you are my dear friend—I will never forget as long as the blood flows through these old veins, that you saved my life. I trust this letter will serve the purpose of calling to mind my case, as you know that I have been more than doubly punished for my indiscretion and am innocent of any grosser crime. Trusting and praying that you will be able to give an early consideration to my case . . .*
>
> *Herman Billik*[691]

Getting no response, a month later, Billik pressed his case:

> *Your Excellency,*
>
> *The hope that I may look forward to clemency at your hands prompts me to again write you, trusting that you will grant me*

some word of encouragement. I am praying for some indication that my case has come to your notice, and that I may look forward with renewed hopes in the advent of your reply.

Yours most respectfully, Herman Billik #1139[692]

This time, he did get a response, but it was definitely not what he had hoped for. The Board of Pardons once again laid out the technical procedures to present an application before the governor. They reminded Billik, "You have a life sentence . . . ," something that was already painfully obvious to him, and then dashed his hopes almost entirely:

As you have received clemency once, the Board cannot hold out very much hope that you will be treated with further clemency, even should you petition at this time. Possibly it would be better for you to wait some years before asking a reconsideration in your case.[693]

Some years? He had been in jail for more than nine years by this time. The suggestion must have been almost unbearable. Father O'Callaghan kept lobbying, but there appeared little promise for the immediate future. Just a few months later, though, a completely unforeseen event would change everything.

46

The End

On May 10th, 1916 Emma's one-time boyfriend, Joe "Tip" Cooney, was shot on the city's West Side in a battle over control of the local Sheet Metal Workers Union. Cooney, who had recently served six months in jail for assault, and was a suspect in the shooting of another man, was described in newspaper accounts as "a handy gunfighter, with one notch in his gat."[694] He was shot through the stomach and rushed to the hospital.

For years Billik had hoped that one day Cooney would come forward to identify the real killer(s) of the Vrzal family. It looked like this might be the chance he had waited for. Assistant State's Attorney John Murphy was sent to the hospital to interview Cooney. Murphy informed him that doctors gave him little chance of survival, and asked him to tell what he knew about the Vrzal case. Cooney couldn't (or wouldn't) talk, and told Murphy to come back the next day.

Before morning, Tip Cooney was dead. Gone with him was perhaps the last chance to prove Billik's innocence once and for all. Billik wept when he heard the news.[695] It wasn't surprising that Cooney wouldn't talk about the case, even on his deathbed. He died stubbornly refusing to even tell detectives who had shot him.[696] Cooney's death eliminated one of the last witnesses who might have been able to clear Billik, but it brought the case back before the public. L. G. Edwardson, who had investigated the Vrzal murders so diligently, ran a story about Billik in the *Chicago Examiner*, and hinted that Cooney had known he was innocent. People began talking about the case again, and the publicity brought forward a long-forgotten witness. A few days after Cooney's death, the warden at Joliet Prison received the following letter:

Dear Sir, in the morning's Examiner *I see an account of Herman Billik who is held there for life. Now I feel it my duty to send you this word for him. Do as you like about it. I am Chief Engineer for the Englewood branch of the Consumer's Co. [Railroad]. Some years ago however I was employed by the C. B. and I. RR Co. at Galesburg, Ill. One night while in the depot there a woman entered and sat before me with her back to me and pulled a pt. flask from her handbag containing a yellow or a white powder (It was at night in electric light and I was not sure). This flask had a skull and cross bone label which she wet with her thumb and erased in my sight. I and a friend of mine saw this. A few weeks after this I picked up a Chicago paper containing the Vrzal murder mystery with photographs of all concerned, among which was the photo of the very woman I saw in the depot at Galesburg. I showed this to a friend who saw the same thing as I did and we both agreed that it must be the woman. After this I lost track of the entire matter [until] after Billik was convicted. I happened to think one morning and link the two affairs, but Billik was convicted then and time had [passed] and I couldn't identify [Emma] Vrzal as the woman for sure. My word in the case was ruled out. My lack of identification was made in the oath stronger than I wished it to be so I said no more. With what evidence I have I could not convict anybody in that case, but I never would have convicted Herman Billik after what I saw. You remember Galesburg is on the same road out of Chicago that Downer's Grove is where these Vrzals used to visit . . .*
                    Resp[ectfully], Gilbert Sellers[697]

Sellers' letter was forwarded to the Pardon Board. Governor Dunne was busy campaigning for re-election at the time, but a special session of the board was scheduled for later in the year. Father O'Callaghan kept pushing Dunne to make sure Billik wasn't forgotten.

November-December 1916

In November, Dunne was defeated by Republican Frank Lowden when the Progressives returned to the Republican party, which still greatly outnumbered Illinois Democrats. Dunne however, still had a few months left in his term to make good on his promise to Billik. In early December, Francis Hinckley received an urgent telegram from Father O'Callaghan. He told him to submit a formal application for Billik's pardon as soon as possible.[698] A hearing was set for December 30th in Springfield. Governor Dunne, who had been a Criminal Court Judge for almost thirteen years before being elected Mayor of Chicago, presided. Dunne biographer Richard Allen Morton said that Dunne, as a judge, was known "for his common sense in dealing with ordinary people caught up in the maze of the law."[699] That certainly fit this case.

Father O'Callaghan came all the way from Washington to attend, as did Jerry Vrzal, who was no longer the meek boy who testified at Billik's trial, but a twenty-seven-year-old man. Jerry told his story of perjury and police intimidation with confidence. Francis Hinckley, now a seasoned attorney, went over the evidence as did L. G. Edwardson, who made a lengthy presentation documenting what he and his reporters had uncovered over the years that pointed to Billik's innocence, including the murder of Henry Niemann and the suspicious death of William Niemann. Dr. Caldwell also appeared on Billik's behalf. He testified as to the timing and onset of the victims' illnesses, which indicated that Billik could not possibly have poisoned them.

1917

The Board said they wanted to interview Billik personally before making a decision. They met with him at Joliet a few days later, then issued their recommendation to the governor:

> It should be taken for granted that after eliminating . . . the testimony of Jerry Vrzal, which was false and perjured, as pointed out by him, that there would yet remain sufficient evidence in the record to justify . . . finding Billik guilty, yet it can not for a moment be conceded that if . . . the many facts and circumstances by him given, indicative of the prisoner's innocence, were substituted therefore, a fair jury could, on the new record, find him guilty. We have an abiding conviction that if the evidence of Jerry Vrzal, as here presented, were substituted for the evidence which he gave on the hearing, all fair minded men, without hesitation or dissent, would conclude that Billik was innocent . . .
>
> The Board of Pardons examined the prisoner at great length . . . We noted particularly his promptness in response, and his thorough candor and frankness. There was no hesitation, apparently no mental reservation. He submitted to the examination with as much docility and simplicity as an unsophisticated child of ten years. He is not possessed of a deep, sly, shrewd, cunning mind as one might suspect because of the life of fraud and deception which he had lived for at least a number of years. On the contrary, he is not an average man in sagacity and cunning. He impresses one as being rather simple, easily to be duped himself. He seems to be devoid of those traits of character, which would make it possible for him to commit so diabolical a crime. He has been confined in the penitentiary for seven years and eleven months; has never even been reprimanded; is at present an inmate of the prison hospital; in poor health, and, as we believe, an innocent man. We think justice requires that he be given an absolute pardon.[700]

On the evening of January 3rd, 1917, in one of his last official acts as governor, Dunne granted Herman Billik a full and absolute pardon. The next morning, Billik shook the hand of Warden Michael Zimmer and, after more than ten years in jail, walked out of the gates of Joliet Prison a free man. Pale and gaunt, with white hair, his mustache shaved clean, he looked far older than his 50 years, and would have been unrecognizable to those familiar with him only from newspaper photos from his trial.

He was met by his recently married son, Herman Jr., and newsman L. G. Edwardson. Billik marveled at the automobile that carried the trio back to Chicago, a contraption which had supplanted the horse and carriage in the years he had been locked away. They enjoyed a nice meal at a downtown restaurant, then stopped at the office of his faithful and now jubilant attorney, Francis Hinckley. When asked of his plans, Billik announced, "I shall go to Cleveland where my sister is and begin life again."[701] His wife Mary, and Edna, now a young lady of nineteen, were also waiting for him there. He said that with the help of his sister Elsa, he hoped to establish a small business, maybe a grocery store. "I'm the happiest man in the world," he told reporters. "My wife has stuck to me all that time. She has worked to support herself and my daughter. Now I am going to work for them."[702]

Not everyone was happy with Billik's newfound freedom, though. "I have nothing in my heart but bitterness for Billik," said Emma. "I could cheerfully stone him to death. It would be a joy to me to pull on the rope that choked his life out."[703] She ridiculed Billik for going back to Cleveland, and even issued a not-so-thinly-veiled threat to the man she claimed hypnotized her mother into murdering her family. "He had better stay away from this town. He might be killed—get what was coming to him—if he tried to live here."[704]

Former prosecutor George Popham called the pardon "an outrage against justice," and Billik a "monstrous murderer," who "killed little children to get their life insurance."[705] Popham, who resigned from the state's attorney's office less than a year after John Healy's election defeat, had been accused of manufacturing false testimony and coaching witnesses in the case, so his statement was no real surprise. Interestingly, John Healy, whose once promising political career ended in no small part because of his handling of Billik's case, apparently made no public statement regarding the pardon. He was enjoying a lucrative private legal practice, in which he was eventually joined by his friend, former Governor Charles Deneen. Though slightly more reserved in his comments than Popham, Judge Barnes also publicly condemned the pardon. He did, however, make one statement that everyone could agree with. "A grave mistake was made," he said, "either when he was imprisoned or when he was pardoned."[706]

Governor Dunne wasted no time responding to criticism of Billik's pardon. "Years ago with S.S. Gregory and tens of thousands of other citizens, I protested to Governor Deneen and the pardon board against his hanging because I honestly doubted then that he was guilty," Dunne said. "The doubts I then had have been more than confirmed by the evidence we heard last week, the evidence of Jerry Vrzal, Mr. Edwardson, and Dr. C.P. Caldwell . . . The evidence before the board of pardons showed that when most of his alleged victims died in Chicago, Billik was in another state. The retraction of Jerry Vrzal of his perjury was not considered by the Supreme Court . . . We did consider it, and believed it to be true and that Billik was the victim of perjury. This is another case in favor of the abolition of capital punishment . . . Billik was indicted for the murder of several persons in the same family by poison. The evidence in all cases would have been practically the same. After Jerry Vrzal had retracted his testimony Billik's friends sought to have Billik tried on the other cases, but the prosecution refused to do so and has never brought any of the other cases to trial, even after Billik had his sentence commuted by Gov. Deneen. The recommendation of the board of pardons was right, and I promptly approved the same."[707]

There were widespread rumors that Edna Billik and Jerry Vrzal had plans to marry. When asked about it, Billik said he had forgiven Jerry for the lies that sent him to prison, and gave the couple his blessing, but both Edna and Jerry tried to downplay the talk. Billik's sister claimed the couple had been engaged for several months, but that Jerry planned to stay away until the public forgot about them.[708] Jerry returned to Washington with Father O'Callaghan, and Edna remained silent.

When a reporter interviewed the family in Cleveland, Billik told of an eerie prophecy years earlier. Though he readily admitted that he had no special powers, he apparently still believed that some people did. "Thirty-five years ago when I was in Prague, a soldier foretold my suffering with dice," Billik said. "He threw the dice down and said, 'Man, I hate to tell you what is before you—long prison term across the water, and you are innocent. You will come out of it, but man you are doomed.' . . . I have thought of that soldier's prophecy so much in prison."[709] Billik took encouragement from the fact that the soldier told him things would eventually turn out alright, and was now optimistic about his future. "My troubles may be over,"[710] he said.

A short time later, the Billiks quietly moved back to Chicago, where they lived on the far West Side under the name Ceicek[711] (a variation of his original name, "Zajicek"). It's not clear if Billik ever realized his dream of opening a small business, but the optimism he expressed upon his release was to be short-lived. Suffering from numerous ailments, including rheumatism, dropsy, and heart disease,[712] he was in and out of the hospital. Finally, on May 20th, just a little over four months after his release from prison, he suffered a heart attack and was rushed by ambulance to the hospital. He languished for several days, often barely coherent. On May 24th, 1917, with family members at his side, Herman Billik quietly passed away at Cook County Hospital. He maintained his innocence to the very end.[713]

Epilogue

•

So, if Herman Billik didn't kill anyone, who did? Emma is the only one who had the opportunity to have poisoned every one of the known victims (including Henry and William Niemann). The basic sequence of events casts more than a small cloud of suspicion over her:

Emma was angry with her family for objecting to her relationship with Cooney and throwing her out of the house. When she was allowed back home, her father became sick and died. Mary suffered a similar fate a few months later. Emma was forced to leave right after Mary died, and went to live with the Niemanns. A week after her arrival there, Henry Niemann died, leaving control of the dairy farm to William. A few months later, Tillie visited Emma at the Niemann farm. She became extremely sick with stomach problems which persisted until she died (while Emma was back home to visit over Christmas weekend).

Later that year, Jerry began losing weight and growing weak. His mother sent him to live with Billik's family in Cleveland and his condition improved dramatically. Then little Rosie started feeling ill. She was first poisoned in July, right around the time that Emma spent the night at the Vrzal home and took her out to Downers Grove for a few days. Emma brought Rosie to see Dr. Caldwell and used a fictitious address. Later, she lied about having taken her, and falsely claimed that Caldwell told her he might have been mistaken about the incident. Rosie died when

Emma came home to celebrate Labor Day weekend and Ella's birthday. When Emma asked if Ella could come visit her, Mrs. Vrzal's response was alarming. Emma herself said, "My mother said when I wanted to take Ella to visit me at the farm, that she would rather have her go with strangers than me."[714] Had Mrs. Vrzal herself become suspicious?

Ella became sick following her sister Rosie's funeral (which Emma attended). Around this same time, someone began poisoning Mrs. Vrzal with arsenic. Within a few months, Mrs. Vrzal sold the house and business to Emma and William. She took Jerry, Bertha, and a critically ill Ella, and moved in with her cousin, into a tiny, already-crowded apartment in the poverty-stricken area around the stockyards. Meanwhile, Emma and William moved into the house on 19th Street. Ella died a few weeks later, when Emma visited them on Thanksgiving.

The night Mrs. Vrzal was called to the police station for questioning, Emma came to the house. When she discovered her mother was being interviewed about the deaths, she went down to the station uninvited and began telling police about her suspicions of Billik. The next day, as her mother lay dying, she told Dr. Caldwell that her mother had poisoned the children. The amount of money police determined was missing from Mrs. Vrzal's effects was $1,900, the same amount that Emma and William were supposed to have given her in cash when they bought the house a few weeks earlier. There is no real proof, other than Emma's word, that that money was actually paid to Mrs. Vrzal.

At the inquest, Emma testified that she and William were married, though they were not. Might she have considered the fact that witnesses cannot be forced to testify against their spouse? A month later, they travelled out to Will County to get married by a justice of the peace. Shortly thereafter, William Niemann cancelled his life insurance policy. He then started showing symptoms similar to those that Martin Vrzal had. Emma went to the State's Attorney concerned that she would be blamed if her husband died suddenly. After she was assured that no suspicion would be cast upon her,

William's health deteriorated. Jerry came from Valparaiso to tell Emma that O'Callaghan and some sort of detective (which he believed Edwardson to be) were looking into the possibility that she and William had murdered the Vrzals. At that point, Emma quit calling the doctor who had been treating her husband, and a few days later William died. On his final day, she saw him grow markedly worse, and even called her brother-in-law to tell him that William would likely die soon. But she didn't bother to call a doctor until William was already dead. When she did, she called Dr. Weiskopf, who had previously misdiagnosed her father's illness. Weiskopf was so suspicious that he refused to sign a death certificate and called authorities.

Emma may well have had one or more accomplices in some or all of the murders. Joe Cooney, William Niemann, and even Jerry himself all seem likely to have had knowledge of the crimes that they never disclosed to authorities. O'Callaghan and Edwardson identified several other possible co-conspirators, though nothing about them is known beyond the names scrawled on the note in Billik's case files.

The final mystery surrounds William's first wife, Louise. She died quite young, with symptoms consistent with arsenic poisoning. If her body were ever exhumed, and it were shown that she died from arsenic poisoning, it could add a whole new perspective to the case.

History has not been kind to Herman Billik. He is discussed in books and articles about crime and killers which, without exception, cast him as a depraved serial killer of the lowest order.[715] The accounts characterize Father O'Callaghan as a simple publicity seeker, call Billik's pardon "inexplicable," and the public outcry to save him the result of "mass hysteria."[716] They fail to mention the Niemann murder(s) at all, and provide only the barest outline of the "facts," many of which have no apparent basis in reality. Even stories from reputable newspapers such as the *Chicago*

Tribune, New York Times, and *Washington Post* are riddled with exaggerations and factual errors, often claiming Billik was convicted of six murders, some even saying he killed several of his wives.[717]

I will address two misstatements, simply because they have been repeated so often that most observers now assume them to be true. Both likely originate from Philip Lindsay's 1958 book *The Mainspring of Murder,* in which the author has crafted a fictionalized account of Billik's case. Lindsay states that Billik's name was originally "Vajicek," presumably a simple typo, either on his part or that of his undocumented source. Billik's original name was, of course, "Zajicek." He eventually started going by "Billik," his stepfather's name, because he thought it was easier for people to say. Lindsay also makes reference to Billik calling himself "The Great Billik." It does have a nice ring, but his professional name was, in fact, "Professor Herman." There is no reference to "The Great Billik" prior to Lindsay's book.

I spent more than six years studying virtually every record even remotely related to the case in an effort to provide a historically accurate document of the events and evidence: thousands of pages of transcripts from the trial, inquests, Supreme Court proceedings, police interviews, sworn affidavits, hundreds of news articles from the time of the events, and countless more legal documents, letters, and files. There are scores of facts and incidents I haven't included which further support Billik's innocence and disprove the wild tales and misstatements that have persisted, but, for fear of burdening the reader, I have tried to be brief. Early in my research, I planned to write a brief story about a long-forgotten serial killer: the surreal tale of a Bohemian fortune teller with a striking persona, who murdered an entire family one by one. But, as I delved further into the facts, I found myself thinking, just as Father O'Callaghan had, "Everything that I discover makes me ever more sure that he is not guilty."

The year after Herman Billik died, the Spanish Flu pandemic that ravaged the world* hit Chicago. In November of 1918, over the course of just five days, Herman Jr., Emil, and Mary Billik were all stricken with influenza, and died. Herman Jr. was the father of a one-year-old baby girl. Edna Billik survived. She buried her mother and brothers just yards from the grave of her beloved father. The much-discussed marriage between Edna and Jerry never took place. There is evidence that Edna was married for a short time and stayed in Chicago, but her trail goes cold after 1920.† Years of research have left me still wondering what became of the girl who helped save her father from the hangman, only to watch her entire family die in the span of a year and a half.

Tiring of his renewed notoriety, a few months after Billik's release, Jerry changed his name to "Jerome Martin Vaughan" and eventually moved to California. He did get married years later and, true to his promise to Judge Barnes, became a lawyer. He practiced in Los Angeles for a number of years, and passed away in 1963.

Emma had two sons, and lived a long, uneventful life after Billik's pardon. She was married to the same man for more than thirty years, until he passed away on Easter Sunday in 1943. Emma lived in the Chicago suburb of Berwyn, and died in 1972 at the age of 90. Bertha Vrzal was raised by Emma and her new husband. She married, had a son, and eventually moved to Michigan, where she died in 1965.

Former Police Chief George Shippy died while Billik was in prison. His health, particularly his mental state, had continued to decline after his retirement, with police eventually detailed to his home due to his frequent outbursts of violence. He was so unstable

---

* Worldwide, some 21 million people died, including 600,000 Americans, and more than 8,500 Chicago residents.

† A marriage license was filed in Cook County on September 22, 1917 for "Edna Billick and William H. Jordan." They were living separately by Sept. of 1918, and Edna is listed alone in Chicago in the 1920 Census, though she still identified herself as married. William H. Jordan re-married in December 1922, but it's not clear if Edna had passed away, or they divorced.

near the end of his life that his wife feared it was "unsafe for him to be at large"[718] and had him committed. He spent the last months of his life in the insane asylum in Kankakee. His condition was described as paresis (a partial paralysis) with softening of the brain.[719] It's commonly associated with syphilis, which likely was the true nature of his long, slow demise.

Governor Dunne returned to his law practice in Chicago. He remains the only man to serve as both Mayor of Chicago and Governor of Illinois. He is remembered today as one of the most honest and reform-minded men to occupy either office. Though he would lament his failure to convince the legislature to do away with the death penalty, Dunne's greatest accomplishments involved standing up for the most vulnerable members of society: improving treatment and conditions for prisoners, the insane, and the sick. The Illinois State Senate summed up Dunne's character when they adopted a unanimous resolution saying, in part, "His honesty was and is proverbial, his fair dealing unquestioned, and his open, appealing democracy such as to make him a real friend of men."[720]

Father O'Callaghan remained prominent in the temperance movement until he passed away in 1931. His obituary recounted how he led a prolonged fight to save the life of an immigrant who had been wrongly convicted of murder and sentenced to death.[721] But they weren't talking about Herman Billik. Amazingly, a few years after Billik died, O'Callaghan became interested in the case of a Chinese student in Washington who was convicted of a brutal multiple murder and sentenced to die. In a seven-year saga that could easily fill the pages of another whole book, Ziang Sun Wan was eventually cleared of the crimes and released from prison.

Bibliography

•

Books

Arey, Leslie Brainerd, William Burrows, J.P. Greenhill, Richard M. Hewitt, editors. *Dorland's Illustrated Medical Dictionary, 23rd Edition.* Philadelphia: W. B. Saunders Company, 1961.

Avrich, Paul. *The Haymarket Tragedy.* Princeton, NJ: Princeton University Press, 1984.

Christison, Dr. J. Sanderson (John Sanderson). *The Tragedy of Chicago: a study in hypnotism, how an innocent young man was hypnotised to the gallows, denouncements by savants.* Chicago: J.S. Christison, 1906.

Dedmon, Emmett. *Fabulous Chicago.* New York: Random House, 1953.

Donnelley, Paul. *501 Most Notorious Crimes.* London: Bounty Books, 2009.

Dreisbach, Robert H., MD, PhD. *Handbook of Poisoning.* Los Altos, CA: Lange Medical Publications, 1969.

Duis, Perry R. *Challenging Chicago: Coping With Everyday Life, 1837–1920.* Urbana and Chicago: University of Illinois Press, 1998.

Dunne, Edward F. *Illinois: The Heart of the Nation,* 5 vols. Chicago: Lewis Publishing, 1933.

Gray, Henry, F.R.S. *Anatomy, Descriptive and Surgical,* Revised American, From Fifteenth English Edition. editors T. Pickering Pick and Robert Howden. New York: Bounty Books,1977.

Hayner, Don and Tom McNamee. *Metro Chicago Almanac.* Chicago: Chicago Sun Times Inc. and Bonus Books, Inc., 1993.

Hayner, Don and Tom McNamee. *Streetwise Chicago.* Chicago: Loyola University Press, 1988.

Johnson, Curt and R. Craig Sutter. *The Wicked City, Chicago From Kenna to Capone.* New York: Da Capo Press, 1998.

Lakeside Annual Directories of Chicago, 1880–1917, Microfilm, Newberry Library, Chicago, IL.

Larson, Erik. *The Devil In the White City.* New York: Vintage Books, 2004.

Lindberg, Richard. *Return to the Scene of the Crime.* Nashville: Cumberland House, 1999.

Lindsay, Philip. *The Mainspring of Murder.* London: John Long, 1958.

Loerzel, Robert. *Alchemy of Bones.* Urbana and Chicago: University of Illinois Press, 2003.

Longstreet, Stephen. *Chicago, An Intimate Portrait of People, Pleasures, and Power:1860–1919.* New York: David McKay Company, Inc., 1973.

Lowe, David. *Lost Chicago.* Avenel, NJ: Wings Books, 1975.

Lyghyt, Charles E., M.D. editor. *The Merck Manual of Diagnosis and Therapy.* Rathway, NJ: Merck Sharpe & Dohme Research Laboratories, 1961.

Lyle, Judge John H. *The Dry and Lawless Years.* Englewood Cliffs, NJ: Prentice-Hall, Inc., 1960.

Morton, Richard Allen. *Justice and Humanity, Edward F. Dunne, Illinois Progressive.* Carbondale and Edwardsville, IL: Southern Illinois University Press, 1997.

Osborn, Albert S. *Questioned Documents,* Second Edition Facsimile. Chicago: Nelson Hall Co., 1974.

Parker, James N., M.D. and Philip M. Parker, PH. D., editors. *Arsenic Poisoning.* San Diego: ICON Health Publications, 2004.

Pietrusza, David. *Judge and Jury: The Life and Times of Judge Kenesaw Mountain Landis.* South Bend, IN: Diamond Communications, 1998.

Roth, Walter and Joe Kraus. *An Accidental Anarchist.* San Francisco: Rudi Publishing, 1998.

Sandburg, Carl. *Smoke and Steel.* New York: Harcourt, Brace, and Howe, Inc., 1920.

Sawyers, June Skinner. *Chicago Portraits.* Chicago: Loyola University Press, 1991.

Simpson, Dick. *Rogues, Rebels, and Rubber Stamps.* Boulder, CO: Westview Press, 2001.

Sinclair, Upton. *The Jungle.* New York: Doubleday, Page, and Company, 1906.

Spink, J.G. Taylor. *Judge Landis and 25 Years of Baseball.* St. Louis: The Sporting News Publishing Company, 1974.

Sullivan, William L., editor. *Dunne: Judge, Mayor, Governor.* Chicago: The Windermere Press, 1916.

Wendt, Lloyd and Herman Kogan. *Lords of the Levee: The Story of Bathhouse John and Hinky Dink.* Indianapolis: The Bobbs-Merrill Company, 1943.

Articles / Essays

"Affections of the Heart and Circulatory System," excerpts from *Orthopathy* by Herbert M. Shelton, Presented by Dr. Stanley S. Bass; website accessed August 16, 2010, http://drbass.com/orthopathy/chapter11.html

Bansal, S.K., N. Haldar, U.K. Dhand, and J.S. Chopra, "Phrenic Neuropathy in Arsenic Poisoning," *Chest* 1991; 100; 878–880, DOI 10.1378/chest.100.3.878; http://chestjournal.chestpubs.org/content/100/3/878

Gorby, Michael S., "Arsenic Poisoning" [clinical conference]. *The Western Journal of Medicine*, 1988 Sept; 149: 308–315; http://www.ncbi.nlm.nih.gov/pmc/articles/PMC1026413/

Gross, C.R. and A.O. Nelson, Insecticide Division, Bureau of Chemistry and Soils, U.S. Department of Agriculture, Washington, D.C.; "Arsenic in Tobacco Smoke," *American Journal Public Health Nations Health*, 1934   January 24; [original scanned version of text] accessed online September 15, 2010, http://www.ncbi.nlm.nih.gov/pmc/articles/PMC1558493/

Greenburg, C., S. Davies, T. McGowan, A. Schorer, and C. Drage, "Acute Respiratory Failure Following Severe Arsenic Poisoning," *Chest* 1979; 76;596–598, DOI 10.1378/chest.76.5.596; http://chestjournal.chestpubs.org/content/76/5/596

Murphy, Martin J., Lynn W. Lyon, and Jerry W. Taylor; "Subacute Arsenic Neuropathy: Clinical and Electrophysiological Observations," *Journal of Neurology, Neurosurgery, and Psychiatry*, 1981; 44: 896–900.

Ratnaike, R.N., "Acute and Chronic Arsenic Toxicity," *Postgrad Medical Journal* 2003; 79:391–396; www.postgradmedj.com

Warner, Kelly L., Angel Martin, Jr., and Terri L. Arnold, "Arsenic In Illinois Ground Water—Community and Private Supplies," U.S. Department of the Interior, U.S. Geological Survey, *Water-Resources Investigations Report 03-4103*, July 2003.

Newspapers

Chicago American, microfilm, Chicago Public Library.
Chicago Daily Journal, microfilm, Chicago Public Library.
Chicago Daily News, microfilm, Chicago Public Library.
Chicago Daily Tribune, microfilm, Chicago Public Library.
Chicago Examiner, microfilm, Chicago Public Library.
Chicago Herald, microfilm, Chicago Public Library.
Chicago Record-Herald, microfilm, Chicago Public Library.
Chicago Tribune, Chicago Tribune Archives, ProQuest Archiver [database online]: http://pqasb.pqarchiver.com/chicagotribune

Historical Newspapers, Birth, Marriage, & Death Announcements, 1851–2003 [database online]. Ancestry.com Operations Inc, 2006.

New York Times, ProQuest Historical Newspapers [database online], ProQuest.com; http://query.nytimes.com/search/query?srchst=p

Springfield News (Springfield, IL) original news clippings, State of Illinois Executive Clemency Files, Herman Zajicek, aka Herman Billik, Illinois State Archives, Springfield, IL.

Washington Post, Washington Post Archives, ProQuest Archiver [database online]. http://pqasb.pqarchiver.com/washingtonpost/search.html

Washington Post online: http://www.washingtonpost.com

Indexes / Databases / Government Records

1900 United States Federal Census [database online]. Ancestry.com Operations Inc, 2004.

1910 United States Federal Census [database online]. Ancestry.com Operations Inc, 2006.

1920 United States Federal Census [database online]. Ancestry.com Operations Inc, 2010. Images reproduced by FamilySearch

1930 United States Federal Census [database online]. Ancestry.com Operations Inc, 2002.

California Death Index, 1940–1997 [database online]. Ancestry.com Operations Inc, 2000.

Chicago Police Department Homicide Record (1870–1930), microfilm, Northeastern Illinois University, Regional Archives Depository, Chicago, IL.

Chicago Police Department Homicide Record Index (1870–1930). Illinois Secretary of State [database online], http://www.cyberdrive-illinois.com/departments/archives/homicide.html

Cook County Coroner's Inquest Record Index (1872–1911). Illinois Secretary of State [database online], http://www.cyberdriveillinois.com/departments/archives/cookinqt.html

Cook County, Illinois, *Cook County Coroner's Inquest Record (1872–1911),* microfilm, Northeastern Illinois University, Regional Archives Depository, Chicago, IL.

Cook County, Illinois, Cook County Recorder of Deeds *Property Tract Books,* Cook County Recorder of Deeds, Chicago, IL.

Database of Illinois Death Certificates, 1916–1950. Illinois Secretary of State [database online] http://www.cyberdriveillinois.com/departments/archives/idphdeathindex.html

DuPage County, Illinois, DuPage County Coroner *Records of Inquest,* microfilm, DuPage County Corner's Office, Wheaton, IL.

Illinois Statewide Marriage Index, 1763–1900. Illinois Secretary of State [database online] http://www.cyberdriveillinois.com/departments/ar-chives/marriage.html

Illinois Statewide Death Index, Pre-1916. Illinois Secretary of State [database online] http://www.cyberdriveillinois.com/departments/ar-chives/death.html

State of Illinois *Executive Clemency File, Herman Zajicek, aka Herman Billik,* Illinois State Archives, Springfield, IL.

U.S. World War I Draft Registration Cards, 1917–1918 [database online]. Ancestry.com Operations Inc, 2005.

U.S. World War II Draft Registration Cards, 1942 [database online]. *Ancestry.com*

Websites

"ADAM Medical Encyclopedia," A.D.A.M., Inc, database online, http://www.nlm.nih.gov/medlineplus/encyclopedia.html

"Agency For Toxic Substance and Disease Registry, Toxic Substances Portal, Arsenic," accessed April 6, 2010. http://www.atsdr.cdc.gov/substances/toxsubstance.asp?toxid=3

"Alchemy of Bones," accessed January 15, 2004, http://www.alchemyofbones.com/

"A Look at Cook," accessed January 28, 2005, http://www.alookatcook.com/

"Chicago Streets Database," Daniel E. Niemiec, accessed June17, 2007, http://www.rootsweb.com/~itappcnc/pipcnstreetfind.htm

"Joliet Prison Photographs," accessed November 10, 2010, http://www.jolietprison.com/publications/catalog.asp

"Medical Discoveries, Chloroform," website accessed February 2, 2011, http://www.discoveriesinmedicine.com/Bar-Cod/Chloroform.html

"MedicineNet.com Medical Dictionary," database on line, http://www.medterms.com/script/main/hp.asp

"New Evils For Old, Chapter X, Soil and Health Library," website ac-cessed June 4, 2010, http://www.soilandhealth.org/02/0201hyglibcat/020134syphilis/020134syphilis-ch10.htm

"Old St. Mary's Catholic Church History," accessed August 4, 2006, http://www.oldstmarys.com/Parish_history.htm

"Paulist Fathers" website, accessed August 4, 2006, http://www.paulist.org/main/whoare.htm

"The Dramas of Haymarket," Chicago Historical Society website, ac-cessed January 25, 2008 http://www.chicagohs.org/dramas/overview/over.htm

"U.S National Library of Medicine, National Institute of Health," PubMed.gov, database on line, http://www.ncbi.nlm.nih.gov/pubmed

Acknowledgments

I would like to express my deep gratitude to publisher Tracy Ertl, for her enduring support and belief that this was a story worth telling. I would also like to thank everyone at Midpoint Trade Books for their amazing work, especially managing editor Megan Trank, cover artist Michael Short, publicist Felicia Minerva, and editors Caroline DeLuca and Rio Santisteban. Their hard work and insight was so greatly needed and appreciated. I would also like to thank my mother, Kathy Shukis, for her never-ending support throughout this project. Lastly, I would like to thank my wife Keisha, the love of my life, and mother of our new baby girl. Her understanding and patience has made this possible.

Notes

•

1 Carl Sandburg, Smoke and Steel (New York: Harcourt, Brace, and Howe, 1920), p 37.
2 Chicago Daily News, December 4, 1906.
3 Transcript of Coroner's Inquest, p 69; Chicago Daily News, July 11, 1907.
4 Chicago Daily Tribune, November 22, 1904.
5 Transcript of Coroner's Inquest, State of Illinois Executive Clemency Files, Herman Zajicek, aka Herman Billik, Illinois State Archives, Springfield, IL; p 43.
6 Ibid.
7 Chicago Daily Tribune, June 2, 1929.
8 Lakeside Annual Directory of Chicago, 1905, microfilm, Newberry Library, Chicago, IL.
9 Chicago Daily Tribune, December 6, 1906.
10 Ibid.
11 Chicago Daily Tribune, December 8, 1906.
12 Chicago Daily News, December 7, 1906.
13 Chicago Daily Tribune, December 8, 1906.
14 Chicago Daily News, December 7, 1906.
15 Chicago Daily Tribune, December 6, 1906.
16 The Newark Advocate (Newark, Ohio), December 18, 1906.
17 Ibid.
18 Chicago Daily News, December 6, 1906.
19 Chicago Daily News, December 7, 1906.
20 Chicago Daily Tribune, December 7, 1906.
21 Chicago Daily Tribune, December 8, 1906.
22 Chicago Daily Tribune, December 9, 1906.
23 Ibid.
24 Chicago Daily Tribune, December 10, 1906.
25 Dr. J. Sanderson Christison (John Sanderson), The Tragedy of

Chicago: a study in hypnotism, how an innocent young man was hypnotized to the gallows, denouncements by savants (Chicago: J.S. Christison, 1906).

26 Chicago Daily Tribune, December 10, 1906.
27 Ibid.
28 Chicago Daily Tribune, December 18, 1906.
29 Ibid.
30 Chicago Daily Tribune, April 14, 1907.
31 Chicago Daily Tribune, April 16, 1907.
32 Chicago Daily Tribune, December 18, 1906.
33 Transcript of Coroner's Inquest, p 52.
34 Ibid., p 55.
35 Ibid., p 58.
36 Ibid., p 57.
37 Ibid., p 71
38 Ibid., p 61.
39 Ibid., p 60.
40 Ibid., p 66.
41 Ibid., p 69.
42 Ibid., p 109.
43 Ibid.
44 Ibid.
45 Ibid., p 112.
46 Certificate of Live Birth, City of Cleveland, June 21, 1893.
47 Transcript of Coroner's Inquest, p 132.
48 Ibid.
49 Ibid.
50 Ibid.
51 Idib. p 128.
52 Ibid., pp 147–148.
53 Ibid., p 152.
54 Ibid.
55 *Transcript of Coroner's Inquest*, p 159.
56 Ibid.
57 Ibid.
58 Ibid.
59 Ibid., pp 159–160.
60 Ibid., p 160.
61 Ibid.
62 Ibid.
63 Ibid.
64 "Chicago History Museum, The Stockyards," website accessed April 3, 2011; http://www.chicagohs.org/history/stockyard/stock2.html
65 *Transcript of Coroner's Inquest*, p 184.

66 Ibid., p 186.
67 Ibid., p 196.
68 Ibid., p 241.
69 *Chicago Daily Tribune*, January 5, 1907.
70 Signed Statement of Dr. Walter S. Haines, dated January 4, 1907; State of Illinois Executive Clemency Files, Herman Zajicek, aka Herman Billik, Illinois State Archives, Springfield, IL.
71 *Cook County Coroner's Inquest Record (1872–1911)*, microfilm, Northeastern Illinois University, Regional Archives Depository, Chicago, IL, Inquest Nos. 40009/250, 40010/251, and 40014/255.
72 *Chicago Daily Tribune*, January 5, 1907.
73 *Elyria Daily Chronicle* (Elyria, Ohio), January 8, 1907.
74 Ibid.
75 *Chicago Daily Tribune*, January 6, 1907.
76 *Chicago Daily Tribune*, January 5, 1907.
77 *Chicago Daily Tribune*, Jan. 15, 1907.
78 *Chicago Daily* Tribune, January 19, 1907.
79 Ibid.
80 Ibid.
81 Ibid.
82 *Chicago Daily Tribune*, December 23, 1906.
83 *Chicago Daily Tribune*, February 16, 1907.
84 Signed Affidavit of Walter S. Haines, February 20, 1907; State of Illinois Executive Clemency Files, Herman Zajicek, aka Herman Billik, Illinois State Archives, Springfield, IL.
85 *Chicago Daily Tribune*, February 19, 1907.
86 *Transcript of Coroner's Inquest*, p 323.
87 *Cook County Coroner's Inquest Record (1872–1911)*, Coroner's Inquest Nos. 40011/252, 40012/253, 40013/254.
88 Dick Simpson, *Rogues, Rebels, and Rubber Stamps* (Boulder, CO: Westview Press, 2001), pp 53–54.
89 Ibid., p 52.
90 Ibid., p 50.
91 Edward F. Dunne, *Illinois: The Heart of the Nation,* (Chicago: Lewis Publishing, 1933), Vol. II, pp 294–295.
92 *New York Times*, July 10, 1914.
93 *Transcript of Coroner's Inquest*, pp 116–117.
94 "Statement of Herman Billik, Jr." taken by Police Attorney Comerford, December 28, 1906; State of Illinois Executive Clemency Files, Herman Zajicek, aka Herman Billik, Illinois State Archives, Springfield, IL.
95 *Transcript of Coroner's Inquest*, p 116.
96 "Statement of Herman Billik, Jr." taken by Assistant State's Attorney Popham, May 13, 1907; State of Illinois Executive Clemency Files, Herman Zajicek, aka Herman Billik, Illinois State Archives, Springfield, IL.

97 Ibid.
98 Ibid.
99 Ibid.
100 *Chicago Daily Tribune* May 9, 1904.
101 *Chicago Daily Tribune*, January 20, 1907.
102 *Chicago Daily Tribune*, July 3, 1907.
103 Ibid.
104 *Chicago Daily Tribune*, July 4, 1907.
105 Ibid.
106 Ibid.
107 Ibid.
108 Supreme Court of Illinois, *Abstract of Record and Bill of Exceptions, No. 5814*, December Term 1907; pp 13–15.
109 *Chicago Daily Tribune*, July 6, 1907.
110 Ibid.
111 Ibid.
112 *Abstract of Record and Bill of Exceptions*, pp 68–77.
113 Ibid. p 72.
114 Ibid., p 91.
115 Ibid., p 84.
116 Ibid. pp 73–74.
117 *The Newark Daily Advocate* (Newark, OH), July 9, 1907.
118 *Chicago Daily Tribune*, July 6, 1907; *Washington Post*, July 7, 1907; and *Chicago Daily Tribune*, July 7, 1907.
119 *Chicago Daily Tribune*, July 7, 1907.
120 Ibid
121 Supreme Court of Illinois, *Brief and Argument For Defendant in Error, No. 5814*, December Term 1907; p 15.
122 *The Newark Daily Advocate*, (Newark, OH) July 9, 1907.
123 *Chicago Daily Tribune*, July 9, 1907.
124 Ibid.
125 Ibid.
126 *Chicago Daily News*, July 9, 1907.
127 *Transcript of Coroner's Inquest*, pp 55–56.
128 Ibid., pp 307–308.
129 Ibid., p 51.
130 Ibid., p 49.
131 *Chicago Daily Tribune*, July 10, 1907.
132 *Transcript of Coroner's Inquest*, p 49.
133 *Abstract of Record and Bill of Exceptions*, p 435.
134 *Chicago Daily News*, July 10, 1907.
134 Ibid.
136 *Transcript of Coroner's Inquest*, p 48.
137 *Brief and Argument For Defendant in Error*, p 9.
138 Ibid., p 16.

139 *Abstract of Record and Bill of Exceptions,* p 266; and *Transcript of Coroner's Inquest,* p 180.
140 *Chicago Daily News,* July 11, 1907.
141 *Abstract of Record and Bill of Exceptions,* p 273.
142 *Chicago Daily Tribune,* July 12, 1907.
143 Ibid.
144 *Abstract of Record and Bill of Exceptions,* p 312.
145 *Chicago Daily Tribune,* July 12, 1907.
146 Ibid.
147 Ibid.
148 Ibid.
149 Ibid.
150 *Abstract of Record and Bill of Exceptions,* p 321.
151 *Chicago Daily Tribune,* July 12, 1907.
152 Ibid.
153 Ibid.
154 *Chicago Daily News,* July 12, 1907.
155 Ibid.
156 Ibid.
157 Ibid.
158 *Chicago Daily Tribune,* July 13, 1907.
159 *Chicago Daily News,* July 12, 1907.
160 *Chicago Daily Tribune,* July 13, 1907.
161 *Chicago Daily News,* July 12, 1907.
162 Ibid.
163 *Chicago Daily Tribune,* July 13, 1907.
164 Ibid.
165 *Abstract of Record and Bill of Exceptions,* p 372.
166 Ibid., p 398.
167 *Chicago Daily Tribune,* July 13, 1907.
168 Ibid.
169 *Abstract of Record and Bill of Exceptions,* p 332.
170 Ibid., p 369.
171 Ibid.
172 *Chicago Daily Tribune,* July 14, 1907.
173 *Abstract of Record and Bill of Exceptions,* p 410.
174 [First Statement of] *Jerry Vrgal* [sic]; Undated Police Interview; State of Illinois Executive Clemency Files, Herman Zajicek, aka Herman Billik, Illinois State Archives, Springfield, IL; p 1.
175 *Abstract of Record and Bill of Exceptions,* p 366.
176 *Hearing By the State Board of Pardons on the Application of Herman Billik,* Transcript, State of Illinois Executive Clemency Files, Herman Zajicek, aka Herman Billik, Illinois State Archives, Springfield, IL pp 104–105.
177 *Chicago Daily News,* July 15, 1907.

178   *Chicago Daily News*, July 16, 1907.
179   *Chicago Daily Tribune*, July 17, 1907.
180   *Chicago Daily News*, July 16, 1907.
181   Ibid.
182   Ibid.
183   Ibid.
184   Ibid.
185   *Abstract of Record and Bill of Exceptions*, p 473.
186   Ibid.
187   Ibid., p 470.
188   *Chicago Daily News*, July 16, 1907.
189   *Abstract of Record and Bill of Exceptions*, p 476.
190   *Chicago Daily News*, July 16, 1907.
191   Ibid.
192   *Abstract of Record and Bill of Exceptions*, p 482.
193   *Chicago Daily Tribune*, July 17, 1907.
194   *Chicago Daily Tribune*, January 9, 1904.
195   *Chicago Daily Tribune*, July 17, 1907.
196   *Brief and Argument For Defendant in Error*, p 70.
197   *Abstract of Record and Bill of Exceptions*, p 526.
198   Ibid., p 527.
199   Ibid., p 525.
200   Ibid., p 538.
201   *Transcript of Coroner's Inquest*, p 55 and p 218.
202   *Brief and Argument For Defendant in Error*, p 3; *Petition For Clemency to His Excellency, Gov. Charles S. Deneen*, April 18, 1908; State of Illinois Executive Clemency Files, Herman Zajicek, aka Herman Billik, Illinois State Archives, Springfield, IL; p 5; and *Affidavit of Retraction of Testimony of Jerry Vrzal*; State of Illinois Executive Clemency Files, Herman Zajicek, aka Herman Billik, Illinois State Archives, Springfield, IL.
203   *Transcript of Coroner's Inquest*, p 56.
204   Ibid., p 57.
205   *Abstract of Record and Bill of Exceptions*, pp 535–536.
206   Ibid.
207   Ibid., p 545.
208   *Chicago Daily News*, July 17, 1907.
209   Ibid.
210   *Abstract of Record and Bill of Exceptions*, p 540.
211   *Chicago Daily News*, July 17, 1907.
212   Ibid.
213   Ibid.
214   *Abstract of Record and Bill of Exceptions*, p 540.
215   *Chicago Daily News*, July 17, 1907.
216   *Chicago Daily Tribune*, July 18, 1907.

217 *Chicago Daily Tribune,* July 19, 1907.

218 *Chicago Daily News,* July 18, 1907.

219 *Chicago Daily Tribune,* July 18, 1907.

220 *Chicago Daily Tribune,* July 19, 1907.

221 *Cook County Herald* (Arlington Heights, IL), July 26, 1907.

222 *Chicago Daily News,* July 19, 1907.

223 Ibid.

224 *Abstract of Record and Bill of Exceptions,* p 370.

225 *Washington Post,* August 2, 1907.

226 *Chicago Daily Tribune,* February 8, 1909.

227 *Chicago Daily Tribune,* September 9, 1907.

228 "Statement of Herman Billik, Jr." May 13, 1907.

229 "Old St. Mary's Parish History," website accessed March 5, 2005;
http:\\www.oldstmarys.com/Parish_history.htm

230 *Marion Daily Star* (Marion, OH) October 8, 1907.

231 Letter dated March 20, 1908 from L.G. Edwardson to State's Attorney Healy; State of Illinois Executive Clemency Files, Herman
Zajicek, aka Herman Billik, Illinois State Archives, Springfield, IL.

232 *1900 United States Federal Census,* Chicago Ward 8, Cook County,
IL, ED 200.

233 *Chicago Daily Tribune,* November 1, 1907.

234 Ibid.

235 Ibid.

236 Letter from Emma Neamann to Jerry Vrzal at Valparaiso; post-
marked October 24, 1907; State of Illinois Executive Clemency
Files, Herman Zajicek, aka Herman Billik, Illinois State Archives,
Springfield, IL.

237 Ibid.

238 *Chicago Daily Tribune,* November 4, 1907.

239 Ibid.

240 *Chicago Daily News.* November 5, 1907.

241 *Chicago Daily Tribune,* November 5, 1907.

242 Ibid.

243 Ibid.

244 *Chicago Daily News.* November 5, 1907.

245 Ibid.

246 Ibid.

247 Ibid.

248 Ibid.

249 *Chicago Daily Tribune* November 6, 1907.

250 Ibid.

251 Ibid.

252 Ibid.

253 Ibid.

254 *Chicago Daily Tribune,* November 7, 1907.

255 *Chicago Daily Tribune* November 6, 1907.
256 Ibid.
257 Ibid.
258 *Chicago Daily Tribune,* November 7, 1907.
259 *Chicago Daily Tribune,* September 1, 1901.
260 *Chicago Daily Tribune,* January 9, 1919.
261 *Chicago Daily Tribune,* November 16, 1907.
262 Ibid.
263 Ibid.
264 Ibid.
265 *Chicago Daily Tribune,* November 17, 1900.
266 Certificate of Death, William Neamann; Cook County, Illinois, issued November 18, 1907; No. 12041; and *Cook County Coroner's Inquest Record (1872–1911),* Inquest No. 43105, November 18, 1907.
267 Robert H. Dreisbach, MD, PhD, *Handbook of Poisoning* (Los Altos, CA: Lange Medical Publications, 1969) pp 169–171.
268 Ibid.
269 C.R. Gross and A.O. Nelson, Insecticide Division, Bureau of Chemistry and Soils, U.S. Department of Agriculture, Washington, D.C.; "Arsenic in Tobacco Smoke," *American Journal Public Health Nations Health,* 1934 January 24, pp 36–42; [original scanned version of text] accessed online September 15, 2010, http://www.ncbi.nlm.nih.gov/pmc/articles/PMC1558493/.
270 "Affections of the Heart and Circulatory System," excerpts from *Orthopathy* by Herbert M. Shelton, Presented by Dr. Stanley S. Bass; website accessed 8 August 16, 2010, http://drbass.com/orthopathy/chapter11.html; "New Evils For Old," Chapter X, Soil and Health Library, website accessed June 4, 2010, http://www.soilandhealth.org/02/0201hyglibcat/020134syphilis/020134syphilis-ch10.htm; and "Love to Know Classic Encyclopedia," website accessed November 14, 2008, http://www.1911encyclopedia.org/Arsenic
271 *Chicago Daily Tribune,* December 4, 1905.
272 *Chicago Daily Tribune,* May 12, 1916.
273 Ibid.
274 Ibid.
275 *Chicago Daily Tribune,* December 5, 1918.
276 *Chicago Daily Tribune,* March 24, 1918.
277 *Chicago Daily Tribune,* December 5, 1918.
278 *Chicago Daily Tribune,* December 8, 1918.
279 *Chicago Daily Tribune,* December 9, 1918.
280 *Chicago Daily Tribune,* December 5, 1918.
281 *Chicago Daily Tribune,* December 5, 1918.
282 *Chicago Daily Tribune,* December 10, 1918.

283 *Chicago Daily Tribune,* December 5, 1918; and *Chicago Daily Tribune,* December 8, 1918.
284 *Chicago Daily Tribune,* December 15, 1918.
285 *Chicago Daily Tribune,* December 10, 1918.
286 *Chicago Daily Tribune,* January 4, 1927.
287 Judge John H. Lyle, *The Dry and Lawless Years* (Englewood Cliffs, NJ: Prentice-Hall, Inc., 1960), p 75.
288 Cook County Recorder of Deeds Original Property Tract Book 486A; "Invty 98/344," dated 1/2/1908.
289 Personal interview with Doris Thygerson, granddaughter of William Niemann, January 23, 2004.
290 Letter from Emma Neamann to Jerry Vrzal, October 24, 1907.
291 Personal interview with Doris Thygerson, January 23, 2004.
292 "Examination of Jerry Vrzal By Judge Barnes, March 7, 1908," State of Illinois Executive Clemency Files, Herman Zajicek, aka Herman Billik, Illinois State Archives, Springfield, IL, p 42.
293 Supreme Court of Illinois, *Opinion of the Court, No. 5814,* February 20, 1908.
294 Ibid.
295 *Brief and Argument For Defendant in Error,* p 88.
296 Ibid.
297 Ibid., p 89.
298 "Examination of Jerry Vrzal By Judge Barnes," p 123.
299 *Abstract of Record and Bill of Exceptions,* p 348.
300 Transcript of Inquisition, DuPage County Coroner, Case 52 017, Henry Niemann, September 25, 1908, DuPage County Coroner, Records of Inquest, Microfilm, Wheaton, IL; p 39.
301 *Chicago Daily Tribune,* February 21, 1908.
302 *Abstract of Record and Bill of Exceptions,* p 372; and "Examination of Jerry Vrzal By Judge Barnes," pp 107–109.
303 *Abstract of Record and Bill of Exceptions,* p 268.
304 Ibid., p 157.
305 *Chicago Daily Tribune,* July 14, 1907.
306 *Chicago Daily Tribune,* February 21, 1908.
307 "Affidavit of Retraction of Jerry Vrzal," State of Illinois Executive Clemency Files, Herman Zajicek, aka Herman Billik, Illinois State Archives, Springfield, IL.
308 *Abstract of Record and Bill of Exceptions,* pp 286–287
309 "Affidavit of Retraction of Jerry Vrzal."
310 Ibid.
311 Ibid.
312 Ibid.
313 Ibid.
314 Ibid.
315 Ibid.

316 Ibid.
317 Ibid.
318 *Chicago Daily Tribune*, February 23, 1908.
319 *The Newark Advocate* (Newark, Ohio), December 18, 1906.
320 *Chicago Daily Tribune*, February 26, 1908.
321 Ibid.
322 *Chicago Daily Tribune*, March 5, 1908.
323 *Chicago Daily Tribune*, March 3, 1908.
324 "Examination of Jerry Vrzal By Judge Barnes," p 22.
325 Ibid., pp 9–10.
326 Ibid., p 39
327 *Chicago Daily Tribune*, July 29, 1899.
328 *Chicago Daily Tribune*, July 29, 1899.
329 "Examination of Jerry Vrzal By Judge Barnes," p 65.
330 Ibid., p 66.
331 Ibid., p 67.
332 Ibid., p 66.
333 Ibid., pp 69–70.
334 Ibid., p 128.
335 Supreme Court of Illinois, *Abstract of Retraction, No. 5814*, June Term, 1908, State of Illinois Executive Clemency Files, Herman Zajicek, aka Herman Billik, Illinois State Archives, Springfield, IL, p 7.
336 Ibid.
337 "Examination of Jerry Vrzal By Judge Barnes," p 92.
338 Ibid., p 76.
339 *Abstract of Retraction*, p 5.
340 "Examination of Jerry Vrzal By Judge Barnes," p 96.
341 Ibid., p 97.
342 Ibid., p 100.
343 Ibid., pp 102–103.
344 Ibid., pp 107–108.
345 Ibid., p 109.
346 Ibid.
347 "Examination of Jerry Vrzal By Judge Barnes," p 118.
348 Ancestry.com. *World War I Draft Registration Cards, 1917–1918* [database online]. Provo, UT, USA: Ancestry.com Operations Inc, 2005, No. 10H 7886, Jerome Vaughan, June 5, 1917.
349 "Examination of Jerry Vrzal By Judge Barnes," p 107.
350 Ibid., p 120.
351 *Transcript of Coroner's Inquest*, p 41; *Abstract of Record and Bill of Exceptions*, p 332 and p 370.
352 "Examination of Jerry Vrzal By Judge Barnes," p 137.
353 Letter from L.G. Edwardson to State's Attorney Healy, March 20, 1908.
354 Ibid.

355 *Chicago Daily Tribune*, March 24, 1908, "Billek's [sic] Friend Is Balked."

356 Walter Roth and Joe Kraus, *An Accidental Anarchist* (San Francisco: Rudi Publishing, 1998).

357 *Chicago Daily Tribune*, March 31, 1908; "Billick [sic] Case Echo In Court."

358 Ancestry.com. *1910 United States Federal Census* [database online]. Provo, UT, USA: Ancestry.com Operations Inc, 2006. Chicago, Cook County, IL ED560, conducted 4/21/1910 shows Bertha living with Emma on 19th St.

359 *Chicago Daily Tribune*, April 11, 1908.

360 *Edwardsville Intelligencer* (Edwardsville, Illinois), April 14, 1908.

361 *Chicago Daily Tribune*, April 15, 1908.

362 *Washington Post*, April 19, 1908.

363 *Chicago Daily Tribune*, April 19, 1908.

364 *Hearing By the State Board of Pardons*, Transcript, p 52.

365 *Chicago Daily Tribune*, April 19, 1908.

366 *Hearing By the State Board of Pardons*, Transcript, p 70.

367 Ibid., p 72.

368 *Transcript of Coroner's Inquest*, p 55.

369 *Abstract of Record and Bill of Exceptions,* p 370.

370 Letter from Emma Neamann to Jerry Vrzal, October 24, 1907.

371 *Chicago Daily Tribune*, April 19, 1908.

372 Ibid.

373 Ibid.

374 Ibid.

375 *Hearing By the State Board of Pardons*, Transcript, pp 104–105.

376 *Chicago Daily Tribune*, April 19, 1908.

377 *People vs. Billik, Transcript of Arguments*, Board of Pardons, State of Illinois Executive Clemency Files, Herman Zajicek, aka Herman Billik, Illinois State Archives, Springfield, IL p 267.

378 Letter to Gov. Deneen from jurors, State of Illinois Executive Clemency Files, Herman Zajicek, aka Herman Billik, Illinois State Archives, Springfield, IL.

379 *Hearing By the State Board of Pardons*, Transcript, pp 162–163.

380 *Chicago Daily Tribune*, April 19, 1908.

381 Ibid.

382 Ibid.

383 Ibid.

384 *Hearing By the State Board of Pardons* , Transcript, p 51.

385 *Transcript of Arguments*, Board of Pardons, p 191.

386 *Abstract of Record and Bill of Exceptions,* pp 172–173.

387 Ibid., p 194.

388 *Hearing By the State Board of Pardons*, Transcript, p 202.

389 Ibid., p 20.

390 Ibid., p 221.
391 *Chicago Daily Tribune*, April 19, 1908.
392 Ibid.
393 Ibid.
394 Ibid.
394 *Hearing By the State Board of Pardons*, Transcript, p 235.
396 *Chicago Daily Tribune*, April 19, 1908.
397 *Hearing By the State Board of Pardons*, Transcript, p 238.
398 *Chicago Daily Tribune*, April 19, 1908.
399 *Transcript of Coroner's Inquest*, p 109.
400 *Abstract of Record and Bill of Exceptions*, p 274.
401 Ibid., p 155.
402 *Transcript of Coroner's Inquest*, p 107.
403 *Abstract of Record and Bill of Exceptions*, pp 273–275.
404 *Transcript of Arguments*, Board of Pardons, p 271.
405 Ibid., p 380.
406 Ibid., p 276.
407 Ibid.
408 Ibid., p 273.
409 Ibid., pp 275–76.
410 Ibid., p 278.
411 Ibid., pp 278–79.
412 Ibid., p 380.
413 Ibid., pp 384.
414 Ibid., p 385.
415 *Chicago Daily Tribune*, April 19, 1908.
416 *Transcript of Arguments*, Board of Pardons, pp 385–86.
417 Ibid., pp 385–86.
418 *Transcript of Arguments*, Board of Pardons, p 286.
419 Ibid., pp 286–87.
420 Ibid., p 287.
421 Ibid., p 288.
422 Ibid., p 397.
423 Ibid.
424 Ibid., p 399.
425 Ibid., p 397.
426 Ibid., pp 390–91.
427 Ibid., p 391.
428 Ibid.
429 Ibid., pp 391–92.
430 Ibid., p 392.
431 Ibid., p 391
432 Ibid., p 394.
433 *Chicago Daily Tribune*, April 20, 1908.
434 *Chicago American*, April 20, 1908.

435 *Chicago Daily Tribune*, April 20, 1908.
436 Ibid.
437 Ibid.
438 *Edwardsville Intelligencer* (Edwardsville, IL), June 9, 1908.
439 *Chicago Daily Tribune*, April 21, 1908.
440 Ibid.
441 Anonymous Letter to Father O'Callaghan, c. April 1908; State of Illinois Executive Clemency Files, Herman Zajicek, aka Herman Billik, Illinois State Archives, Springfield, IL.
442 Ibid.
443 *Cook County Coroner's Inquest Record*, Coroner's Inquest No. 45049, Vol. 86, Page 115; May 8, 1908.
444 *Chicago Daily Tribune*, May 10, 1908.
445 *Chicago Daily Tribune*, May 9, 1908.
446 Letter to William E. O'Neill from W.A. Drake, June 1, 1908, State of Illinois Executive Clemency Files, Herman Zajicek, aka Herman Billik, Illinois State Archives, Springfield, IL p 1.
447 Walter Roth and Joe Kraus, p 150.
448 Albert S. Osborn, *Questioned Documents,* Second Edition Facsimile (Chicago: Nelson Hall Co., 1974) pp 390–399.
449 Letter to William E. O'Neill from W.A. Drake, June 1, 1908, p 2.
450 Ibid., pp 3–4.
451 Ibid., pp 5–6.
452 Letter to Governor Deneen from Father O'Callaghan, June 4, 1908; State of Illinois Executive Clemency Files, Herman Zajicek, aka Herman Billik, Illinois State Archives, Springfield, IL.
453 Ibid.
454 *Chicago Daily Tribune*, June 6, 1908.
455 *Chicago Daily Tribune*, June 8, 1908.
456 Ibid.
457 Ibid.
458 Ibid.
459 Ibid.
460 *The New York Times*, June 9, 1908.
461 Ibid.
462 *The Elyria Chronicle* (Elyiria, Ohio), June 8, 1908.
463 *Steven's Point Daily Journal* (Stevens Point, WI), June 9, 1908.
464 Ibid.
465 *Washington Post*, June 9, 1908.
466 *Chicago Daily Tribune*, June 9, 1908.
467 Ibid.
468 Ibid.
469 *Steven's Point Daily Journal*, June 9, 1908.
470 *Chicago Daily Tribune*, June 9, 1908.
471 *Chicago Daily Tribune*, June 10, 1908.

472 *The Marion Daily Star* (Marion, Ohio), June 10, 1908.
473 *Washington Post*, October 31, 2006, "Infamous Piece of Chicago History Goes on Block," online: http://www.washingtonpost.com/wp-dyn/content/article/2006/10/30/AR2006103000984.html
474 Paul Avrich, *The Haymarket Tragedy* (Princeton, NJ: Princeton University Press, 1984), pp 391–398.
475 *Chicago Daily Tribune*, June 10, 1908.
476 Ibid.
477 Ibid.
478 Ibid.
479 Ibid.
480 Ibid.
481 *Chicago Daily Tribune*, June 11, 1908.
482 Ibid.
483 Ibid.
484 Ibid.
485 Ibid.
486 Letters in State of Illinois Executive Clemency Files, Herman Zajicek, aka Herman Billik, Illinois State Archives, Springfield, IL; including: Letter to Governor Deneen from William M. Bradley, Village of Lake Villa June 10, 1908; and Letter to Governor Deneen from Catherine Stanton, Woodlawn Station, June 1908.
487 *The Marion Daily Star* (Marion, OH), June 12, 1908.
488 *Chicago Daily Tribune*, June 12, 1908.
489 Ibid.
490 Ibid.
491 *The New York Times*, June 12, 1908.
492 Ibid.
493 Ibid.
494 *The New York Times*, June 12, 1908.
495 *Chicago Daily Tribune*, June 12, 1908.
496 Ibid.
497 Daniel E. Niemiec, "Chicago Streets Database," 2003 [database online], accessed June17, 2007, http://www.rootsweb.com/~itappcnc/pipcnstreetfind.htm
498 *Chicago Daily Tribune*, June 12, 1908.
499 *Evening Telegram*, (Elyria, Ohio), June 12, 1908.
500 *Chicago Daily Tribune*, June 12, 1908.
501 Ibid.
502 Ibid.
503 Ibid.
504 Ibid.
505 Ibid.
506 Ibid.
507 Ibid.

508 Ibid.
509 Ibid.
510 *The New York Times*, June 12, 1908.
511 *Chicago Daily Tribune*, June 12, 1908.
512 Ibid.
513 Ibid.
514 *Chicago Daily Tribune*, June 13, 1908.
515 *Chicago Daily Tribune*, June 13, 1908.
516 *New York Times*, June 13, 1908.
517 *Chicago Daily Tribune*, June 13, 1908.
518 *Chicago Daily Tribune*, June 13, 1908.
519 Ibid.
520 *The Mansfield News* (Mansfield, Ohio), June 12, 1908.
521 *Chicago Daily Tribune*, June 13, 1908.
522 *Marion Daily Star* (Marion, Ohio), June 12, 1908.
523 *Chicago Daily Tribune*, June 13, 1908.
524 *New York Times*, June 13, 1908.
525 *Washington Post*, June 13, 1908.
526 *The Mansfield News* (Mansfield, Ohio), June 12, 1908.
527 *Chicago Daily Tribune*, June 13, 1908.
528 Ibid.
529 Ibid.
530 *Washington Post*, June 13, 1908.
531 Ibid.
532 *Chicago Daily Tribune*, June 13, 1908.
533 Ibid.
534 *Washington Post*, June 13, 1908.
535 *Chicago Daily Tribune*, June 13, 1908.
536 Ibid.
537 Ibid.
538 *Marion Daily Star* (Marion, Ohio), June 12, 1908.
539 *The Mansfield News* (Mansfield, Ohio), June 12, 1908.
540 *Chicago Daily Tribune*, June 13, 1908.
541 *Chicago Daily Tribune*, June 13, 1908.
542 *Chicago Daily Tribune*, June 28, 1908.
543 *Chicago Daily Tribune*, July 2, 1908.
544 *Chicago Daily News*, July 2, 1908.
545 Ibid.
546 *Chicago Daily Tribune*, July 2, 1908.
547 *Chicago Daily Tribune*, July 31, 1908.
548 *Chicago Daily News*, July 30, 1908.
549 Ibid.
550 *Chicago Daily Tribune*, July 31, 1908.
551 *Chicago Daily News*, July 30, 1908.
552 *Chicago Daily Tribune*, July 31, 1908.

553   Ibid.
554   Ibid.
555   Ibid.
556   *Chicago Daily Tribune*, August 1, 1908.
557   Ibid.
558   *Chicago Daily Tribune*, July 31, 1908.
559   *Chicago Daily News*, July 31, 1908.
560   Ibid.
561   *Chicago Daily Tribune*, July 31, 1908.
562   Ibid.
563   Ibid.
564   *Chicago Daily News*, July 31, 1908.
565   *Chicago Daily Tribune*, August 1, 1908.
566   *Chicago Daily Tribune*, July 31, 1908.
567   *Chicago Daily News*, July 31, 1908.
568   Ibid.
569   Ibid.
570   Supreme Court *Opinion, No. 5814.*
571   *Chicago Daily News*, August 1, 1908.
572   *Chicago Daily News,* August 4, 1908.
573   *Chicago Daily Tribune* August 2, 1908
574   Ibid.
575   *Chicago Daily News,* August 4, 1908.
576   Ibid.
577   Ibid.
578   Ibid.
579   Ibid.
580   Ibid.
581   Ibid.
582   Ibid.
583   Ibid.
584   Ibid.
585   *Chicago Daily News*, August 1, 1908.
586   Transcript of Henry Niemann Inquisition, pp 9–11.
587   Ibid., p 12.
588   Ibid., p 26.
589   *Chicago Daily Tribune*, August 5, 1908.
590   Curt Johnson and R. Craig Sutter, *The Wicked City, Chicago From Kenna to Capone* (New York: Da Capo Press, 1998), p 29.
591   *Chicago Daily News,* August 5, 1908.
592   *Chicago Daily Tribune*, August 5, 1908.
593   Ibid.
594   Ibid.
595   Ibid.
596   Ibid.

597 Ibid.
598 *Chicago Daily News*, August 5, 1908.
599 *Chicago Daily Tribune*, August 5, 1908.
600 *Chicago Daily News*, August 5, 1908.
601 *Chicago Daily Tribune*, August 6, 1908.
602 Ibid.
603 *Chicago Daily Tribune*, August 8, 1908.
604 Ibid.
605 *Chicago Daily Tribune*, August 6, 1908.
606 Ibid.
607 Ibid.
608 *Chicago Daily Tribune*, July 31, 1908.
609 *Chicago Daily Tribune*, August 6, 1908.
610 Ibid.
611 *Chicago Daily News*, August 6, 1908.
612 *Chicago Daily Tribune*, August 5, 1908.
613 *Chicago Daily Tribune*, August 7, 1908.
614 Ibid.
615 Ibid.
616 Ibid.
617 Ibid.
618 Ibid.
619 Ibid.
620 Ibid.
621 *Chicago Daily Tribune*, August 9, 1908.
622 Ibid.
623 *Chicago Daily News*, August 10, 1908.
624 *Chicago Tribune*, July 13, 1907.
625 Transcript of Henry Niemann Inquisition, pp 20–21.
626 *Chicago Daily News*, August 11, 1908.
627 *Brief and Argument For Defendant in Error*, p 3; *Petition For Clemency to His Excellency, Gov. Charles S. Deneen*, April 18, 1908; State of Illinois Executive Clemency Files, Herman Zajicek, aka Herman Billik, Illinois State Archives, Springfield, IL; p. 5; and *Affidavit of Retraction. Chicago Tribune* July 13, 1907.
628 Transcript of Henry Niemann Inquisition, pp 43–45.
629 Ibid., p 44.
630 Ibid., p 45.
631 *Chicago Daily News*, August 11, 1908.
632 Transcript of Henry Niemann Inquisition, p 50.
633 Ibid.
634 Personal interview with Doris Thygerson, January 23, 2004.
635 Transcript of Henry Niemann Inquisition, List of Witnesses.
636 Ibid., p 67.
637 *Chicago Daily Tribune*, August 21, 1908.

638 *Chicago Daily News,* August 22, 1908.
639 *Chicago Daily Tribune,* August 22, 1908.
640 Transcript of Henry Niemann Inquisition, pp 73–74.
641 Ibid., p 81.
642 Ibid., p 82.
643 Ibid., p 85.
644 Ibid., pp 79–80.
645 Ibid., p 90.
646 *Chicago Examiner,* September 26, 1908
647 *The Washington Post,* October 20, 1908.
648 Ibid.
649 *Chicago Daily Tribune,* October 20, 1908.
650 *Decatur Daily Review* (Decatur, IL), October 22, 1908.
651 *Decatur Review* (Decatur, IL), October 21, 1908.
652 *Chicago Daily Tribune,* November 18, 1908.
653 Ibid.
654 *The Washington Post,* November 22, 1908, p E4.
655 *Chicago Daily Tribune,* November 18, 1908.
656 *The Washington Post,* November 29, 1908.
657 *Ft. Wayne Journal-Gazette* (Fort Wayne, IN), November 23, 1908.
658 *Ft. Wayne Journal-Gazette* (Fort Wayne, IN), November 25, 1908.
659 Dunne, Vol. II, p 479.
660 *Decatur Daily Review* (Decatur, IL), December 2, 1908.
661 *Lima Daily News* (Lima, Ohio), November 27, 1908.
662 *Chicago Daily Tribune,* December 4, 1908.
663 Ibid.
664 Handwritten Letter from Albert Barnes to Governor Deneen, December 5, 1908; State of Illinois Executive Clemency Files, Herman Zajicek, aka Herman Billik, Illinois State Archives, Springfield, IL.
665 *Decatur Daily Review* (Decatur, IL), December 2, 1908.
666 *Chicago Daily Tribune,* December 7, 1908.
667 *Chicago Daily Tribune,* December 8, 1908.
668 Letter from Albert Barnes to Governor Deneen, December 5, 1908.
669 *Cook County Herald* (Arlington Heights, IL), January 29, 1909.
670 Chicago Daily Tribune, January 24, 1909.
671 *Nevada State Journal* (Reno, NV), January 29, 1909.
672 *Chicago Daily Tribune,* September 30, 1909.
673 *New York Times,* May 28, 1909.
674 *Chicago Tribune,* January 12, 2003, p 1, "Clemency For All;" Chicago Tribune Archives, ProQuest Archiver [online database] http://pqasb.pqarchiver.com/chicagotribune/advancedsearch.html
675 *1910 United States Federal Census,* 2006, Chicago, Cook County, ED 153, image 393.
676 Dunne, Vol I, p 187.
677 Simpson, p 53.

678 Dunne, Vol I, p 187.
679 Ibid., p 184.
680 *Chicago Daily Tribune*, August 8, 1912.
681 Dunne, Vol II, p 353.
682 Edmund N. Allen, Warden, "Report of the Commissioners of the Illinois State Penitentiary at Joliet, For the Two Years Ending September 30, 1914;" Springfield: State of Illinois, 1915, pp 7–10, Joliet Prison Photographs website accessed November 11, 2010: http://www.jolietprison.com/publications/catalog.asp
683 Handwritten Letter to Governor Dunne from Herman Billik, July 12, 1914; State of Illinois Executive Clemency Files, Herman Zajicek, aka Herman Billik, Illinois State Archives, Springfield, IL.
684 Ibid.
685 Ibid.
686 Letter to State Board of Pardons from J.P. Benson, Sept. 5, 1914; State of Illinois Executive Clemency Files, Herman Zajicek, aka Herman Billik, Illinois State Archives, Springfield, IL.
687 Handwritten Letter to Governor Dunne from Herman Billik, December 6, 1914; State of Illinois Executive Clemency Files, Herman Zajicek, aka Herman Billik, Illinois State Archives, Springfield, IL.
688 Letter to Herman Billik from State Board of Pardons, December 18, 1914; State of Illinois Executive Clemency Files, Herman Zajicek, aka Herman Billik, Illinois State Archives, Springfield, IL.
689 Letter to State Board of Pardons from Prison Physician, Illinois State Penitentiary, Joliet, IL, April 17, 1915; State of Illinois Executive Clemency Files, Herman Zajicek, aka Herman Billik, Illinois State Archives, Springfield, IL.
690 Ancestry.com. *World War I Draft Registration Cards, 1917–1918* [database online]. Provo, UT, USA: Ancestry.com Operations Inc, 2005, No. 10H 7886, Jerome Vaughan, June 5, 1917.
691 Handwritten Letter to Gov. Dunne from Herman Billik, Dated February 17, 1916; State of Illinois Executive Clemency Files, Herman Zajicek, aka Herman Billik, Illinois State Archives, Springfield, IL.
692 Handwritten Letter to Gov. Dunne from Herman Billik, Dated March 19, 1916; State of Illinois Executive Clemency Files, Herman Zajicek, aka Herman Billik, Illinois State Archives, Springfield, IL.
693 Letter to Herman Billik from Thomas M. Kilbride, State Board of Pardons, Dated March 21, 1916; State of Illinois Executive Clemency Files, Herman Zajicek, aka Herman Billik, Illinois State Archives, Springfield, IL.
694 *Chicago Daily Tribune*, May 11, 1916.
695 *Chicago Daily Tribune*, June 2, 1929.
696 *Chicago Daily Tribune*, May 13, 1916.
697 Letter to Warden Zimmer, Joliet State Prison, From Gilbert Sellers,

May 15, 1916; State of Illinois Executive Clemency Files, Herman Zajicek, aka Herman Billik, Illinois State Archives, Springfield, IL.

698 Letter to State Board of Pardons From Francis Hinckley, December 7, 1916; State of Illinois Executive Clemency Files, Herman Zajicek, aka Herman Billik, Illinois State Archives, Springfield, IL.

699 Richard Allen Morton, *Justice and Humanity, Edward F. Dunne, Illinois Progressive* (Carbondale and Edwardsville, IL: Southern Illinois University Press, 1997), p 4.

700 *Recommendation of the Board of Pardons of the State of Illinois, Special October Session 1916, In the Matter of the Application of Herman Zajicek, alias Herman Billik for Pardon*, State of Illinois Executive Clemency Files, Herman Zajicek, aka Herman Billik, Illinois State Archives, Springfield, IL.

701 *Chicago Examiner*, January 4, 1917.

702 *Chicago Daily Tribune*, January 5, 1917.

703 Chicago Daily Tribune, January 8, 1917.

704 Ibid.

705 Chicago Daily Tribune, January 7, 1917.

706 Chicago Daily Tribune, January 6, 1917.

707 *Chicago Daily Tribune*, January 7, 1917.

708 *Chicago Daily Tribune*, January 9, 1917.

709 Ibid.

710 Ibid.

711 *Chicago Daily News*, May 25, 1917.

712 *The Daily Northwestern* (Oshkosh, WI), May 25, 1917.

713 *Chicago Daily Tribune*, May 25, 1917.

714 *Abstract of Record and Bill of Exceptions,* pp 369–370.

715 The two most well-known are Philip Lindsay's, *The Mainspring of Murder* (London: John Long, 1958) and Stephen Longstreet's, *Chicago, An Intimate Portrait of People, Pleasures, and Power:1860–1919* (New York: David McKay Company, Inc., 1973). The most recent is *501 Most Notorious Crimes* (London: Bounty Books, 2009) by Paul Donnelley.

716 Philip Lindsay, *The Mainspring of Murder* (London: John Long, 1958), pp 128–129.

717 *Washington Post*, June 2, 1924.

718 *Chicago Daily Tribune*, February 6, 1913.

719 Chiago Daily Tribune, April 13, 1913.

720 Dunne, Vol II, p 372.

721 *Washington Post*, August 12, 1931.

Index

•

NOTE: Page numbers in *italics* indicate a photograph or artwork. An *italicized "n"* following
a page number indicates a note on that page.